Laurence Marks, tele[...] north London and edu[...] next door to the prison[...] co-writer Maurice Gr[...] successful television seri[...] recent years including: *Shine On Harvey Moon*, *The New Statesman* (winner of the 1988 International Emmy Award, Popular Arts category) and *Birds of a Feather*. He is a director of Alomo, a leading independent television production company.

His interest in the Ruth Ellis story began when he was working as a freelance journalist and was asked to write a lengthy article for the now defunct *Nova* magazine. A chance meeting with Tony Van den Bergh enhanced his interest and the idea of a book was born.

Tony Van den Bergh was educated in misery at Repton School, Derby, and then trained for the stage at RADA. He began writing for radio immediately after the Second World War, and is the author of over 1,000 radio plays and documentaries including *The Ruth Ellis Story*, *Jack the Ripper*, *The A6 Murder* (with Alan Burgess), *Dead on Arrival* and *Hanratty*. He has also had a varied and interesting journalistic career, including work for the *Sunday Times* as journalist 'on the run' with Charles Richardson, when the south London gang leader escaped from prison. He has presented medical programmes for both radio and television, and received a World Special Award in 1988 for *Treat Me Gently* in which, under spinal anaesthetic, he gave running commentary as he underwent a hip-replacement operation. For seven years, until 1988, he was joint presenter and author of the Central TV series *Getting On*. His books include *The Jack Johnson Story*, *The Padded Ring*, *The Trade Unions: What are They?* and *Diminished Responsibility* (with Laurence Marks).

He is a former inspector for the British Boxing Board of Control and has been a boxing commentator for ITV and BBC radio and television. He was also co-founder and managing director of Four Square Books.

... television and screen writer, was born in ... educated at Holloway County – the school ... where Ruth Ellis was executed. With ... he has created some of the most ...

RUTH ELLIS

A case of Diminished Responsibility?

LAURENCE MARKS
AND
TONY VAN DEN BERGH

PENGUIN BOOKS

PENGUIN BOOKS

Published by the Penguin Group

Penguin Books Ltd, 27 Wrights Lane, London W8 5TZ, England

Viking Penguin, a division of Penguin Books USA Inc.

375 Hudson Street, New York, New York 10014, USA

Penguin Books Australia Ltd, Ringwood, Victoria, Australia

Penguin Books Canada Ltd, 2801 John Street, Markham, Ontario, Canada L3R 1B4

Penguin Books (NZ) Ltd, 182–190 Wairau Road, Auckland 10, New Zealand

Penguin Books Ltd, Registered Offices: Harmondsworth, Middlesex, England

First published by Macdonald and James Publishers 1977

Published in Penguin Books 1990

1 3 5 7 9 10 8 6 4 2

Filmset in Monophoto Times

Printed in England by Clays Ltd, St Ives plc

'When any child is murdered in England today, I am the subject of attack. They say that if it weren't for my sister, we would still have the death penalty . . . and then that child would have lived.'

Muriel Jakubait (the sister of Ruth Ellis), to whom this book is dedicated.

To the living we owe our respect, to the dead we owe nothing but the truth.

VOLTAIRE

Diminished responsibility was introduced in the Homicide Act, 1957. It applies only to those charged with murder, and if successful reduces the charge to manslaughter. To succeed in the defence, the defendant must prove (on the balance of probabilities rather than beyond a reasonable doubt) that he was suffering from such abnormality of mind (whether arising from a condition of arrested or retarded development of mind or any inherent causes or induced by disease or injury) as substantially impaired his mental responsibility for his acts or omissions.

ACKNOWLEDGEMENTS

A very great number of people helped the authors, either individually or collectively, in the collection of material for this book. To the following the authors are indebted:

The late Mr Justice Havers
The late Mr Christmas Humphreys
The late Mr John Bickford
Lord Mishcon
Mr Leon Simmons
Mr George Rogers, CBE
Mr Fenton Bresler
The late Dr William Sargant
The wife of the late Dr T. P. Rees
Mrs Gladys Yule
Mr Cliff Davis
The late Mr Conrad Nockolds
Mr Granville Neilson
Mr Andrea Clare Neilson
The late Robert Craddock
Mr Jack Dunkley
The late Mr John Chandos
Sergeant Alan Thompson
Mr Colson
Mr Albert Pierrepoint
Ms Faith Roberts
Ms Tony Frith
Mr Nick Townsend
Mr Harry Harris
Mr Peter J. Edwards
Miss Kim White
The late Mr Edgar Lustgarten
Mrs John Winstanley
Ms Heather Jenner

Mrs Tom Steele
Mr Kevyn Rees
Ms Hazel Jones of Syndication International

The staff that gave us help and assistance at:

New Scotland Yard
Warlingham Park Hospital
HM Stationery Office
The Daily Mirror Library
The British Museum Newspaper Library

The article by 'Cassandra' is reprinted by permission of the *Daily Mirror*; the article 'The Death Penalty' by permission of *The Lancet*. Extracts from *The Trial of Ruth Ellis* are reproduced by kind permission of Ms Tina Miruzzi of David and Charles (Holdings) Ltd.

The authors also wish to thank the good offices of the Director of Public Prosecutions.

Five people warrant a 'special' thank you:

Mr Peter Dunk for encouraging us to write a story that deserved to be told.
Ms Helen Wright for her tolerance and time in typing the manuscript which was often presented to her in nothing more than cipher.
Ms Susan Marks whose encouragement and good food kept one of the authors going in times of desperation.
Mr Paul Flattery who many years ago suggested that the Ruth Ellis story was worth investigating.
Muriel who, as Ruth Ellis's sister, was able to give the authors an insight into her family's life that had, to date, never been infiltrated. Also for her unselfish help in answering questions at all times that sometimes were of such a personal nature that the authors had no right to ask them.

Finally, the authors would like to thank three people without whose help, guidance and assistance this book would never have been written. To them we owe more than they will ever know.

Mr Peter Williams
Mr Christopher Goddard
Ms Alex Sumner

FOREWORD

It was in 1973 that Tony Van den Bergh approached the BBC proposing that they commission him to write a programme based on the post-war London afternoon drinking clubs. It was a period when men who had been pilots or tank commanders were finding it difficult, if not impossible, to integrate with normal, everyday civil life. Many of them chose to become commercial travellers – misnamed 'Knights of the Road' – rather than resume office work as clerks or buyers. Usually they discovered that being a traveller did not mean rushing about Britain in smart cars and wining and dining customers in the fleshpots, but rather spending evenings in dreary commercial hotels and the days in flattering men of little worth and much conceit to keep their order books respectable for examination.

To them the afternoon drinking clubs – usually basement premises – were refuges where they could fantasize about their halcyon days. There would be hostesses to hang on their every word and laugh all too readily at the stories picked up on their rounds; stories that the hostesses had no doubt heard many times before. But it was easy to laugh when they were paid to do so and easier still to reburnish the egos of ex-war heroes. For a few hours a night the former soldiers, sailors and airmen could relive their past.

Ruth Ellis ran such a club and the BBC suggested that Tony Van den Bergh should concentrate on her case, for, after all, her execution undoubtedly helped the anti-capital punishment lobby, so wide was the revulsion of feeling amongst ordinary people at her execution for a crime of passion. In France, no doubt, she would have served only a nominal sentence.

At the same time Tony Van den Bergh was starting out on his researches, so was Laurence Marks for a lengthy magazine feature. It would be over a year before the two of them were to meet and swap notes.

The coincidences which were to tie Van den Bergh to the case were almost supernatural. The first was at dinner. John Chandos, actor and writer, had been a close friend of Van den Bergh's since they were at the Royal Academy of Dramatic Arts. John wanted to know what the author was writing at the time.

'The story of Ruth Ellis,' he answered.

'Who better than you?'

'I don't understand,' Van den Bergh replied.

'Well,' Chandos said, 'she shot her lover because he was having an affair with another girl.'

'Yes, I know that.'

'That girl,' exclaimed Chandos, 'was Faith. You knew her very well!'

And he did. Faith was a beautiful and warm girl who was introduced to Van den Bergh by Chandos many years before. Now she was running a small hotel in south-west France. She was written to and in her reply she stressed that not enough notice had been taken at the time of the kind of person Ruth Ellis was. Little mention had been made of her taking drugs.

This information was stored away, only to be resurrected a few days later whilst dining with Dr William Sargant, the famous psychiatrist, who had done more than anyone else in the world to bring the mentally sick out of the revolting Victorian asylums to live as out-patients rather than merely exist on large doses of Largactyl.

His books *Battle for the Mind* and *The Mind Possessed* are both best-sellers. Dr Sargant had absolutely no idea of what Van den Bergh was writing, because as far as he was concerned, the author was a medical journalist with his own radio series: *New Lifelines In Medicine*.

He began talking about injustice and how he believed that judges, having spent most of their lives cosseted in the cotton wool of the legal profession, should not be allowed to inflict sentences on people whom they could not begin to understand. As an outstanding example he cited Ruth Ellis, saying that his partner, the late Dr T. P. Rees, had treated Ruth Ellis for mental illness and that he had been amazed that she had not been called to give evidence in her defence, for according to Dr Sargant if she had been taking drugs and then given pastis by her 'alternative' lover,

Desmond Cussen, she would not have been responsible for her actions.

On the last day of her life, Ruth Ellis had discharged her solicitor, Mr John Bickford, after a most acrimonious scene. She had then turned to the solicitor who had handled her divorce from George Ellis, Mr Victor Mishcon. His clerk, Mr Simmons, had in fact dealt with her and for him she had the greatest respect, and it was to him she wrote the last letter of her life.

Naturally, Van den Bergh went to visit Mr Mishcon and was delighted to discover that they had met previously when the former had written an article for the Jewish Board of Guardians, of which the solicitor was a member. This made his investigation as to what happened at those last moments much simpler.

Studying the trial transcript it was learned that she had been prosecuted by Mr Christmas Humphreys, later to become a judge. Many years earlier Messrs Humphreys and Van den Bergh had, in fact, edited an anthology of poems.

Humphreys explained that as far as the prosecution was concerned there was really only one question of importance. This he put directly to Ruth Ellis: 'Mrs Ellis, when you fired that revolver at close range into the body of David Blakely, what did you intend to do?' Her answer: '. . . I intended to kill him', settled the prosecution's case. Today, Mr Humphreys has little sympathy for Ruth Ellis. He says it was one of the most cold-blooded murders in which he was the prosecuting counsel.

For many years Hugh Oloff de Wet, the sculptor of the author's closest friend – now alas dead – had lived in a studio in Church Street, Kensington. He paid no rent and this he owed entirely to Conrad Nockolds, a commercial photographer of great kindness and generosity. Conrad had for a time concentrated his abilities on photographing racing cars, as his brother Ray, a superlative artist, painted them and the third brother, Harold, wrote about them as editor of a motor magazine. Conrad 'Twinky' Nockolds was fascinated by the author's project.

'You must go and see my sister Gwen,' he said. 'She was the manageress of the Steering Wheel Club at the time of the murder. Only a few nights before she had thrown Blakely and Ellis out of the club following a row, which culminated in Blakely punching his companion in the face.'

Gwen Nockolds was one of several witnesses to Blakely's assault of Ruth Ellis, and she was surprised not to be called to give evidence for the defence. Gwen was also an old friend, but she preferred not to talk about the instance, saying that she felt everyone connected with the case was so grubby that she wanted to hear no more about them. Following the investigations the authors knew exactly what she had meant.

The next coincidence must have been the most remarkable. Van den Bergh was staying with friends at their home in the New Forest. The hostess's daughter was ill and on the Sunday the local Catholic parish priest came in to administer her communion. Afterwards he chatted over a glass of wine with the author. He had absolutely no idea who Van den Bergh was or that he was researching the case of Ruth Ellis.

The priest said that he had been a prison chaplain for some years. Then he related how one of the saddest moments of his life had been when he had sat on a Home Office committee to decide whether Ruth Ellis was fit to hang! On the committee had been a Home Office psychiatrist, a civil servant and himself. He had been outvoted and she hanged.

Van den Bergh had known several of the afternoon drinking clubs, and had several times met Morris 'Maury' Conley, the man who put Ruth into one of his clubs as manageress. He was an unprepossessing creature who had more than one conviction for living off immoral earnings. If he could be found he would make an interesting contributor to the programme.

The author explains: 'Some years ago I was writing an interview for a radio series, *It Takes All Sorts*. One of my subjects had been Tony Frith, the button queen, who, at that time, had the smallest shop in London, just off Carnaby Street. There she sold buttons, many of great historical value. Now she had moved into a larger premises off Wigmore Street. We had kept in touch and one afternoon she and I were drinking coffee outside a street café when we were joined by one of her friends, a total stranger to me. In conversation the stranger learned about my interest in Conley. "That's easy," she said, "he lives in the same block as I do."'

When more was learned about the story of the love between Ruth Ellis and David Blakely, it was realized how tremendously motivated she was by jealousy. Certainly she had sound cause for it, for he had many lovers. His parents lived in Penn, Buckinghamshire, where he had embarked on an affair with a married woman.

This was yet another in the long line of coincidences, for not only did Van den Bergh's parents live at Penn, but he had met and married his wife in the village and they had lived the first four years of their lives together in a charming Tudor cottage there.

In the BBC office which Van den Bergh was allowed to use by grace of Allan Burgess, a producer, was a board with a list of programmes in production. Although Bob Craddock was to be the producer for The Ruth Ellis Story, the programme was listed under the name of Tony Van den Bergh. Also for the *It Takes All Sorts* series, the author was interviewing Heather Jenner, the doyenne of marriage bureaux proprietresses. She walked into the BBC office in use by Van den Bergh and glanced at the notice board. 'Ruth Ellis!' she exclaimed. 'Well, you must come and see my hairdresser. He supplied the peroxide to dress her hair for her trial.'

This was not unimportant. The defence depended almost entirely on the impression the defendant made in the witness box. By the time of the trial her hair had lost its brash peroxide blondness. But the hairdresser was allowed in so that Ruth appeared as the archetypal brassy tart. It did nothing to help her case.

By this time Laurence Marks's feature had appeared in a magazine and he was now concentrating his efforts on getting a television drama of the case into production. So, one year after the two had begun separate researches, they met for the first time and swapped notes. Many were identical. Some were unbeknown to each other. It was suggested by their agent that the two of them should go away and write a true account of what *really* happened in the strange, fated, and mixed-up life of Ruth Ellis.

Together they went to meet Ruth's sister, Muriel, who had looked after Ruth in their early teens. Muriel proved to be a delightful woman, entirely loyal to her sister's memory. She knows the coincidences mentioned in these pages and clearly believes the real story of Ruth Ellis should be told and that those who were largely to blame for the tragedy should not escape their share of the limelight.

To her we say, we have done our utmost.

Tony Van den Bergh and Laurence Marks.
January 1977.

1

The body of Ruth Ellis, the last woman to be hanged in the United Kingdom, today rests in the country graveyard of St Mary's parish church at the old town of Amersham in a valley of the Chilterns.

But her mortal remains have not been moved from her first sepulchre in the grounds of grim Holloway prison because the sense of public outrage had belatedly percolated through into the consciences of the Home Office hierarchy. On the contrary, from the outset of her trial, it was patently clear that the then Home Secretary, Major Gwilym Lloyd George, and his senior civil service officials were intent not only on her being found guilty, but on the retributional aspect of maintaining a death penalty; a macabre hangover from past centuries.

The murder had been enacted during a period in which the anti-hanging brigade, led by the dedicated Mrs Van der Elst, were campaigning raucously to sweep away what they believed to be a medieval obscenity.

The Home Secretary appeared totally convinced that any show of mercy might be interpreted as weakness; as giving way to new, untried theories. He was backed up by the whole Establishment who – no doubt equally sincerely – were convinced that if the death penalty, which they visualized as the ultimate deterrent, were swept away, the floodgates would be open for violence if not mass murder.

Their contention was that if the blonde, drinking club hostess was spared, then inevitably the next woman found guilty of murder would also be pardoned . . . and the next. They also believed that from there the next small step would be to the reprieve of male killers. The Victorian concept, of the virtue of punishment for punishment's sake, still prevailed.

At that time anyone who was sentenced to death came before a special committee – a secret committee – appointed by the Home Secretary himself. The committee's function was to consider all aspects of the case and also to examine the mental state of the convicted felon. They would then recommend to the Home Secretary whether or not he should advise the Sovereign to show clemency. The theory was sound. The practice, however, proved pragmatic rather than idealistic. Small committees can be 'carefully selected'. Dr William Sargant, former head of the Department of Psychology at St Thomas's Hospital, and author of *Battle for the Mind* and *The Mind Possessed*, claims that if a psychiatrist chosen to sit on these committees revealed overmuch sensitivity towards the accused's mental state, he was never again invited. Instead, doctors who could be 'relied on' to dowse any pangs of conscience were appointed in their places. The felon under examination rarely escaped the noose. Those psychiatrists who claimed that in many cases the offender was mentally ill rather than wantonly criminal were blacklisted.

So it was that when the Home Office committee of three met to consider whether Ruth Ellis should live or die, the chairman was a Home Office official, the psychiatrist 'reliable' as far as the pro-hangers were concerned, and the third member must have proved a disappointment to those who appointed him for he urged clemency, but was, not surprisingly, outvoted by the other two.

Now her only chance of reprieve lay with the Home Secretary. But on the eve of her execution, when solicitor Victor Mishcon had taken over the case from John Bickford at the condemned's urgent request, the brave Major was conveniently studying form at a race meeting. Even the senior civil servant at the Home Office was unavoidably absent from his office and when Victor Mishcon and his clerk, Mr Simmons, went to make the last possible appeal, they found nobody with the authority to take any positive action at the Home Office. It must have been like trying to wrestle with an octopus. Unfortunately the prize for the winner meant life or death to the girl (for she was little more than that) who sat in the condemned cell.

So Ruth Ellis was hanged. Most of the ordinary people in Britain plus the executioner, Albert Pierrepoint, were shocked, disgusted and many of them felt a personal share in the guilt engendered. Nevertheless, despite the controversy which has raged ever since, Ruth Ellis's grave in Amersham has attracted meagre attention. The reason is easy to establish. On the headstone is carved the name: Ruth Hornby. Few people would associate 'Hornby' with the woman who fired four bullets into her lover outside the Magdala public house in the respectable north London suburb of Hampstead. That her grave is not overgrown and neglected is due solely to the regular visits and care of her elder sister Muriel, and Muriel's two daughters, Marlene and Pauline.

The only reason that permission was given for the removal of the body from Holloway to the rolling Buckinghamshire country-side was the rebuilding of the prison. It would have been embarrassing if the bulldozers had disinterred such remains.

A new sense of enlightenment, coupled with the urging of penal reformers, has now, at last, persuaded those who rule over the ever-growing prison population, that Holloway should be trans-formed into a hospital to house women offenders. Over seven hundred and fifty women are incarcerated in Holloway – about half the total number sent to prison in the whole country. Mrs Wing, a former governor, once estimated that the public needed protection from only thirty or forty of those under her charge; the rest of the inmates were either inadequate, mentally or physically handicapped or defective, or were the outcome of appalling en-vironments. So, reluctantly, those who, like the Victorian upper classes, believed in retribution, gave way. Holloway is in the process of being rebuilt, though whether it can ever shed the memories or exorcize the shades of the pitiful women who were hanged there is an entirely different question. Certainly nobody who served on the staff at the time of the execution of Edith Thompson or Ruth Ellis will ever be the same again.

When permission was given for the disinterment, Ruth's il-legitimate son, Andy Clare, was her next of kin. He it was who decided that she should be reinterred under her maiden name of Hornby, rather than Ellis or her family name, Neilson. Her sister Muriel, brother Granville, and their families, however, still hope that one day her real name will be inscribed over her grave. Ruth Ellis was outspoken. Brash but honest. She would never have wished for her identity to be hidden.

Today psychologists, psychiatrists, and sociologists are forever arguing whether genes, inherited from parents, or environment

9

have the greatest influence on a person's character and life. However, not even the most ardent geneticist would disagree that to a large extent the life in the home during childhood can mould the future adult's personality and approach to work and pleasure. So it is important, if one is going to understand Ruth Ellis and why she killed in a mania of jealousy, to appreciate her background and the insecurity of the years in which she grew from child to womanhood.

Ruth Ellis's paternal grandfather was a well-known Manchester-based musician. He not only taught the piano but also played the organ in the cathedral. His was a middle-class family who had made their money out of weaving. His son – Ruth Ellis's father – Arthur Hornby, became a talented cellist. When Ruth was born the large orchestras were seeing the end of a halcyon period. Conductors of jazz bands were household names: Harry Roy, Roy Fox, Carrol Gibbons, Geraldo, Billy Cotton and Ernie 'Snake Hips' Johnson.

At a slightly higher stratum, small groups of highly talented musicians played 'palm court' music for afternoon teas in the larger hotels or in clubs for the now forgotten *thé dansants*. Such groups also played in cinemas to help create the apt moods for the silent films. 'The March of the Gladiators' often heralded violent action, whilst 'Hearts and Flowers' warned of a sentimental episode and much eyelash fluttering.

A good musician was seldom out of work. Arthur Hornby was a good musician and so long as he was prepared to travel, earning a living for his family had not been difficult. This golden age for musicians did not grind to a halt. Al Jolson, crooning 'Sonny Boy' in *The Singing Fool* from what was inaccurately described as the silver screen, almost stopped it in mid-note. When the cinema managers dismissed their players, Ruth Ellis's father was ill-prepared to cope with the stresses and uncertainties of poverty. This might not have mattered overmuch, for he was often away, had his wife been practical and efficient. But Bertha, Ruth's mother, was even less equipped to deal with difficulties.

She was half-French, half-Belgian. Her mother had died when she was only two. Living at different times in Brussels, Antwerp, and Liège, she had been raised by nuns. She was a Catholic Jewess, as is reflected by the names of her three aunts who were her only relatives: Rachel, Miriam, and Olga. When the Germans invaded Belgium at the outset of the First World War she became a refugee. In a small boat she was brought to England, wrapped only in a blanket and without shoes.

To say that she was ill-prepared to face life, let alone to deal with a family when money was short and her husband out of work, would be a gross understatement. Her religious grounding had been so strict and traditionally Catholic that when her own daughters grew up, she was incapable of explaining even the simplest fact of life. It is hardly surprising that after the execution of her daughter, Ruth, she should lose interest in life and should exist today in a home for the mentally ill.

When she married Arthur Hornby, he was a kind, considerate man. He was successful, with much self-respect. But out of work, his pride bruised, he became churlish and bad-tempered. Often he was violent.

After she had come to England, Bertha had worked at the only job available to foreign girls without specific qualifications. She had gone 'into service'. It is rather surprising that Arthur Hornby had married someone so unsuited to his way of life.

This ill-matched pair had six children. The eldest, Julian, was to die in the mid-sixties from wounds received in the Second World War. The second child was Muriel, who for reasons which will follow, became for all intents and purposes 'mother' to the younger children. Granville, 'Jim', was the next in line. He loved Ruth deeply and on the very last night of her life went in search of her wealthy lover who, he believed, was responsible to a large extent for the killing. Granville hoped that he could persuade the man, Desmond Cussen, to give fresh evidence to the Home Secretary and so secure a stay of execution.

Ruth was the next child, being born on 9 October 1926. In her drinking club years she would often claim – jokingly – that she was a Mancunian, being conceived in Manchester, though born in Rhyl. The reason that the family moved from the Lancashire industrial town to the North Wales sea-side resort was that Granville contracted sleeping sickness. The family doctor recommended sea air. With work growing more of a rarity, one outlet for musicians was the cruising ships on which small orchestras entertained the holiday-makers. Rhyl was conveniently near to

11

Liverpool, from which the cruisers sailed for the Canaries and North Africa.

The fifth child, Jackie, died when only eighteen months old. The last infant was Elizabeth who, being brought up in infancy sleeping in damp air-raid shelters during the Blitz, contracted asthma. She died only three months after Ruth's execution and though the death certificate may have stated the cause of death as 'cardiac failure following asthma', her sister, Muriel, to this day believes a broken heart was the cause.

Many actors and musicians, clowns and music hall artists, have assumed sobriquets, feeling that perhaps their baptismal names and surnames were too banal or unromantic to grace an artistic performer. Few film stars have succeeded under their own names. It was, no doubt, for this reason that Ruth Ellis's father, though retaining his Christian name of Arthur, took Neilson as his surname, and it was as Ruth Neilson that his second daughter was registered at birth.

Ruth's first home was at 74 West Parade, Rhyl, a holiday town which was to make the headlines over forty years later, when James Hanratty, who was later to be hanged for the A6 murder, sited his alibi in a lodging house in a narrow lane on the hillside of the town.

Muriel was five years old when the family moved to Rhyl. She was sent to the local elementary school, where she was joined five years later by younger sister, Ruth. The children seldom saw their parents, for Arthur Hornby had to travel to find work and whenever possible his wife would join him. So it fell to Muriel, though little more than a child, to play the part of housekeeper and mother to the family. She dressed, washed, and fed little Ruth, who at that time showed few signs of the pretty woman she was to become. She was myopic, which caused her to wear glasses from an early age, and pudgy.

They may have stayed in Rhyl indefinitely had Arthur Hornby not found work which offered security playing in a cinema at Basingstoke in Hampshire. It was work he might formerly have rejected, but now he accepted with alacrity. The family followed him to Basingstoke where they lived in a variety of homes. But although he had gladly accepted the work, he felt it beneath his talent. Frustrated and bitter, whereas many men might have turned to drink for solace, Arthur Hornby turned on his wife and children. He ordered, argued, and berated them all. He used his fists on his wife, sons, and eldest daughter. Ruth was fortunate, because Muriel would interpose between her father and her sister whenever he was in one of his rages.

Muriel herself was showing signs of becoming a beauty, and this seemed to enrage him even more, so that she suffered not only violence but considerable indignities from him. When he lost his job at the cinema he became even more demented. The two girls found their days at Fairfields Senior Girls School a relief from home life, so that both were reasonably happy, Muriel leaving when she turned fourteen. At home it was row after row, little food, and no money for pleasure. Their mother reverted to her convent days, doing little except knit, crochet, and pray, though she occasionally occupied herself in good works looking after invalids in the locality.

Under his professional alias, Arthur Neilson found work at last. It was not as a musician, let alone a cellist. Park Prewett Mental Hospital needed a telephonist-cum-hall-porter. He applied and was briefly grateful for the job. With her father irrational and her mother opting out of life, now more than ever Muriel had to accept total responsibility. Certainly she sacrificed herself to the family. Ruth was the most difficult of her charges. The younger girl was now showing clear signs of precociousness. She was cheeky and resented discipline. When out with her brothers and sisters she would run off without warning. Muriel, for her pains, would be torn between wanting to go after her and having to stay as guardian to the younger members. No one ever found out where Ruth went, and, if questioned, she would become sullen and refuse to explain. As for Muriel, when she returned without her younger sister, her father would fly into a rage, abuse her, and even on occasion strike her. She grew to hate and fear Arthur Hornby.

Naturally these scenes could not be kept secret. Neighbours became aware of what was going on and watched with interest from behind their lace curtains. The angry father noticed the movements in the windows and would swear at the onlookers. But though he pretended not to care what they thought of him, he was basically a sensitive man, and he solved the problem by moving.

13

But wherever they went, a similar situation arose. As a result the family never had a settled home, and this insecurity no doubt had its effect on Ruth's development. Eventually they took a house way out of town where there were no neighbours to interfere.

Unfortunately, even then, he did not confine his ill temper to the family. He spoke sharply to the relatives of patients in hospital who telephoned to make inquiries after their sick ones. They complained. Doctors and nurses were antagonized by his moroseness. It was not surprising that he was discharged.

By now war had been declared. Many companies, fearing air-raids, moved further afield. As a result Hornby was able to find work as a caretaker in Reading. This was another step down the social ladder and it did little to raise his spirits.

Ruth, now fifteen, hated her home and had little respect for her parents. Leaving school, she started work as a waitress. This took her out of the repressive atmosphere of the home and brought her into contact with people who, generally, were amused by her chattiness and pertness. But for Muriel there was no escape. Her mother could not begin to cope with the family, so sheer force made her remain at home as 'mother' to the other children.

There was no jealousy in Muriel's heart as she watched her younger sister blossom out into an attractive if slightly brassy woman. Already Ruth had several boy-friends and most likely had already had a first lover. Her earliest serious affair was with a Scot, Bill Bailey, who often boasted of his 'castle' on his Highland estate. These efforts to impress Ruth were doomed to failure. She merely laughed at him.

Muriel, five years older, had no affairs. However, she had met and fallen in love with a man who was to become a successful engineer. His origins were Lithuanian and his family were East End cabinet-makers. He must have been a very patient man, because four years were to pass before Muriel could break out of the tentacles of the family octopus, which enmeshed her so tightly. Arthur Hornby took his eldest daughter's sacrifice for granted. Why should he have to pay for any help for his wife when Muriel was strong, if not willing?

In 1941, Arthur Hornby's fortunes took a decided turn for the better. He got work in London as a chauffeur centred in South-wark, where he was provided with a flat. He would be alone in

London and there were two large rooms at the flat. Naturally, Ruth leapt at the chance of moving to London, despite the considerable dangers of air-raids. She had one close friend, a rather coarse girl called 'Mac'. At first her father refused to allow her to bring her friend with her, but eventually gave way. Unfortunately his decision was not selfless, for his wife, paying an unheralded visit, found her husband and Mac in what the popular press could have described as a 'compromising situation'. For once the wife acted decisively. She threw Mac's suitcase out of the window and the girl through the door. For once Arthur Hornby was the silent partner.

Deciding that her husband was not to be trusted on his own, Bertha moved to London to look after him, leaving Muriel once again to act as substitute mother. Eventually, after a further three months, Muriel was allowed to follow and so the family were once again united. Muriel was at last free to live a life of her own. She found work in a munitions factory, where she was later joined by Ruth.

Ruth had now shed all her puppy-fat. She was still myopic but was so vain that she refused to wear glasses. Her hair was growing darker, and she resorted to the peroxide bottle to remedy this. For the rest of her short life she was to be inordinately proud of her peroxide blonde hair. She believed the popular saying that 'gentlemen prefer blondes'. It would not be an exaggeration to say that her fixation to remain blonde was a contributory factor to the poor impression she made when giving evidence at her trial.

With Mac departed, Ruth turned to Muriel for company. Her elder sister could make up a foursome without endangering Ruth's role as queen. They went to dance clubs and south London cafés and restaurants. Often Muriel had to wait on street corners late at night while her younger sister courted in various doorways. Sometimes Ruth would tell her sister to go home alone and to cover for her until she returned when dawn was breaking. When Muriel, still pathetically innocent, complained of Ruth's behaviour, Ruth would jeer at her and mock her virgin state. She would tell Muriel: 'You may be my elder sister, but I'm ten bloody years older than you in experience.' There is little doubt she was telling the truth.

When the Blitz broke on London from the skies, Southwark was a major recipient of the bombs as the Nazi pilots followed the river to the centre of the capital. The Ellis house received a direct hit, and Ruth, returning home from a party, dug her father out of the rubble. She saved his life but not his health. Arthur Hornby never again worked full-time. After a short period during which the family split up in various lodgings, they eventually found a home at 19 Farmers Road in Camberwell.

Tragedy had not finished with the Hornby family. Julian, the eldest son, had been called up. He was severely wounded and although he survived, he was to die from his wounds twenty-six years later. Now the earnings of the daughters were of vital importance to the family, for Granville was also serving in His Majesty's army. He too was wounded. Shot in the eye, he was taken prisoner and was to spend the rest of the war in German POW camps.

The munitions work was noisy and allowed little time for social contact. That certainly did not suit young Ruth, who, on the excuse to her family that she should earn more money, gave in her notice and went to work in the Oxo factory in Southwark. But for her, work was only a filling-in period between parties, flirtations, and affairs. She was dancing mad. Every night while the rest of the family sought shelter in the underground stations, Ruth was out living dangerously and not caring whether or not she was courting tragedy. She would say: 'A short life and a gay one,' whenever anyone tried to reproach her. Her words were to prove ironically prophetic.

Yet another member of the family was to suffer from the war, for the youngest daughter contracted asthma. But Ruth remained untouched. London was thronged by Allied soldiers, many of whom – especially the GIs – had money to burn. They were greedy for excitement as an emetic after fear and watching friends die on the battlefield. They needed companionship and sex. Ruth was pretty, gay and confident. She thought she knew everything. Night after night she stayed out until the early hours. Some nights she did not return home. Her friends took her dancing and to restaurants and clubs in the West End. This she looked upon as *really* living. Few soldiers have strict morals when they are far from home. There is little doubt that Ruth Ellis was a most sought-after girl.

However, nature took its revenge. She contracted rheumatic

fever – acute rheumatic arthritis. This condition is not necessarily very serious, but it is debilitating and needs long treatment. She became an in-patient at St Giles Hospital, Camberwell. Altogether she remained in bed over eight weeks. Often doctors give advice which they believe will benefit their patient, but which can well become an excuse for what the patient wants to do. The young houseman, no doubt attracted by her gaiety even when feeling unwell, recommended that on her discharge she should try and take as much exercise as possible. Exercise? What better exercise is there than dancing? So Ruth Ellis started dancing. We all accept advice readily when it fits in with our own wishes.

So, on her discharge, she became a dancing *aficionado*. Hair peroxided, glasses abandoned, with her sensual but slim figure, she had no difficulty finding servicemen to take her to dance clubs.

Factory work seemed beneath her now. Men kept asking whether she was a professional dancer or if she were on the stage. Ruth inhaled their words. Although without any stage experience, she left her work and enrolled at a small drama school at Richmond. But the drama school required fees to keep solvent, and Ruth was no longer a wage-earner. For a short time she managed to find evening work singing with a band. The pay was meagre, but she felt herself a star and relished being the centre of attraction. Her voice was not at all bad, but there is little evidence of any substantial talent. When the band moved on, she took work as an usherette in a cinema. That, too, lasted only a matter of weeks. The work was not exciting enough to retain her interest. Then she was employed as a photographer's assistant. This was much more to her taste. She liked the importance of telling people where and how to stand.

One of her assignments was to help photograph dancers at the Streatham Locarno ballroom. Afterwards she would take orders from couples who liked the results. It was at the Locarno that Ruth met a young French–Canadian soldier, Clare. It was a brittle affair. He was a long way from home and was immediately enchanted by the blonde, well-busted Londoner. She was swept off her feet by his natural pugnacity and his determination to get whatever he wanted. He had money to spend and delighted in showing her what she considered to be a 'good time'. Ruth

17

accepted straight away that he would expect her to sleep with him; indeed, it is probable that she initiated the affair. He told her many tales about the beauty of his native Canada, but omitted to tell her of his wife and three children waiting for him at home. Ruth genuinely believed he would take her back to Canada with him when the war was over.

Ruth was so confident as to the future, that she took Clare home with her to meet her family. Everyone liked the young soldier and nothing was done to put any obstacle in her way. The fact that he was a Catholic reassured any doubts her mother might have harboured. With memories of her own upbringing by the Belgian nuns, she believed everything he told her.

Bertha cannot be blamed for misplacing her confidence. Clare was most convincing. Yet, the Canadian was hardly an outstanding romantic figure. He was short and stocky, but full of confidence verging on the arrogant. Like so many servicemen far from home, he spent generously. Although not as well paid as the American GIs, he was able to spend more freely than his British counterparts. He made women feel that he respected their opinion, for he was experienced and had learned the value of listening as well as talking.

Naturally, in war-torn London, there were hundreds upon thousands of romances which were based on little more than mutual sexual attraction. But there is little doubt that, even though it eventually proved to be transitory, Ruth Neilson and the Canadian soldier were genuinely in love. He was completely captivated by her youth and enthusiasm for life as well as her pertness; she by his air of authority and generosity. Whatever Ruth admired in the West End shop windows, Clare bought for her without hesitation. Dresses. Jewellery. Flowers, especially red carnations. The latter were to become a theme of her life and, indeed, would even be associated with her after her body was cold.

Bertha was ill-equipped by her education and environment to advise, let alone control, so high-spirited a daughter. Ruth's mother could talk of heaven and the rules of the Church, but little of life and certainly nothing of contraception. Almost inevitably, Ruth became pregnant. It was a fearful shock to her, for she told herself repeatedly that although others might 'fall', it would not happen to her. Young girls frequently place their faith in a fairy

18

godmother who doesn't exist. It was by no means to be Ruth's only pregnancy.

In her fear, she asked herself whether there was any reason why Clare should not marry her. She was seventeen, old enough to be married. He was ten years older and as far as she was concerned there was no reason for his commanding officer to withhold his permission for their marriage. But she was nervous when she broached the subject to Clare. She told him that her parents, far from objecting, saw it as an ideal solution. Not only did they like the Canadian, but Bertha, as a Catholic, was horrified at the concept of an illegitimate child. Clare appeared enthusiastic. He would approach his CO that very week.

Apparently the CO raised no objections, so Ruth began to make arrangements as to what she would wear and where they would be married. However, whenever she tried to fix the date, Clare had to plead that he was under orders and, what is more, he wanted to have a real honeymoon and that meant arranging leave.

It is somewhat odd that it was the unworldly Bertha who first felt the gnawings of doubt. If confirmation as to his freedom to marry were so tardy, then she would write to the commanding officer herself. She would not tell the happy couple what she was doing. The CO's permission would come as a welcome surprise for them. The commanding officer's reply to her inquiry exploded the family's complacency. Clare was not only married, but had three children in Canada.

Ruth, feeling not only cheated but cheap, attacked her erstwhile fiancé violently. Clare did his utmost to placate her.

'Yes, I'm a married man. I didn't like to admit it because I love you so much. Can't you understand that? But I'm glad it's out in the open now. I don't love my wife; I never have. Of course, I'll look after the kids, but I'll divorce her. It's you I love. Surely you know that. We'll get married, even though it may take a little time . . .'

While Bertha was aghast at the realization that even if Clare meant what he said, her grandchild would be born out of wedlock, Arthur, her husband, by now an invalid and almost totally self-centred, took the news as yet another blow by fate aimed entirely against him. Muriel alone offered comfort and reassurance.

Ruth might well have accepted her fiancé's protestations

because, afraid of being thought an innocent, she desperately wanted to believe him. But the whole problem was taken out of her hands when one morning the florist delivered a large bunch of red carnations and a letter. Both had been dispatched from the ship taking Clare back to Canada. Perhaps it was a routine posting. More likely the CO had decided to extricate one of his soldiers from a web of Clare's own weaving. No doubt the officer told himself that once back home Clare would forget Ruth, besides which there was nothing rare in girls bearing unwanted children at that time.

Rather surprisingly, Clare sent Ruth money for the birth so as she should keep the child. This went on for over a year. Then the money stopped. Ruth heard no more. Perhaps by this time she had become for him an overseas episode which he preferred to forget. So Ruth went back to work as a cashier whilst she waited for her child to be born. But it was only a makeshift arrangement, for her waist was beginning to expand. For the last month she stayed with Muriel, who by then had two sons and a daughter of her own. In fact, she was to bear five children in four years. With Muriel's family filling the house, Bertha and Arthur Hornby had moved into furnished rooms close by.

Ruth went for advice to a social society which looked after and tried to help unmarried mothers. It was a time when London was emptying of anyone whose work was not essential to the war effort, so Ruth was dispatched north, to have her baby at Gilsland Nursing Home some eighteen miles from Carlisle. This had the advantage of taking her away from London and the amused and malicious comments of her former friends in the club world. In Northumberland, no one knew her and she was able to tell anyone who inquired that her husband, an American pilot, had been killed only two months after their wedding. Her son, whom she christened Clare Andrea, was to be called by his family the more prosaic name of Andy; and Andy he remains to this day.

Returning to London, she was nervous when she took her newborn child for her parents to see. She had good reason. Her father turned his back and her mother cried. But by now Muriel was the mother of two sons and a daughter, Pauline. Muriel welcomed her sister and admired the robust little boy. It was just as well she took to the child because she was to spend more time looking after him

20

than his mother. Ruth would never have admitted to herself for a moment that she was using her sister, but she noted the warmth of Muriel's welcome and realized that here was a home where she could safely leave Andy. She was still young enough to shrug off the past and dismiss as a nightmare anything which might cause her embarrassment.

Her figure soon returned to normal, in fact her breasts were now a little fuller and more voluptuous. She noted how men eyed her as she passed them in the street. Men would often find excuses to speak to her. She was amused at the obviousness of their approaches. She had spent enough time in the clubs to appreciate that many men were prepared to pay for sex, and though she was no whore, she could not see why she should not capitalize on an activity which she enjoyed so fully herself. She kept telling herself that she would go back to being a hostess, but it was difficult to do that and feed her child.

It was an advertisement in a local newspaper which started her on her new career: a career which was eventually to lead her to heartbreak, murder, and the gallows. Many of the greatest tragedies of literature have a prevailing sense of inevitability about them. From the first page the reader realizes that there can be no escape from the eventual tragedy. It is almost as if a metronome were started which would tick away the moments until the characters at last destroyed themselves. Twist endings seldom happen except in comedies. So it was with Ruth. Her story was, indeed, to be tragic, and from the moment she read the advertisement she was committed to her own destruction.

Wanted. Model for Camera Club. Nude but artistic poses. No experience required. Highest references available. Confidential.

Ruth enjoyed the admiration of men, so why not? She was no prude and she had been to parties where nudity had been accepted. She applied for an interview. She stripped without embarrassment in front of three club members who watched intently. She was engaged on the spot. They forgot about the references.

Far from being in the least shame-faced, she found it exhilarating to pose nude before seven or eight men at a time. She smiled at the hunger in their eyes as they tried to conceal their emotions behind a camera. She relished the sense of power she derived from making them ask her to turn towards them so they could get 'artistic' photographs. The fact that most of the 'photographers' had no film in their cameras was neither here nor there. If they tried to press her to go out with them, she laughed at them, telling the others aloud what had been whispered into her ear. If any of them mauled her, she would stare straight into their eyes making no effort to conceal her contempt. Then she would laugh and make a joke about it to the others. Many of the photographers grew to hate her, but even though they might, they still could not resist her blatant physical attractions.

If any of them were young and attractive – and the combination was rare at the Camera Club because such men did not have to stoop to such devices to get female companionship – she would accept their offer. She would go out dancing and dining. She would kiss them and allow a farewell fumble in the taxi on the way home. That was as much as she would allow until she had recovered from the memory of Clare. Later, when she was a fully fledged club hostess, she would laugh at her seventeen-year-old puritanism.

Morris 'Maury' Conley was a club owner. He had no need to pretend to be an enthusiastic photographer to see girls in the nude. However, he was a dealer in flesh and found such clubs fertile sources of merchandise. So it was that he visited the Camera Club, saw Ruth, and was impressed by what he saw. He noticed not only the fullness of her figure, but also the aplomb with which she handled the aggressive photographers. He was not interested in her as a model, but realized at first sight that she could well become an asset to him in one of the four clubs he owned – and his other activities! He invited Ruth to meet him for a drink that very night at his Carroll's Club in Duke Street. Although he was a most unprepossessing specimen, Ruth had been told by the secretary of the Camera Club that Conley was a most influential impresario in clubland. So, without hesitation, she accepted.

Maury Conley was no stranger to trouble or prison. His record was followed with interest by the Press. In 1936, when only 34 years old, he went to a charity gambling house with £8 and by the end of the evening was £342 the richer. Four days later he closed his West End shop – Caplan and Conley Costumiers – went bankrupt and made £10,000 out of his failure. A few days after the closing of his business about £700 worth of raw skins were found in his father's cellar in Stepney. Conley's explanation was that he had put them there as a surety for a loan of £1000 from his father. Whether or not this was true, it certainly made Conley very rich. But Conley was not the type of man to keep a good old-fashioned 'fraud' to himself and soon it was known in his social circles that the closure of his shops had made him an immense amount of cash. Unfortunately not only his social circle heard of it. The trustees of his bankruptcy case had their ears open. They made inquiries for seven months, and then charges under the Bankruptcy Acts were made against him.

He appeared at the Old Bailey and after a week-long trial, Maury Conley must have thought the gods were smiling on him. Twice the jury returned unable to agree on a verdict. The third time Conley's luck ran out. He was found guilty of fraud and sentenced to two years' imprisonment. This experience did not deter his activities and he was soon back in unethical action again. He became a pioneer in making one-arm bandits work for him.

At West London magistrates' court, Chief Inspector Bye told the bench that the gaming machines supplied by Maury Conley were 'so rigged that the jackpot could never be won if the machines were played on for a hundred years'. Conley was returned to prison for a further four months.

Bankruptcy, fraud, and gambling machines were innocent occupations compared to his other activities. In 1956, Duncan Webb, crusading crime reporter, named Conley in the *People* as: 'The vice boss.' The article began: 'Right at the centre of corruption in the West End of London stands the figure of Morris Conley.' He goes on to say: 'I hereby name him as Britain's biggest vice boss and the source of tainted money which nourishes London's night life.' Webb described Conley as: 'A monster with the Mayfair touch.'

Conley, behind the façade of being a smooth, jolly, middle-aged night-club king and darling of society, was, in fact, running an immensely profitable vice racket. According to Duncan Webb, Conley foresaw a modern trend in that business executives enjoyed visiting massage parlours where as often as not the customer massaged the masseuse instead of vice versa.

Whilst researching for this article, Duncan Webb witnessed at first hand the ferocity of Conley's viperous reaction to danger. Seeing a photographer taking a photograph outside the flat of one of his female agents, he leapt from a taxi, strode across the crowded pavement, and launched a savage attack on the pressman. Conley settled this little contretemps out of court.

After Ruth Ellis's execution, the interest of the vice squad into his activities resulted in his having to close the Little Club and the Hollywood Club. Subsequently he appeared in court for running a brothel and was fined £100 and twenty guineas costs. When charged Conley said: 'I did not know what was going on.' It would be interesting, if he were telling the truth, to learn where he got the £400 which was found in his pocket. It was stated in court that both clubs were known as the haunts of hostesses where they would sit with clients for £5 so long as they could also pay £3 for a bottle of champagne. The Little Club closed immediately after Duncan Webb's exposure, but not before the brash Conley had tried to sell it to band-leader Harry Roy for £15,000.

Some men and women do not set out intentionally to break the law. A series of circumstances arise which, if manipulated skilfully, will result in making the strategist wealthy. They act in what they believe to be a logical manner. Moral reservations do not enter their deliberations. Indeed, frequently the perpetrators are not even aware that they are doing anything which their fellow citizens might consider offensive or evil. Not everyone is born with a moral sense; is aware what is right and what is wrong. Some are able to ignore or turn a blind eye to any tiny shaft of conscience. Others have no conscience to grapple with. Perhaps the latter should be pitied more than condemned.

Unrest, lack of security, broken homes, and the need to change the whole approach to life and death impaired the judgement of those trying to re-adapt themselves to civilian life. Conditions created flocks of human sheep only too vulnerable to the manipulator and ready for shearing.

Morris 'Maury' Conley was a shearer. He would have been quite incapable of resisting the opportunities his shrewd mind detected in the turmoil of the post-war years. Hotels, houses, apartment blocks, flats, and factories stood mere shells, if they had not been completely destroyed. Many residential areas were little more than wasteland. The side streets of the capital were rubbed with broken kerbstone and brickwork. Servicemen were being reunited with their wives. WRNS, ATS and WRAF were either returning to their parents or were bringing their new husbands home. The first requirement of all these homeless ones was a roof over their heads.

Maury Conley watched the rebirth of London through his shrewd little eyes. He appreciated the problems and realized that fat profits could be amassed out of other people's distress. Someone would do it anyway. Why not him? So he became one of the first property developers. Indeed, it was men like Morris Conley who were to give this most necessary activity such a notoriety that decades later men of good will were to be unfairly branded.

He bought and negotiated for new blocks of flats. He patched up derelict buildings. With so many without homes such flats could be auctioned ... even if not in the respectable salesroom. Exorbitant rents could be charged to those whose desperation overruled their commonsense. Soon Maury Conley owned several West End establishments and, like others who were to become notorious in the fifties and sixties, he was not too particular in the methods he used to enforce payment, or the staff he employed to evict those who did not meet his conditions. This investment in property was the first link in his chain.

The second link was Maury Conley's appreciation that many would find routine civil life irksome. Some were bachelors, others married men who found settling down into home life a bore after being the liberators of France, Holland, Belgium, and the Nordic capitals where they had been received as conquering heroes and suitably fêted. Conley, as a property dealer, could readily find premises suitable for development in clubland. Soon he owned several clubs in the West End, each covering different opening hours.

The returned warriors wanted, if not needed, the hostesses who staffed the clubs. Providing the girls was, perhaps, the easiest link he had to forge to complete his chain of success. Girls also found peacetime London less exciting than the war years. Routine office work or plying potential customers with goods in shops could be both tiring and boring. The clubs offered them a tinsel attraction. No early morning work. Being paid for something they enjoyed doing. Maury Conley, as a club owner could bait his hook with the club attractions. He could also supply them with somewhere to live so long as they were ready to be accommodating. The rent for his flats would be far higher than any working girl could possibly afford, but he could ensure they would have ample opportunity for augmenting their wages and tips.

Maury Conley had an appetite for women and considered himself to be an experienced and ardent lover. He was certainly not sexually attractive to women, but if sleeping with the owner of the clubs resulted in having a flat, a reasonably well-paid job, tips, expenses, and free evening dresses, most of them found it a small price to pay.

It is quite probable that a substantial majority of his hostesses did not realize that in sleeping with the boss they were making the first moves into prostitution. Even after weeks at one of the clubs, by which time they had accepted that it was the done thing to take a club member home after closing time, they still would have rejected the word 'whore'. After all, it was their own business what they did. After all, it's a free country!

They were helped in their self-deception by the traditional behaviour pattern well-established in the relationship between hostess and club guest. They were not being paid for sex. That would have been selling themselves. Rather, they were being given a present for their company or a token of gratitude for being 'nice' to the man, who felt he was preserving his manliness if, instead of hiring a prostitute, he was only paying something towards the rent or to keep the girl's aged mother. After a few weeks, the hostesses lost their earlier misgivings and accepted it as a way of life. No longer would they suggest a tip afterwards; the price was negotiated before.

Ruth Neilson knew men. She liked and enjoyed them. By the time she went to work for Maury Conley she had few reservations and certainly no misconceptions as to the services she was expected to supply. At first, no doubt, she restricted herself to the members she liked. But her flat was expensive and she spent freely. So if a member wanted something a little more sophisticated than straight sex, she would consider it. The voyeurs – and many men do enjoy watching women make love – told each other of the blonde hostess who would always give them their money's worth.

One friend of Ruth, who had known her since the days she worked as a photographer's assistant, recalled how she visited Ruth and how she was taught the facts of club life. The girl had always envied Ruth's ability to be the centre of attraction. When they had gone out to dances together in the war years, Ruth had been able to stay on whilst she had had to go home to be in by eleven. They had kept in close touch even though their lives had gone different ways. Whilst Ruth had gone into club business, had married and divorced, she had married and had four children. Now she found herself disillusioned with married life. Leaving her children with her mother she visited the Little Club where Ruth was then manageress and living in the flat provided for her by Maury Conley over the club.

She was most impressed by the way the members treated Ruth and how the blonde manageress, whilst maintaining a bright if brittle conversation, still managed to see that the members' glasses were never empty and that each time one of them would buy a round. She noted how readily Ruth laughed at the anecdotes, however salacious, and how the men were seldom listening to the talker but usually clearly thinking about how they could cap the story. She listened to Ruth using language that would have graced a fishwife. Despite a puritanical upbringing, neither the language nor the tales shocked her. As the till rang again and again, she thought how wise Maury Conley, who was present, had been to promote her old friend to be manageress of his club.

Ruth respected her friend, knowing that her morals were on a higher plane than her own. When after the club had closed and the members and Conley had gone out into the night, her friend asked her why she should not become a hostess, Ruth just laughed as if the very idea was impossible.

'But why not? My figure has gone back to what it was despite my babies.'

'Your figure's smashing. But it's just not for you.'

'I'm just as pretty as you, aren't I?'

Ruth laughed. 'Not conceited are you!'

'I didn't mean it that way. But I do look OK?'

'You do. You look years younger than me though you're older.'

'Well, why not then? I can look after myself.'

'It's just not your line.'

'Why not? I can get them to buy drinks and listen to their stories just like you.'

'You're just not fit for it . . .'

The more Ruth tried to discourage her, the more she persisted. While they argued the radio blared out jazz, so they had to shout to each other to make themselves heard. Ruth always liked a noisy background.

At last Ruth became desperate. She strode across the room and with a somewhat dramatic gesture, switched off the radio. From above came the clear sounds of bedsprings under strain.

'There you are. That's why this life isn't for you.'

'But . . .'

28

'And Maury . . . what did you think of him?'

'He was horrible. Quite horrible.'

'Well, he's part of the deal.'

'You have . . . with him!' The voice was incredulous.

Ruth gave a bitter laugh. 'Yes we all have. We have to.'

The friend still remembers the shock with which she discovered the truth about Ruth Ellis and Maury Conley.

When he first opened his clubs, Maury Conley acted as a male madam. Not only did he arrange assignations for the club members with his girls for outside club hours, but he expected his hostesses to entertain him and his business confederates whenever requested; whatever the age, character, or appearance of his friends, some of whom had criminal records, most of whom were unprepossessing.

It is not surprising that money poured into the club owner's capacious pockets. Rent from the flats. Membership fees for his clubs, though this was a comparatively minor resource for it was more important that guests went to the clubs and bought drinks than that they kept their memberships up to date. There was the profit from drinks. A share of the girls' presents earned at his flats. Extra payments for being so open-hearted and understanding as to allow the girls to take his friends home into their beds. It was a most profitable spider's web that he had skilfully woven. No doubt he believed there was no reason it should not continue indefinitely.

Unfortunately for him the police became aware of what was going on. Even in those days a number of the police were corrupt and there is little doubt that for a considerable time Maury Conley was able to buy indemnity. But the net was closing in on him and he realized it.

Maury Conley was nothing if not a realist. Any further convictions would carry heavy sentences. Over the years he had become accustomed to good living, women's company, and what the fleshpots of the West End had to offer. He found prison life little to his liking. Apart from the appalling prison food, the discomfort of sharing a tiny cold cell, more than anything he missed his girls and being the centre of attention. Prison communities have little affection for those convicted of sexual offences against the young or pimping. He had had a rough time serving his sentences and did not intend to return to prison if he could humanly help it. At the same time it would have been illogical – for him – to turn away from his gold mine. He therefore decided that though the halcyon days might be over, there was no reason he should not continue to make good profits even though on a reduced scale. There was nothing against his taking rents as a flat owner. There was nothing illegal in his receiving the membership money nor the profit on drinks from his clubs. The only problem was 'his girls' and the profits they assured him. He gave little or no thought to the welfare of the girls he had recruited, or corrupted. Such unrealistic matters had no place in the tortuous labyrinth of his mind. He realized that if the girls no longer took men home, his clubs would lose their major attraction. The members would look elsewhere for diversion and already clubs were sprouting up like mushrooms.

Of course, he found a solution; the Maury Conleys of this world always do. He could well afford to pay others to take the risks for him.

At the time Ruth Neilson went to work for him, Conley owned four clubs. He also had other irons in many far less savoury fires. He was a ponce. A shrewd operator, he did not intend to repeat the experience of prison if he could help it. But equally surely he did not want to forgo the substantial profits earned for him by his call-girls. He solved his problem by poncing by remote control. He bought blocks of flats and registered them in his wife's name. The flats were let at high rents to girls who worked in his clubs as hostesses but were not averse to augmenting their pay in less reputable ways. At his clubs, the members would find a middle-aged friendly woman to whom they felt they could talk without being hampered by any inhibitions. This woman would be Conley's madam. She would ask them what they wanted and when. She would then arrange for one of her girls to go to the member's home or hotel or to entertain him in one of Conley's flats. If she did not have any girl suitable at her club, then a telephone call would ensure a subcontract from another of Conley's establishments. The older woman would profit by a percentage of the 'present', but the lion's share would find its way into Maury Conley's capacious pocket.

Today, one of Maury Conley's former manageresses – a large, warm, friendly blonde – lives out her retirement on her small yacht moored in a warm Mediterranean harbour. She will hear nothing against Maury Conley. His standards became hers. She accepted the risks as she accepted the profits.

The one exception to this pattern was the Little Club. Ruth was young and one of Maury Conley's favourite girls. It was not big enough to carry an older woman, Ruth, and a couple of hostesses. Fortunately Ruth was intelligent. She had become hardened by the club life and was not shocked by anything asked of her. Besides, as she was still in great demand Maury Conley would have the best of both worlds. Ruth would run his club for him. Her bar profits would be high because of her warmth of character. She herself would do much of the after-hours entertaining so that two payments would not be necessary. But she would also have to contribute by being 'nice' to Maury Conley, and he retained a key to the flat above the club.

When a girl is young and attractive and living in the unreal, tinsel world of the post-war afternoon clubs, self-deception comes easily. Few of Conley's hostesses thought of themselves as tarts; indeed, they would have been highly indignant at any such suggestion. Tarts stood on street corners or in shop doorways soliciting custom from unknown men. For their part as hostesses they were sexually aware and had 'modern' ideas. Already the word 'permissiveness' was creeping into the English language. What could be wrong in accepting a 'present' after a pleasant, athletic hour or so with a grateful member of the club, who had stood one several drinks and whose name one knew? That surely did not make them into prostitutes? And if their employer asked one of them 'as a favour to me' to entertain one of his friends from out of town, would it not be churlish to refuse? Quite apart from which it might cost her a remunerative and enjoyable job.

The clubs were full of servicemen waiting for their discharge from the forces. They were bored; frustrated. Maury Conley grew rich out of their frustration without apparently suffering any pangs of conscience. Indeed, if tackled, no doubt, he would have claimed to be supplying a social need.

Some of the more jaded club members who had travelled the world and seen most deviations and excesses, demanded something more than a brief affair with only one girl, however willing she might be. In such instances it was merely a question of settling the fee. The Club madam would be undeterred however outlandish the demand. Some of the less experienced hostesses were frankly amused the first time another of the hostesses pretended to make love to them to entertain their guest. They soon learned to conceal their amusement because the laughter had little place in the commercial bed. A few were disgusted and refused to have anything to do with such actions. Inevitably they became known as 'difficult' on the club circuit and found work as hostesses unavailable. The majority cheerfully accepted such demands as 'part of the game' and more than a few grew to prefer the caresses of their own sex, which at least carried no danger of infection or pregnancy.

When Ruth Neilson accepted a job as a hostess in Maury Conley's club, she was no innocent; but she had not realized quite what would be expected of her. His offer seemed on the face of it to be generous. A factory worker with a large family to keep would be lucky to earn over four pounds a week. And by now Ruth was having to pay the rent for her parents, Muriel having her own family to look after. Ruth was to receive five pounds plus ten per cent commission on food and drinks consumed by her customers. She was also allowed, or rather encouraged, to accept tips for keeping the customers contented. If a member asked a girl: 'What will you have?' the invariable reply was: 'Just a small glass of bubbly,' or 'I think I'll take a teensy gin.' Cider was cheap and looked like champagne. Water and tonic looks like gin and tonic, so the profits were high, as were the hostesses' commissions. There were also fringe benefits. The girls had to look sophisticated and attractive. Evening dresses were provided, the fittings usually being supervised by Conley, personally.

Within weeks of starting work at the Court Club – later to be renamed Carroll's – Ruth was earning over twenty pounds a week, quite apart from the personal presents she accepted. It was not solely money which attracted Ruth to the glittering club life. With an unhappy and impecunious background, she was easily impressed by money and what she interpreted as 'style'. At the Court Club she did not only meet servicemen on leave or ex-servicemen reliving their former glories, she was also entertained by wealthy black-marketeers, socialites, and titled people whose names made weekly news in the society colums of the national Press.

When club members, guests who were famous or who performed

on stage, film, or the radio spoke to her by name, she was not only illogically flattered, but reassured herself that she had come a long way from Rhyl and Basingstoke.

To comply with the inane British licensing laws, which not even Adolf Hitler's raiders could disrupt, the Court Club was forced to close every night at 11 p.m. 'Why finish the night so early?' Ruth would ask herself. Muriel would look after Andy. She always had done and always would. There was no shortage of men who wanted to go on with her to other clubs. She usually accepted their offers and within a comparatively short time became known at other clubs. She delighted in the fact that wherever she went she was greeted by hostesses and members as 'Ruth'. Her own favourite club was another of Conley's haunts called the Hollywood in Welbeck Street. The Hollywood opened as the Court closed. Here she could dine, dance, and flirt until nearly three in the morning.

Every Sunday she would make a special point of visiting Muriel to see young Andy. After all, the club doors and windows were shuttered on the sabbath. This is not to suggest that Ruth was completely shallow. She was capable of deep love, as was to be starkly revealed when she shot her lover out of jealousy. But against her love for her son and her elder sister, had to be set the relish for excitement. She compared her former home life and her parents' with the witty, noisy, self-confident members of the Court and Hollywood. Her family had little money to spend on essentials, let alone luxuries. Ruth had seen club members spend as much in an afternoon as her father had earned in a year. Her mother was a simple, continental woman, believing in God and forever citing His commandments and her Church's instructions. Most of the hostesses – especially Conley's manageress – were cynical, agnostic, and sophisticated. At home Ruth was quickly bored. At the clubs she had no time for introspection in the frenetic hunt for excitement.

Ruth was meeting an ever widening circle of hostesses and club guests. Some of the men would ask her to go down to their country houses for the weekend. To ask in advance about the sleeping arrangements would have been to appear naïve, and that was unthinkable. She soon acquired a veneer of sophistication. Her laugh became more strident, her voice more confident. She learned how to order food and what wine to drink with which course. She pored over the society columns in the papers so she would recognize anyone she met during the weekend. She even read the news so she would not be thought ignorant during the after-dinner discussion. She also realized that many men were amused at obscenities when uttered by a pretty young girl. 'Fuck' and 'fucking' became her favourite noun and adjective.

With the end of the war, one might well have expected the boom in afternoon drinking clubs to lag. The contrary was the case. Young men, no longer needed to defend the country, were thrown on to the labour market ill-equipped – except for the pinstripe suit, blue shirt, and trilby hat – to earn their livings. Many of them could have returned to jobs as office boys, which by law had had to be kept open for them. But to sit at a desk casting figures when one was used to firing at 'bandits' from the cockpit of a plane or training one's tank gun on a Panzer Tiger, was unexciting to put it mildly. Many of them, looking for alter-native work, became commercial travellers. 'Knight of the Road' had a romantic ring to it. Only too quickly did they discover that far from being romantic and involving a series of flirtations with frustrated married women as one toured the country by car, it usually involved evenings of indescribable boredom. Commercial hotels – which were all most of them could afford – were dingy and depressing. The barmaids were more likely to be middle-aged and stout, than young girls yearning for the masculine visitor who would wait until closing time before dragging them into bed.

The work was hard and repetitious. There was a queue for such jobs so that sales figures had to be maintained or one was on the dole. Some companies, to their shame, made a policy of sacking the salesman with the lowest monthly return, no matter what. They believed that this kept their sales-force on their toes . . . what it did to the representatives as human beings did not enter the minds of those who sat in the boardrooms.

Such men felt betrayed and lost. On their rare visits to London – visits often covered by false sales reports, for, after all, why should they feel loyalty towards such employers? – they could recapture a taste of their former glory in the afternoon drinking clubs. Surrounded by men with similar pasts they could recall the great events of the war, without their wives interrupting with: 'Oh, not that story all over again!' They could relate dirty stories and have them acclaimed instead of being received with a shrug. Hostesses would collapse in spasms of simulated mirth at tales they had heard a dozen times before. Most important of all, even though they might surreptitiously finger the few remaining coins in their pockets to see if any with serrated edges remained, they could feel men again.

The boom, far from fading, took on a new lease of life. The more men who came to the club to forget the present, the more flatterers there were for Ruth and her fellow hostesses. Yet, despite her experiences at weekend parties and in entertaining Maury Conley's friends, Ruth in some respects was still extraordinarily innocent. For someone who feigned sophistication, she was amazingly ignorant of methods of birth control. Either because of this ignorance or because she was so highly sexed she failed to take the necessary precautions. Once again she became pregnant. This time the father was a wealthy club member, who disappeared from the scene the moment he heard the news.

Fortunately for Ruth by this time she knew hostesses who were able to offer practical advice from their own experiences. Ruth went to a private, albeit expensive, home where she had the first of several abortions.

3

It was in 1950, at the height of the club boom, that Ruth met George Ellis. George Ellis was a qualified dentist. He was also an alcoholic. He was an unhappy man, who was incapable of relaxing without a glass in his hand. He also suffered from 'clubitis', the disease of drinking men which makes it impossible to stay at home so long as a club remains open acting as a magnet to him. He was a member of the Court Club, the Nautical Club, and a dozen other such establishments. He was also well known in many West End public houses, where he would seek companions when the clubs were not open.

Because of his drinking habits, his wife had left him to live with another man. Lonely, and dreading the hour when he would have to go home alone, he sought companionship and sex in his clubs. The hostesses were bored with his mawkish dwelling on past glories, but so long as he was prepared to buy round after round, and so inflate their commissions, they concealed their yawns.

From the first moment George Ellis was introduced to Ruth in the Court Club, he was obsessed by her. Again and again, he invited her out. He mentioned dinner, the theatre, dances, night clubs. But although she would drink with him in her capacity as club hostess, she refused every invitation. She had many younger, more attractive men with whom she could wile away her spare time. Eventually, however, his persistence paid off. More to gain respite from his pestering than from any enthusiasm, she agreed to meet him for dinner. He would wait for her outside the Hollywood Club at 7 p.m. He had baited his hook with the suggestion of dining at the Savoy Grill. It was not to be. That very afternoon at the Court Club she met Hank, a young, good-looking American sergeant, who was in London for one evening only and wanted to 'paint the town red'. She forgot all about her rendezvous with George Ellis. The American would return to the States without any realization that he had unknowingly played a major role in the tragedy of Ruth Ellis.

George Ellis waited with ever growing impatience for the blonde hostess to come tapping down the street. Even when she was half an hour late, he reassured himself that she must have been delayed. After an hour, however, he had to admit to himself that he might have been 'stood up'.

He was well known to all the members of the afternoon clubs which were adjacent to the Hollywood. Some of them had a clientele far less respectable than the Court Club. Indeed, one basement club in the area catered almost entirely for the strong-arm men who, a few years later, would be working for the property developer and criminal, Rachmann.

Three villains noticed Ellis standing on the kerb. They knew and disliked him for his background. They had contempt for him because of his drinking. They guessed what had happened and mocked him.

'How's our boy, then? Got 'imself stood up 'as 'e? No crumpet for George?'

Ellis was impatient and angry. Instead of ignoring them or jeering back, he answered unpleasantly. A scuffle broke out. One of his tormentors came from Bethnal Green and was a member of a gang of tearaways who always carried razors to enforce their opinions on others. The result of this casual fracas was that the dentist was slashed savagely across the cheek; a wound that required eight stitches when he was delivered by ambulance to St Mary's Hospital, Paddington. Indeed, the stitches were inserted in the very same casualty ward where a few years later, John Christie was to seek treatment for a strained back; an injury inflicted by carrying women's bodies out into the garden or into the alcove of his kitchen at 10 Rillington Place.

Ruth had had little compunction in jilting George Ellis, whom she did not even particularly like. But when she learned of the outcome of her preferring the American sergeant, she was overcome by remorse. She considered herself – somewhat illogically – to be the authoress of Ellis's misfortune. She told herself that if she had kept her appointment, Ellis would not now sport a livid weal across his face. When a week later he returned to the Court Club she was determined to make up to him for what he had suffered.

Night after night she went out with him when the Court Club closed. They dined in West End restaurants and then went on to the Gargoyle to dance. She pictured herself as a latter day saint, crusading to stop a man destroying himself by drinking. Certainly, in those early days of their relationship, when he was with her he was not lonely and so did not find it so difficult to say no to a whisky.

A month after the slashing, Ruth joined him on holiday in Cornwall. For him it was the happiest time for years. Already he was showing the ravages of alcohol. Now he was staying at a four-star hotel with a girl ten years younger than himself. Whenever other hotel guests looked at them, she would make a point of kissing him or putting her arms around him as if to ensure that they all realized that she was not a casual good-time girl on a dirty weekend, but a girl in love with her man.

Her actions were not mere show for others to appreciate. She felt flattered when he allowed her to take the glass of whisky from his hand and return it untouched to the bar. To have a middle-aged man, a professional dentist, obey her slightest whim gave her a sense of power, similar to that she had felt when posing at the Camera Club.

At the end of that week they returned to London, where he had agreed to act as a locum for a Hampstead dentist wishing to take a holiday. But the Cornish memories were strong for both of them and when a month later the Hampstead dentist returned, Ellis took Ruth away again to stay at the Selsdon Park Hotel in Surrey.

Ruth's love for Ellis at this time was not an act. To this day, her sister, Muriel, recalls how Ruth told her again and again how much she was in love. For Ruth this was the 'real thing'. There were, perhaps, practical reasons for her self-delusion. George Ellis was an educated, cultivated man. His drinking problem was a challenge to her. If she could save him from himself, everyone would give her the credit. He would be dependent on her. Under his shell of sophistication lurked a very naïve boy. But Ruth did not see this naïve youth, she saw instead the self-assured man of the world. She told Muriel again and again that now she had grown up she much preferred the mature man to the callow youths who came into the Court Club with the sole intention of finding a bed companion for the night. Ellis represented security – class.

'He respects me. He doesn't mind about my past. He knows it was all before I grew up. And Muriel,' Ruth would say, 'I do respect him . . . and love him. It really is the real thing . . .'

It was all very common and predictable. A story which has been played out many times.

By now Andy was six, and the prospect of marriage to George Ellis offered Ruth a secure home for her son. She was an emotional woman, capable of deep motherly love when there were no alternative attractions. She told herself that club life was no suitable atmosphere for a responsible mother. Married to George Ellis, she would not have to satisfy other men. There would not be any more surreptitious weekends, whilst her son stayed with Muriel. She convinced herself that she would not miss her former life. As a respectable married woman with a professional man as her husband she would take her position in society.

As if to convince herself that she could confine herself to one man, she went to live with George Ellis at Sanderstead. It was the post-war period of permissiveness. Sociologists writing in women's magazines recommended that the 'new woman' should test out her prospective fiancé before agreeing to the ceremony. Trial marriage had become à la mode, so Ruth was doing nothing outrageous by the standards of her day.

George Ellis, despite playing the man of the world at the clubs, was still tied to his mother's apron-strings. These strings were more financial than emotional. He explained to Ruth that when his mother died, he would inherit a substantial sum of money. But his mother was one of the older generation. She would not understand their more enlightened views, so Ruth agreed to pretend to his mother that they were truly married.

At Sanderstead, George showed few signs that marriage would cure his drinking habits. Ruth's reaction to his drinking had changed considerably now she was contemplating marriage. At the Little Club she had welcomed his generosity, indeed she had benefited from it financially. Now his drinking meant he was spending *their* money. That was an entirely different proposition. Now she became angry when he was drunk, demanding whether they could have any future if he would not restrain his drinking to make her happy. To try and cure him of his excessive drinking, Ruth persuaded him to go into Warlingham Park Hospital as an

39

in-patient under Dr T. P. Rees. There Ellis was treated and, apparently cured, discharged.

With all the enthusiasm of the new convert, Ellis assured Ruth that he would never drink again. He would start a new life. He was a good dentist. It was only a matter of finding a temporary job so as to get his hand in again. Then he would buy a practice in some pleasant country area and they would live blissfully together for the rest of their lives. She would settle down. She would never again have to work in a club or be at the beck and call of members. They would marry. Have children. She would be accepted everywhere as the wife of a popular local dentist. Of such things are dreams made.

Thousands of alcoholics have made similar resolutions. Few have succeeded in keeping their promises. Ruth, however, was convinced that George Ellis meant every word of it. To show she was equally determined that they should make a success of their future lives together, she pressed him to set a date for their marriage. Perhaps at the back of her mind she could not dislodge the memory of asking Clare the self-same question.

They were married at Tonbridge Register Office on 8 November 1950. There Ruth Neilson became Mrs Ellis. At the wedding Ruth described her father as a 'professional musician', whilst George Ellis gave 'wholesale fish merchant' as his father's trade. She told nobody of her plans, neither members of the family, nor her friends in the clubs. Their witnesses were two casual passers-by invited in off the street. The after-effects of her early illness were manifested when Ellis tried to put the ring on her finger. The joint was so swollen from rheumatoid arthritis that he had to go out to buy a larger one. It is possible that she was afraid that the excitement of the occasion would drive George Ellis to the bottle, and after all her brave words she would be unable to bear the indignity of such a happening.

The first her family knew of her wedding was when she brought Ellis to Muriel's home to introduce him to the family. They – especially Granville Neilson – were far from impressed.

Marriage did not have the desired effect of keeping George Ellis off the bottle. Ruth had hoped that having a young wife might instil a sense of responsibility. Unfortunately, it had the opposite effect. Now he felt he had got Ruth, he found her constant company a hampering of his social life. Once again he began haunting the clubs, buying everyone drinks, recalling the past.

Ruth was nothing if not a fighter. She urged him to start working again, believing that he would find himself in his professional work, besides which working would curtail his drinking hours. But it was all to no avail. Once more he was accepted into Warlingham Park to be dried out. Visiting in hospital, Ruth continued to press him to get work. Eventually, more to please her than with any real enthusiasm, he wrote in answer to an advertisement wanting a dentist to join one of several practices owned by a Mr Ronald Morgan, in Southampton. To account for his not having worked for several months, George Ellis told his prospective employer that he had suffered a minor breakdown through overwork. To his amazement he was the successful applicant and on his discharge from hospital the ill-assorted pair moved south. With the job went a flat at Warsash, on Southampton Water. So George Ellis began work. But all Ruth's hopes and plans were doomed to fail.

In Southampton, Ellis the dentist soon made new friends, who introduced him to new clubs. At the clubs he found a new audience for his anecdotes, which became more and more repetitive the more he drank. He stayed out late most nights. Ruth, who had foreseen that her marriage would raise her on the social ladder, found herself condemned, like many wives from poverty-stricken East End families, to sitting at home watching the food she had cooked grow stone cold. She grew to accept the stumbling of feet up the path and the almost incoherent excuses. Ruth was a girl of spirit and not inclined to endure such treatment. She berated him loudly, using her considerable vocabulary of abuse.

George Ellis, sober, loved Ruth. Drunk, he hated her for trying to tie him to the home. He responded equally viciously. At first he only attacked her with words. Later he used violence on her. Neighbours began to whisper about her black eyes and cut lips. One cannot help but wonder if there was not some twist in Ruth's mind which made her invite violence. In her all too brief life she was to have three deep emotional involvements with men: George Ellis, Desmond Cussen, and David Blakely. Of these, only Cussen did not strike her. On the other hand it could be that she felt guilt and invited expiation by provoking physical attack. After all, she

41

had seen her father repeatedly hit her mother and her sister, Muriel. Perhaps subconsciously she was trying to identify with them or, in Ellis's case, to pay him back for his slashing.

Ruth was transformed by her husband's drinking bouts into a virago. She would spit at him in anger, he would retaliate by hitting her. Eventually she would run away and go and stay with Muriel. George Ellis would follow Ruth to London. Before going to Muriel's to try to persuade Ruth to come back to him, he would pour out his sorrows to anyone who would listen to him in his old club haunts. Usually he went along to the Astor where his generosity guaranteed him a willing listener. Then he would go to Muriel's and promise Ruth that if she returned to him he would never again drink.

Inevitably, Ruth gave way and returned to Warsash, where the pattern would be repeated. That Ruth was contrary in character is shown by her great jealousy if he so much as dared to look at another woman. Their home became a battleground for charge and counter-charge. Ellis would reel home drunk. Ruth would call him a 'drunken sod'. He would lose his temper and would close her mouth in the only way he knew . . . with a punch.

Their rows and shouting matches became the talk of the neighbourhood. Eventually the stories reached Mr Morgan. He could not have his reputation and the reputation of his practices endangered by this drunken dentist whose wife frequently bore the scars of their battles for all to see. In April, only five months after their marriage, George Ellis was again out of work.

Ruth was always at her best at times of crises. Once again she put her bitterness behind her and went out with her husband to stay with his mother in the Welsh beauty spot of Betws-y-coed.

After another drying-out period, Ellis obtained a position with a partnership in Cornwall. That none of his employers required references is one of the minor mysteries of the whole story. There was no home provided, so Ruth decided to return with Andy to London. It is doubtful if she would ever have returned to Ellis had she not discovered that she was pregnant. Probably she would have had another abortion had her mother and father not been so enthusiastic at the prospect of becoming grandparents to a legitimate child. They urged Ruth to 'make up' with her husband so that the child in her belly should have a stable family home.

Though beset with doubts, Ruth heeded their advice and went to live in rooms with her husband. But by now Ellis, having been alone, was in no fit state to do his work. Once again he went into Warlingham Park Hospital under Dr T. P. Rees.

If the jury at her trial had heard of what transpired there, it is extremely likely that they would have added a recommendation to mercy. Ruth followed her husband to London. She was pregnant and in a highly emotional state. Her husband was in hospital surrounded by nurses, and one of the woman doctors was attractive. Someone suggested to Ruth that George Ellis was having an affair with the doctor. It is extremely unlikely that there was any truth in the rumour, but Ruth was in no mental state to apply logic. She stormed into the hospital shouting that her husband was a 'fucking adulterer'. She approached complete strangers and demanded to know if they had seen her husband making love with the doctor, or whether he had made a pass at *them*.

The hospital staff tried to reason with her. She would not listen to them. She knew her husband was having an affair, and she was going to put an end to it. Eventually she had to be physically restrained and given sedatives. For the remainder of her life she was to take drugs as treatment and Dr William Sargant recalls his partner Dr T. P. Rees expressing his surprise that he was not called for the defence at the trial. He believed that with Ruth Ellis on drugs and being given pastis to drink prior to her shooting David Blakely, she would not have been responsible for her actions. But he was not called, and a psychiatrist who knew nothing about her mental history was put into the witness box instead and did her case far more harm than good by his testimony.

Ruth went to Muriel's to have her baby, Georgina. The baby was only three and a half when her mother was executed, yet this did not stop her, many years later, writing an article in the Press about her mother's case and suggesting that if the story be filmed she was the natural choice to play the lead, even though she had neither stage nor screen experience.

Ruth never returned to George Ellis despite his pleas. He was a drunkard and years later committed suicide in a hotel in Jersey.

Ruth's figure soon regained its shape and there was only one choice of employment open to her: the one in which she was experienced. Maury Conley welcomed her back. She had been popular and earned him money. Furthermore he liked her for herself . . . not to mention *himself*. So whilst Muriel looked after Georgina, Ruth returned to club life to become, in time, the manageress of the Little Club.

It is all too easy for those sympathetic to Ruth Ellis to cast David Blakely in the role of the villain. But those who knew him well generally liked him and today speak affectionately of his charm and friendliness.

One girl who was introduced to him by his friends, the Find-laters, slept with David Blakely only six weeks before he was shot dead. She was amazed to find his back scarred with knife marks and general wounds which he said he had suffered when Ruth was in an uncontrollable fury. Today the girl writes: 'No one has written about Ruth Ellis's drug taking. When she was on drugs and drink she was very violent.' However, it must be noted that this girl's information is second-hand because she never met Ruth Ellis herself.

David Moffat Drummond Blakely was a Yorkshireman, having being born in Sheffield at the expensive Oakdale Nursing Home on 17 June 1929. That he was born in such a high-class establish-ment was not surprising, for his father was a highly respected general practitioner.

David Blakely had two elder brothers and a sister, Maureen, with whom he was extremely close. The Blakelys were a well-to-do middle-class family. And, as was customary in those pre-war days, his mother was able to afford a 'nanny' to look after him. For her it was to be a lifelong employment, for she was still looking after him at his flat in Penn when he was murdered.

His close relationship with his nanny was not unusual in the thirties; indeed, in middle-class families, the nurse was frequently closer to the child than were the parents. Nurses would sometimes absorb the affection which more naturally should have been con-centrated on the mothers. The mother – with a human screen between her and the child – became a remote, godlike creature, whom the child saw first thing in the morning and sometimes in the afternoon when paraded to impress the mother's friends. Many mothers have impressed on their grown-up sons how they brought them up, when, in fact, they really handed over their offspring to a surrogate mother – the nanny.

David grew up to respect his mother, but he reserved his love for his nanny and his sister. Annie Blakely was a very social-minded woman. She was one of the queens of the Sheffield morning-coffee belt and was happier in her role as well-to-do hostess than in romping around with her children.

The nominal head of the family, Dr John Blakely, was far less socially inclined. He was a 'born' doctor, looking upon his responsibility to his patients as more important than making money for his wife to spend. His large practice covered a cross-section of the inhabitants of the steel-town. For every wealthy patient who paid his substantial fees, he had a dozen out-of-work patients whom he would treat whilst they for their part promised to pay when they were in work again. He never questioned their intentions and treated rich and poor with equal courtesy and care.

In view of how David was to make the headlines after he was killed in Hampstead, it is somewhat odd that his father, the respectable and respected doctor, should also have been involved in a murder charge. When David was only five years old, his father was accused of having murdered an out-of-work waitress, Phyllis Staton. The prosecution alleged that the 49-year-old doctor had had illicit relations with the waitress and that when she became pregnant he had given her drugs to induce the abortion. Subsequently the girl died of acute septicaemia.

The doctor never concealed that he had had intercourse with Phyllis Staton, but pleaded that if this were a criminal offence, most of Sheffield should have stood in the dock with him. He also admitted prescribing medicaments for her, but swore on oath that what he had prescribed could have done her no harm. He also pointed out to the magistrates that he could prove that he was only one of the girl's several lovers. Despite his disclosures as to intercourse and drugs, the Sheffield magistrates decided that the prosecution's evidence was so flimsy that no jury in the world was likely to convict.

Dr Blakely returned home an innocent man in the eyes of the law and of the majority of his patients who had stood by him loyally. But in his wife's opinion he had, in sleeping with a girl of working-class origins, committed a far graver crime than murder. She was sure that her coffee-morning friends were laughing at her and smirking over his need to seek elsewhere for sexual satisfaction. She took no immediate action, but from the moment he returned home there was always friction, with her speaking as little as possible to her erring husband. It did not make for a healthy or stable family atmosphere. In later years, David Blakely often mentioned that the final rift between his parents when he was eleven was a relief rather than a shock. At last the split became definite. The guerrilla war was over.

Annie Blakely sued for divorce and was granted a decree nisi on the grounds that the doctor had committed adultery. On the decree being made absolute on 2 December 1940, Annie Blakely was granted the custody of her four children of the marriage.

Mrs Blakely was not a gay divorcee for long. On 14 February of the following year she married Humphrey Cook, a very wealthy car-racing enthusiast. He and his bride set up home just off Park Lane in the heart of the West End. By now the family was breaking up and growing up. The doctor remained in Sheffield treating his patients. The two older boys had enlisted in the services, whilst David had been dispatched to Shrewsbury, the West Country public school.

With nurses caring for the sons in childhood and the public schools taking over in the teens, it is not surprising that so many middle-class youths failed to become mature adults. The hall table at their flat was always covered with racing-car journals, for racing was Humphrey Cook's *raison d'être*. It was this mutual enthusiasm – if not fixation – which bound David Blakely closer to his stepfather than to his own father.

David was never to fulfil his dream of becoming a star driver, but all his waking thoughts were of cars and he quickly became known on the fringe of the racing circuit. Indeed, Cliff Davis, a much more successful racing driver in the 1500cc class in which Blakely was to race, sums up what most successful drivers thought of him: 'Charming, smooth-talking, educated, and a shit!'

He and his stepfather would tour the tracks within easy reach of London, talking of little except cars and how David would one day develop his own. If he had not been so bound up in the sport, he would probably have escaped his untimely death, for his friend Ant Findlater says that it was because Blakely was depressed by the failure of their car, the Emperor, that he declined to talk to Ruth during the fatal weekend, and that, far from hearing him laughing in the background when she telephoned 29 Tanza Road, he was more likely to be sobbing. The money was running out, the car had a broken crankshaft, and it was extremely unlikely that David would be able to sort things out in time to race at Le Mans as he had planned. He was in no mood to laugh, nor could he be bothered in his depression to soothe Ruth Ellis's hurt feelings. So he refused to talk to her. She misunderstood the reasons for his avoiding her and, out of her mind with jealousy and fury, she shot him. But that part of the story comes later.

At Shrewsbury School, David Blakely's career was undistinguished – to put it in the best possible light. The Shropshire public school has a fine academic and sporting tradition. David Blakely contributed to neither. His sole interest, even in his public school days, was taking machines apart and reassembling them. Far from censuring Blakely for his lack of achievement, his stepfather sympathized. He understood better than anyone the boy's racing ambitions. It is probable that in David's few successes on the track, Humphrey Cook relived his own boyhood dreams. Certainly when David Blakely left school his main interest was to become a mechanic or a driver. Nothing else was of any interest to him.

He was essentially weak. He needed to get drunk frequently in the company of men to whom he could boast of his skill as a driver or brag about his sexual conquests. And there were many excuses for his boasting about women. He took sex almost as casually as he accepted a drink. It was all very schoolboyish, as if he needed to prove his manhood to himself as well as to everyone else. He would get into drunken brawls, but never came well out of these because, basically, he was a coward and having provoked trouble would run away from it, if it looked like culminating in a fight.

In discussion he was boring, for he only liked talking about cars and had a hatred for all men and women whom he considered to be 'intellectuals'. If, as often happened, a subject went beyond his range, he would sulk like a ten-year-old child. If, however, the

48

conversation veered to cars, his face would become animated and enthusiasm would surge into his voice.

The army was very much public school orientated when it came to officer selection. How a candidate spoke and which school he had attended were still much more important than intelligence or character. Too many clever officers might have proved an embarrassment to the colonels! So it was that, as an Old Salopian with a good accent and having been trained in the school ATC, David Blakely was immediately selected and commissioned when his age group was called up. He was posted to the Highland Light Infantry.

His army career was a facsimile of his school record. He did nothing outstanding, but managed to remain out of trouble. On his discharge he had to find work. There was still a hangover from the Second World War, and there were few jobs in motor sport. At this stage of his life his stepfather chose a job for him. Through influence with the board of the Hyde Park Hotel, Humphrey Cook persuaded them to accept David Blakely as a management trainee. He told David: 'Sometimes a sport is popular, sometimes it isn't. But there will always be a need for caterers.'

David Blakely received so modest a wage as a trainee that it was barely enough for him to live on, let alone to indulge his taste for wine, women, and song. However, his mother, who was thoroughly enjoying playing the role of hostess for her wealthy husband, decided to augment her son's salary by five pounds a week. In those days five pounds would pay for several rounds of drinks and allow him to take a girl out to dinner.

His career as a caterer was doomed to failure from the outset. David Blakely had not the character to buckle down to the discipline and long hours demanded of him by the hotel management. He had little ambition except to make money; and the prospect of eventually becoming a manager of a first-class hotel did not excite him. He preferred the smells of oil in the racing pit to the aromas of the kitchen.

To please Humphrey Cook, the hotel management had accepted young Blakely. It did not take them long to realize they had come off with the worst half of the bargain. Their trainee showed neither enthusiasm nor gratitude for the chance they were offering him. He did as little as possible and rejected any suggestion that involved him going to evening classes. On the positive side, he was presentable, had a pleasant personality and a well-modulated, public school accent. His diffidence appealed more to women than men; and more to the woman between thirty and forty than to girls of his own age. For his part, he was happier in the company of the older woman, whom he could rely on to take the initiative. He was very vulnerable and unsure of himself and always feared rejection by a younger girl. The thirty to forty year olds whom he met when acting as receptionist were flattered by his attentions and the respect and interest they saw in his eyes. Many of them were susceptible. Often they were holidaying in London whilst their husbands remained at work in the North or West. They were not averse to a little discreet sex during their stay in the anonymity of the capital. David Blakely was only too anxious to please. He was quite prepared to be spoiled, to be bought drinks and taken out to fancy restaurants. His pride was not easily bruised, and in his job as a trainee he needed no excuse if he were found entering or leaving a guest's bedroom.

Humphrey Cook not only liked David personally, but was anxious to do everything he could to please his new wife by helping her son. So when his friends on the Hyde Park Hotel board expressed their disappointment at his stepson's attitude to work, he made excuses for him, promising to 'have a word' and that David would 'buckle down' if only they gave him time to settle in. He also met his stepson's bills and lent him money whenever he needed it; which was frequently. As a special birthday present he gave him a second-hand sports car. This was a mistake, for from then onwards David took even less interest in his work – if that were possible – and resented every minute that he was not behind the wheel of the car or tinkering in its engine. Petrol would have been a problem if David had not known he could always charge it to his stepfather's account.

With the financial help of his mother and stepfather, he was able to spend most of his spare time at race meetings. He was even able to enter his car in modest events. Not surprisingly, with a second-hand car and little real driving experience, he had little or no success.

That David Blakely was not completely selfish was shown by his treatment of his father, for whom he had a sincere affection.

Whenever time allowed he would drive to Sheffield to see the doctor. His father was most gratified by his son's visits because he had nursed a suspicion that when David became used to the well-to-do life his stepfather could offer him, he might well forget his real father. His son's loyalty delighted him, and he seldom allowed David to leave without a financial present as a token of his pleasure. Though David Blakely never refused the money pressed into his hand, his love of his parents was genuine and he deeply regretted the break-up of their marriage even though at the time it was an emotional relief after years of tension.

The Steering Wheel Club was not far from the Hyde Park Hotel and it was to become a magnet for the car-mad David Blakely. It consisted of only two rooms, a bar with a restaurant leading out of it up a few stairs. Here could be found Mike Hawthorne, surrounded by his admirers, Stirling Moss, Pete Collins, and all the other top drivers of the day.

The manageress of the club was Gwen Nockolds. The entire Nockolds family was connected with motor racing. Roy was an excellent artist whose paintings of racing cars and impressionist pictures of speed adorn the walls of the RAC and other clubs connected with cars. Harold, now retired, was the editor of a group of motor-racing magazines, whilst Conrad 'Twinky' Nockolds was an outstanding photographer of the sport.

David Blakely found the Steering Wheel provided him with the ambience he most enjoyed. All the members shared his interest in cars and racing, so that the talk seldom soared beyond his capacity. He was able not only to join in, but also to air his opinions. At the Steering Wheel he met most of the stars of the track. If a famous driver spoke to him by name, it was a moment to be treasured and to be retold at the Hyde Park, where the other trainees could not avoid his bragging.

With a few notable exceptions, the car-racing set were heavy drinkers. David Blakely, however, did not have a strong head for drink and he frequently became drunk and obstreperous. When drunk he would behave as if he were still at Shrewsbury, indulging in adolescent horseplay. Usually he ended the evening by squirting members with a soda-water syphon, though he sulked if anyone treated him in a similar manner.

It was at the Steering Wheel, only three nights before he was shot, that David Blakely, after a blazing, strident, and public row, punched Ruth Ellis full in the face. Several of the members, sickened by his action and knowing that it was not the first time he had hit her, moved to intervene, and undoubtedly there would have been even more unpleasant scenes had Gwen Nockolds not taken immediate action, ordering them both to quit the premises.

The club manageress, a much respected and sensible woman, could have given evidence of several occasions on which Blakely struck Ruth Ellis at the club, but, to her surprise, she was never called by Ruth's defence counsel. Desmond Cussen – Ruth's 'other' lover – did refer to the occasions on which he had helped her to camouflage the visible evidence of the assaults, but had others been called at Ruth's trial, it is likely the jury might have viewed Mrs Ellis in a very different light when she took her place in the witness box to give evidence on her own behalf. There were many others who also could have borne witness to his attacks on her. They, too, were not called. The jury made no recommendation to mercy.

David Blakely soon got the taste for club life and became a natural club man. If he had money in his pockets he was only too pleased to play the host, thinking, like so many other young men have done, that popularity can be bought. He would always buy his round and was quite content to stand in a group guffawing at the endless, dreary, dirty anecdotes.

From the waiters and the chefs at the Hyde Park Hotel, he collected his own library of dirty stories, even going to the trouble of noting down any especially salacious joke in his diary so that he would not be lost for words when it came to his turn. Though on the surface popular, most of the members saw through his mask. They detected the 'little boy lost' behind the veneer of self-confidence. The older members recognized the inherent inadequacy behind the braggadocio.

The Little Club in Knightsbridge, very conveniently situated opposite the Hyde Park Hotel, became his second favourite haunt. Here he met Ruth Ellis for the second time, making no better impression on her than on their first encounter at Carroll's Club. Then his bluster and rudeness nauseated her, so that she told one of the hostesses that: 'I hope never to see that little shit again.' Once more he was offensive in his remarks about the club and its hostesses, thinking it was clever to insult those who, because of their employment, were in no position to answer in a similar tone. Yet though she avoided him on that first visit to the Little Club, within a fortnight she was sleeping with him, whilst for his part he was urging Cliff Davis, a close friend, to accompany him to the Little Club to see 'one of the finest fucks in town'.

In February 1952, Dr Blakely died from coronary thrombosis. Out of his father's estate, David Blakely received the grand sum of £7000. With this capital, he was able to entertain ostentatiously; calling to his fellow members at the Steering Wheel to: 'Drink up . . . the next round's on me.' Basically not very intelligent, he could not understand that even if he were buying, it did not necessarily guarantee him a captive audience.

Blakely was extremely proud of his reputation as a womanizer. With his new-found wealth in the bank, he could now afford the luxury of being seen with a pretty woman on his arm. Soon he had two regular girl-friends to accompany him on his drinking sprees. They could not have been more dissimilar. One was a dainty, extremely pretty, cinema usherette. She had a ready smile, platinum hair, and a provocative figure. She was also totally unsophisticated and looked upon Blakely as if he were a god from another planet. The other girl was much more robust, both physically and mentally. This girl, to whom he became engaged, was the daughter of a wealthy Yorkshire businessman. She had been raised in the sporting world. Like the usherette, she fell in love with Blakely's act of being the well-to-do playboy. She regularly took him home to the North so that her family could get to know him. There she boasted to her friends about capturing such an attractive 'man of the world'.

But not even these two girls could satisfy his enormous ego. Even whilst engaged to Mary Newton Dawson, the Yorkshire lass, he slept around, mostly with older women. One of these was to play an important role in the tragedy.

Carole Findlater was the wife of another car-racing enthusiast, whom David Blakely was to refer to as 'quite my best friend'. However, his friendship for the husband did not prevent Blakely sleeping with his wife. The two men had a blazing row, but eventually a relationship was established in which the two men never mentioned the past. Today Anthony 'Ant' Findlater is

53

remarried and living in the South of France. He says: 'After Blakely's death there were suggestions that Carole had been having an affair with him. I don't really know if it was true or not. But if he'd had the opportunity David wasn't the sort of man to pass it up.' There was no rancour in the statement.

The older women who slept with Blakely must have been attracted by his spoiled child act, because from a sexual point of view he was no lion. Several of them have spoken of his ineffectiveness as a lover. This is not surprising. David Blakely's outstanding characteristic was selfishness; and selfishness does not make a good lover. He was too intent on his own pleasure to worry about a woman's needs. Thus he usually left the more experienced women unsatisfied. Most of them spent only one night with him, and then, disappointed, looked elsewhere for company.

Now he had money, he no longer took the trouble to be polite to hotel guests or management. He looked upon the hotel as a convenient place to pass the time until the Little Club opened. Then he had only to slip out of the door to reach the club in a matter of seconds through the Knightsbridge subway. He may have thought the management was unaware of what was going on, but if so, he was very wrong. The hotel manager sent for him and informed him that he was not suited to the catering trade which demanded attention to work and some signs of enthusiasm. As far as the hotel was concerned he could collect his cards and leave that very day. David Blakely was not surprised. Yet though he was bored with the job and did not mind leaving, his pride was sorely hurt. Surely his stepfather's influence could . . .? But the manager seemed unimpressed by Blakely's suggested threat and there was nothing for him to do but to collect his odds and ends and depart.

No doubt the management thought they had seen the last of him, but David Blakely reacted typically to the sack. The following morning he lounged into the bar as it was opening, and, playing the wealthy guest, ordered himself a double gin and tonic.

Humphrey Cook was still the indulgent stepfather and attributed David's failure to 'high spirits'. Perhaps he had been asking too much in expecting David to settle down to hotel life when he had only recently come out of the army. Instead of insisting that David should apply for work elsewhere, he decided that his wife and her son should go on a world tour. No doubt the holiday would do the young man good. Certainly his theory proved valid because, on his return, David did get a job; and one far more to his liking than training at the Hyde Park Hotel.

By this time Humphrey Cook had bought the Old Park, a very large house in Penn, Buckinghamshire. He converted the house so that David should have a flat of his own. He also invited David's old nanny to come down and look after his stepson. It was not far from home that David found work at Silicon Pistons Ltd. Here he worked with his hands and found his interest in machines of considerable value.

As the family still had a flat in London, David could now enjoy the best of both worlds. He liked the Penn life. The Chiltern village is beautiful and there were many people from the theatre living in the area. The Crown, the centre of social life in the village, was full most nights with a chattering throng. There David Blakely could play the successful racing driver; though he had still to win a race. Almost inevitably he started an affair with a married woman living in the village. This affair was to be one of the main reasons for Ruth Ellis's violent jealousy.

In London there was by this time another woman in his life, a tall American model. He took her around the clubs, amongst them the Little Club. He and Ruth started sleeping together again. By now she had forgotten her earlier antagonism and was genuinely in love with him. Soon he had no time for the American model . . . but at Penn the other woman was still available. The ingredients were ready for the explosion that was to result in his dying outside the Magdala with four bullets in his body.

5

Most of us need to identify ourselves with individuals involved in a case if we are to appreciate fully the train of events leading up to the crime and the passions aroused in those who committed the offence or suffered from it. It is difficult for the ordinary 'man or woman in the street' to identify with any of the main characters in the crime which resulted in the death of David Blakely and the hanging of Ruth Ellis.

To many people, certainly most women of strict upbringing, Ruth Ellis was patently the villainess. She was, to them, a foul-mouthed club hostess who whored on the side; an unmarried mother whose man left her to bring up her child alone; a murderess who had two lovers and killed one of them when he wanted no more to do with her. To others, David Blakely was the villain of the tragedy. Weak, boastful, drunken, cowardly, inadequate with a schoolboy sense of humour, he slept around without any thought of the hurt or harm he might be inflicting on the minds or bodies of the women he used so casually.

But there is a third group – evidence has come to light both after the execution and many years later, which lends weight to their opinion – who believe that Desmond Cussen was really responsible for the murder. They believe that even though he did not fire the gun personally, he it was who made sure that Ruth Ellis knew how to fire it and that she found David Blakely while she was in a state of mind when all reason had fled.

These critics of Desmond Cussen claim that not only did he give Ruth Ellis the gun with which she shot Blakely, but that he also first oiled it, taught her how to hold and aim it, and even took her down to Epping Forest for target practice. Having done his best to ensure she could handle the weapon, there is evidence that he drove her first to 29 Tanza Road, the home of the Findlaters, and after that to the Magdala where the victim was run to earth.

It is remarkable, if she were not tutored in firing the gun, that she hit Blakely at all, let alone four times. She must have been shaking at least inwardly, with terror at what she was about to do, apart from being affected by the drugs and pastis she had consumed. It must also be remembered that from early childhood she had suffered from extremely weak eyesight. Indeed, to focus closely on anything she had to screw up her eyes. Even wearing glasses, without Cussen's training she surely would have placed *all* the passers-by in jeopardy and not merely wounded one woman. Desmond Cussen, despite knowing she was taking drugs for her mental state, plied her with Pernod until she could not have been responsible for what she was doing. Had the judge and jury known these facts it is extremely doubtful that she would have hanged, for she would certainly have been a strong candidate for a recommendation to mercy. Had the judge and jury also known of the beating up she had received at Blakely's hands directly after having an abortion for his child and shortly before the shooting, their attitude would have been very different.

Mr Justice Havers, the trial judge, has since said that although an execution decision rests in the end with the Home Secretary, in his opinion had all the above-mentioned information been brought forward to the attention of the jury, it is extremely unlikely that she would have been executed: she would certainly have qualified for a reprieve.

Dr William Sargant, the former head of the Department of Psychology at St Thomas's Hospital, has said: '. . . if she had been filled with Pernod, on top of her mental illness, for the whole weekend, almost anything could have happened. Partly mad and filled up with one of the most violent drinks that could have been given . . .!'

What sort of man was this who, even though inflamed by jealousy, could provoke a drunken, half-crazed woman into shooting his rival whilst he stood watching safely on the sidelines?

Both physically and mentally Desmond Cussen was an un-inspiring specimen. He was short, rather chunky, with dark hair growing down on to his forehead in a widow's peak; hair which he sleeked back like a Brylcreem model of that period. His eye-brows were prominent and he sported a pencil-thin moustache which stretched from corner to corner of his full, rather sensual

He was well-educated and moderately intelligent. He had ~~n~~othing outstanding academically or sportingly at school or ~~afterw~~ards in the Royal Air Force. One of the strange links he shared with David Blakely was his dependence on an older woman – in his case his mother, in Blakely's the nanny.

There was never any question as to what career Cussen would follow. He had no particular talent and no specific ambition. His family owned a wholesale and retail tobacconist chain which had its head office at 93 Peckham High Street, in south-east London. Desmond Cussen was not the kind of man to strike out on his own. He had no unrealized dreams to be fulfilled, no need to take risks. So, as was usual in those days, after paying lip-service to the theory – and theory it was – that the budding executive should learn the trade from the bottom up, he duly became a director of the family business.

Desmond Cussen had two other characteristics which he shared with Blakely; a love of motor racing – he drove a Ford Zodiac with considerable verve and skill – and a deep love of alcohol. Also, like Blakely, he became Ruth Ellis's lover. The man who, in the trial at the Old Bailey, was to be referred to as 'her alternative lover' was a bachelor, which, in view of his reliance on his mother, was not wholly surprising.

He lived in a well-furnished and comfortable flat at 20 Goodwood Court, a private block in Devonshire Street, midway between the BBC's Broadcasting House and the green belt of Regent's Park. It was to Goodwood Court that he brought Ruth Ellis after she had been sacked by Maury Conley from the Little Club. Generously, he also found room for Andy Clare during the child's Christmas holidays. It was not altogether surprising that Maury Conley had discharged Ruth. A casual study of the books revealed that since her obsession with David Blakely, the takings had nose-dived from over two hundred pounds a week to between seventy and eighty pounds, and Maury Conley disapproved of charity.

Desmond Cussen and David Blakely knew each other long before Ruth Ellis appeared on the scene. Both inadequate, they found confidence in the braggadocio of the fringe of the car-racing scene. Although from the outset they disliked each other, they managed to hide their feelings as each of them relaxed in the company of the 'stars' of the racing world, especially pin-up boy Mike Hawthorne.

Hawthorne, the six-foot-two, blond lion of the course, died soon after Ruth Ellis shot Blakely. He crashed his Jaguar on the Guildford bypass. Hawthorne was a star of radio, television, and films. Indeed, he represented motor racing on the first night of commercial television.

Hawthorne did not like either Desmond Cussen or David Blakely, but like many conceited men, he was vulnerable to sycophancy and he only objected when any of his lickspittles presumed on his good nature and went too far. When on one occasion Blakely, with his infantile sense of humour, put the soda syphon on the world champion and followed this childish act by putting an ice cube down his neck, Hawthorne reacted violently. He went after Blakely threatening to 'break his fucking neck'. Blakely went scrambling behind the bar appealing for someone to help him. He knew the damage that Hawthorne would inflict upon him. Indeed, Hawthorne would have caused considerable damage had not Cliff Davis intervened. In the general mêlée which followed, Cliff Davis lost his glasses, but nevertheless managed to discourage Hawthorne with a swift right hook. Cliff Davis was a close friend of Blakely's, even though they were rivals on the track.

There were many uncharming aspects of Desmond Cussen's character, even though they were not uncommon traits in the members who haunted the West End clubs. Cussen needed reassurance. He needed praise. He expanded when people sought his advice. Normally he was withdrawn and tended to sit watching the world from a side seat. But if encouraged he would brag of his sexual prowess and boast of his conquests over women who were anyway available to those who had funds. At the clubs, though generally reticent, he allowed himself to be drawn on subjects which reflected his virility. And once he had fallen in love and become obsessed with Ruth Ellis, there is no evidence that he was attracted by any other woman. Indeed, until the trapdoor swung open breaking Ruth Ellis's neck, there is no suggestion that despite his previous history, he ever made a pass at any other woman.

But after her execution, when it might be thought he would hide under a cloak of anonymity, he could not resist bragging of his sexual expertise. He told Robert Hancock, author of the excellent book *Ruth Ellis* published in 1963, that Ruth's performance in between the sheets was 'sexually very mechanical, but she was great fun to be with at a party.' This is, indeed, in stark contrast to the memories of many of her club friends, not least Cliff Davis, the racing driver, who recalled quite dispassionately that the only time they 'hit it off' she was 'the best fuck ever created. An artist!' Cussen's derogatory comment comes somewhat unconvincingly from a man who could well have stood beside her in the dock.

The contrasts between the origins of Ruth Ellis and Desmond Cussen, their environments and their inherent tastes, makes their relationship and his intense possessiveness extremely hard to appreciate. His declaration, on several occasions, of his love for her – on more than one occasion he publicly offered to marry her – stands in bold contrast to his behaviour both at the trial and in the days preceding and after her execution.

After Ruth Ellis was arrested, Desmond Cussen showed all the tendencies of the devoted lover. He showered her with flowers, scent, make-up and books. Never had the bleak prison received such rich presents. He wrote to her daily declaring his undying love. But from the moment the foreman of the jury declared in court that they had found her guilty and the judge sentenced her to death, he acted as if at one turn of the switch, he had excised her from his life.

After the sentence, not only did Desmond Cussen make no effort to see her or even write to her, but as far as he was concerned she did not exist. No more flowers. No more scent. No more make-up. No more dyes to retain the platinum blonde hair he had so long praised.

On the penultimate night of Ruth's life, Granville Neilson, her brother, had searched desperately for Desmond Cussen. Neilson had hoped that he might persuade his sister's 'alternative lover' to reveal his own share in the events leading up to the murder, and, by so doing, might gain at least a temporary reprieve. The public at large were appalled by what was happening but as always, needed a period of gestation before their sorrow could have any impact on the authorities. But, by then, Cussen had brought down a curtain on this most sordid episode in his life. From the moment Ruth was given the death sentence, Cussen was erasing her memory. He was able to draw on inward resources which enabled him to forget the past and rebuild his life. Ruth Ellis was thrust into the background and eventually, to eliminate any reminder of her existence, he emigrated to Australia in 1964.

It is only too easy to condemn. It is more difficult to comprehend. It is possible to sympathize with Cussen's emotions, if not to admire his ethics. His motivation was, perhaps, as much rooted in jealousy and hatred for David Blakely as in love for Ruth. And surely, his jealousy and hatred for his rival was justified?

Desmond Cussen was a mature businessman. He earned a substantial salary. He had proved himself a successful man of commerce. David Blakely, his rival, was younger and a ne'er do well. Whilst Cussen always met the bill, Blakely was always short of money and often 'on the knock'.

Desmond always treated Ruth like a lady. He was considerate and attentive towards her. He helped her on with her coat and opened the car door for her. Blakely treated her like a tart. He shouted at her, and if she angered him when he was drinking, did not hesitate to punch her. Desmond Cussen was the only witness to Blakely's violence on Ruth who was called to give evidence at the Old Bailey.

Living with Ruth at Goodwood Court and visiting her at Egerton Gardens, Cussen had repeatedly seen the scars of Blakely's assaults. At the trial he was asked by Mr Melford Stevenson QC:

'Have you ever seen marks or bruises on her?'

Cussen replied: 'Yes.'

'How often?' asked Counsel.

'On several occasions.'

Then, after establishing that only a few weeks before the shooting and shortly after she had an abortion, Cussen had seen scars before taking her to a dance, the defence counsel asked:

'Did you help disguise bruises on her shoulders?'

'Yes.'

'Were they bad bruises?'

'Yes. And they required quite heavy make-up.'

Cussen added that Ruth came back to his flat and, when he arrived back late, he found her in a very bad condition. To find a woman with whom you are obsessed bruised and beaten by another man is surely a reason for deep hatred?

Desmond could and did offer Ruth Ellis security. First he took her into his Goodwood Court flat and later helped her to find a large room at Egerton Gardens, off Brompton Road. Blakely offered her marriage, but only when she was pregnant and when she knew he was already engaged to another girl. At the time he knew she would not and *could* not accept. It was a safe offer. Cussen continued to care and look after her even when he discovered she was lying to him and sleeping with Blakely when she was pretending to be visiting her daughter, Georgina, in the North of England.

Besotted, he had not been able to bring himself to sever the knot which bound them together. But lying awake in the desolate hours of the early morning, when he knew she was cuddling up beside his rival in a bedroom of a Kensington hotel, must have eaten his soul. To lose the woman one loves is difficult enough, but to lose her to a man one considers despicable is beyond imagination.

Here, perhaps, is the clue to his behaviour. When he was with Ruth Ellis he was a mere puppet manipulated by his own irrational emotions and the fixation which beset his imagination. Logic fled his mind. Like a punch-drunk boxer he kept returning to soak up the insults and rebuffs he suffered second hand from the arrogance of David Blakely. He released his hatred publicly only once when, with Ruth, he cornered Blakely at the Bull, Gerrards Cross, *en route* to Penn. He challenged Blakely to 'come outside', but true to his reputation, Blakely ran away refusing to fight, saying that to resort to violence was a sign of immaturity.

Desmond Cussen could offer Ruth Ellis, a mere club hostess, everything he thought she could possibly want. David Blakely offered her nothing except insult and assault. It is not surprising that jealousy, which John Milton described as the 'injured lover's hell', drove all more rational thoughts from his mind. There is little doubt that Desmond Cussen grew to hate and detest Blakely. This hatred gradually magnified until it became an even greater obsession than his love for the club hostess.

When David Blakely was dead and Ruth Ellis sentenced to death, perhaps then – and only then – did Desmond Cussen's jealousy die. With Ruth Ellis separated from him by the grey walls of Holloway prison, her attraction for him may also have waned.

It may be that, as if awakening from a nightmare, he began thinking as a rational businessman again; and thinking rationally, he thanked God he had not stood beside her in the dock on a charge of murder.

What had transpired must have seemed to him like an episode from a horror film. He, a well-established and respected man of commerce, had become involved with a cheap tart who slept around, acted as a manageress for a notorious pimp, and was known as an expert in fulfilling the kinkiest fantasies of her clients. He, a man of judgement, had allowed his mind to become eroded by jealousy for a wastrel who was not worthy to share a room with him, and out of his hatred he had risked trial by jury through handing Ruth Ellis the weapon of death. As if waking from a bad dream, perhaps, Desmond Cussen stretched himself and decided on the day after the verdict to start a new day and a new life.

On the other hand, his reasons for severing all connections with Ruth Ellis once she had been condemned may have been even less admirable . . . if that were possible. Until the foreman of the jury had uttered the word 'guilty', Cussen had been in peril. At any moment Ruth Ellis might have decided to tell the whole truth and in so doing might have pointed at him and said: 'There is the man who gave me the gun. There is the man who plied me with pastis when he knew I was already taking tranquillizers. He could see I was in no fit state to know what I was doing. He knew I could not see very well, so he had to teach me how to fire and aim the gun. He encouraged me to kill David. He urged me to fulfil my boasts. Indeed, he drove me to Tanza Road to find David and when he was not there, drove me to the Magdala. He only drove off when I was arrested. I want to die for I believe in an "eye for an eye and a tooth for a tooth", but I want the truth told. How the Findlaters enticed David away from me and how he, Desmond Cussen, urged me to kill him.'

Certainly when Ruth Ellis was found guilty, Desmond Cussen had no further reason to reassure her of his support. There could be no second trial. He was safe. So the presents to Holloway ceased, as did the correspondence. Today Cussen lives in Australia where he recently told a newspaper reporter when confronted with those accusations that Ruth could so easily have pointed at him from the witness box at the Old Bailey: 'I won't say she's a liar.'

6

Cliff Davis was the only person in the story of Ruth Ellis who really *knew* the three leading characters well. Today he runs a successful second-hand sports-car business in London. A tall, ebullient character, Davis dominated the 1500cc class during the early part of the fifties. At first sight he strikes one as being the archetypal RAF fighter pilot based at Biggin Hill in endless war films. Although now middle-aged, there are still strong intimations of the cavalier sports-car driver of the post-war period.

As a young man, his entire life was centred on cars, racing, and the racing throng. It was David Blakely who introduced him to Ruth Ellis. For weeks Blakely had been pressing him to go to the Little Club to see this 'smashing blonde . . . what a girl!'

Recently he recorded with affection his memories of those days generally and of Blakely, Ruth Ellis, and the Little Club specifically. When asked how well he knew Blakely, he smiled and answered: 'I knew him a lot longer than I knew Ruth, but I did get to know Ruth very well later. You see we used her club a hell of a lot. We used to go there almost every night after a spell at the Steering Wheel.

'We used to have a real laugh at the Steering Wheel, but that club used to shut at eleven, so, of course, we wanted somewhere else to go on to. Rather than go to an expensive night club, we started going down to the Little.' Davis always used to refer to Ruth's club as 'the Little'.

'We had a good time, or I suppose we wouldn't have kept going back. Besides, the Little didn't worry over-much about licensing laws, it kept open virtually until we were ready to leave.'

Davis described the club as being merely an upstairs drinking club on the first floor of a building just off Knightsbridge. There was one room and a bar. It didn't serve food, and everyone associated with it was very amenable. The racing fraternity really used to have a good time with the girls and there would always be a couple of prostitutes hanging around expecting to pick up business. Davis also knew Maury Conley. He only met him twice, but quickly formed an opinion of him. 'Frankly, he was a typical West End spiv; not a man you would particularly want to consort with.'

Blakely and Davis met at the track. David would race a lot in those days, racing a Cooper while Blakely had an HRG. Both were in the same class, so it was inevitable that they would get together both on and off the track. 'You see, motor racing in those days was completely different from what it is today,' explained Davis. 'You could go to a club meeting and all of the boys would be there: Stirling Moss, Mike Hawthorne, Peter Collins . . . the whole scene. An ordinary club meeting. Then next week there could be an international event at Silverstone and we'd all go there. It would be the same mob. There wasn't this differentiation there is today between club racing and professional racing drivers. We were all being paid more or less as professional racing drivers, but only bloody few of us made a living at it. Most of us were subsidized by parents or businesses.'

His very first meeting with Blakely had been at the Steering Wheel Club: 'In those days racing drivers weren't like they are today. You lived at a very fast rate; booze, women . . . everything. All the things they shudder about today. That was the name of the game. And all of us used to meet at the Steering Wheel. It was a super place. Just two rooms – the bar and a few steps up to the restaurant. So you could walk into the Steering Wheel and one glance round would tell you who was there. You'd be bound to find some of your mates. That's why the place ticked. It was home to anybody who was anybody in the racing world. So I used to see a lot of David. If we'd go to Silverstone we'd have piss-ups in the local pub either before or after the meeting. He liked his booze; he was really a drinker.'

Asked of David Blakely's character, Davis smiled, rubbed his RAF-style moustache and said: 'David was a good-looking, well-educated, supercilious shit! He wasn't averse to poncing, and he certainly ponced on Ruth. His parents kept him and he had a flat just off Park Lane paid for by them. He was looked after by a housekeeper, and his stepfather paid her wages too. That housekeeper was like a mother to him.

'I went round there several times, though he didn't encourage too many visitors there. I don't know if he even took the odd bird there. I liked David, no mistakes about that. You see, we've all got our faults. You don't go about looking for a man's faults if he's a good drinking mate and you can have a laugh with him. Ruth would go down to a race meeting and she'd bring a bloody great holdall full of champagne and delicious food. She'd lay on a banquet picnic. Of course we all used to dive in. She was tremendous fun.'

His recollections do not correspond with those of Ant Findlater, who said just as recently that at race meetings: 'Ruth did not fit in. She stuck out like a sore thumb.'

If Davis considered Blakely a supercilious shit, what did he make of Ruth Ellis's character? 'She was a typical club girl you'd meet in an after-hours drinking club. She was very attractive. Mind you, she was not a girl I'd personally have gone for, because she was too clued-up, too sharp. She'd been around. She had the sort of qualities some men look for, but not me. On the other hand as a woman – not to marry but to fuck – she was wonderful. She was the best fuck that has ever been created. She was out on her own. The only woman I can honestly say in my life who had – as far as sex was concerned – no equal!'

He admitted frankly that he had made love with Ruth, or rather, that she had made love to him. 'It was just one of those things. The boys used to lark around and the language was always very heavy. It just clicked one night. I always used to pull her leg. I used to say: "I think you'd make a real good fuck, Ruth," and one night she said "Come on then, let's go."'

It has often been said that Ruth Ellis was a whore. That she accepted money for sex. This certainly isn't Cliff Davis's impression. 'As far as the boys of the racing world were concerned, Ruth always bought her round. She never ponced on anyone; not once. There was no argument about that. We all used to go in there and she'd set us up as soon as we arrived, no matter how many of us there were. And as far as I know she didn't take money for sex.

'But what an artist! She started at your toes and she went all the way up with her tongue. She gave you the full treatment, and by the time you got through, you felt out of this world. She really developed her potentialities to the limit as a sex symbol. Terrific! I

66

only ever had the experience once, because it was the only time I clicked with her, but I was never short of birds in those days.

'But apart from sex I rated her very highly as a person. OK, they all say today that she was this and that, but she had a hard life and she kept her principles. She had a bloody sight more principles than Blakely. With all good things going for her she was nuts about him. After all, he was a good-looking boy who spoke very well indeed. You couldn't help but like him. Ruth was a placid person, and I never knew her to get angry or blow her top. I wouldn't have thought she was an explosive person. But put the two of them together and it could be something completely different. She wouldn't have gone to bed with anyone who was paying, but if she *fancied* someone, it was OK.'

Cliff Davis was asked if he thought it was just sex that kept Blakely and Ruth together. 'I think it went a lot deeper than that. I used to go down the Little some nights with Blakely. If it was a quiet evening, she'd come over and have a chat with us. She'd make a great do over him.'

At her trial, evidence was given as to Blakely's assaulting her in public. This did not sound as if they enjoyed quiet chats together. 'Well, he never hit her at the Little or in front of me. He wouldn't have dared. But just the same I knew he used to knock her around because she used to have black eyes and bruises. Theirs was the absolute in the love-hate relationship. They were two people who should never have been allowed to meet because they reacted like dynamite to each other. They wanted each other – and the feeling was so diabolically strong that it excluded everybody else. If she was talking to somebody else or flirting with someone it immediately sparked off an explosion. And of course she felt the same over his behaviour.

'But just the same I never saw him hit her in public. They were usually very good, for after all David was basically a gentleman, although he could be a bastard on occasion. But outwardly he'd control himself.

'At that time, Blakely had a girl-friend, a very sweet girl, and at the end of every season we used to go to dinners and dances together. David used to come with his girl-friend; never with Ruth. Of course that just wouldn't have been on. Usually he took this one girl; after all, he was engaged to her.'

What sort of driver was Blakely? 'He did quite well, though I don't think he won an awful lot of races. But in those days I used to win most of the races in the 1500cc class.'

So, if Blakely was 'quite good' why didn't he do better? 'The usual problems: money, development, time, and knowledge. Of course he had a certain amount of money, but it was never enough. He had quite a good mechanic, too, in Ant Findlater. But it's not quite as simple as that. To be fair, he did drive at Le Mans. I think he drove for the works. He wasn't a member of the British Racing Drivers' Club, you have to qualify for that. You've got to win three international races within a set period. I joined in 1952. There are only about 500 members today.'

Davis went on to describe the explosive nature of Blakely's and Ruth's love-hate relationship and how he took it when he heard the news of the shooting. 'I never thought it would end like that. You meet people in life who have arguments and rows with their wives, swear and curse at them. Then they're all lovey-dovey the next minute. Nothing really serious comes of it. But this was a time when things went too far. She was incensed; out of her mind.

'And you know, the real villain of the piece was Desmond Cussen. He was a snaky bastard. I knew him well. He was well-dressed and suave. Not so young as most of us. Thick-set chap. He always used to sit in the corner of the Steering Wheel and drink on his own. That is, unless he could get somebody to talk to him. He wasn't a popular man at all. Yes, I spoke to him many times. I knew him well, but he was a cagey character.'

The last time Davis saw Blakely was shortly before the shooting. When the news filtered through to Goodwood, where Davis was racing that day, he was not overly surprised. Of course, it caused him a shock, but nothing more. Racing drivers are used to seeing their best friends killed on the track and they come to accept death as second nature. Because of all the fights between David and Ruth, Davis was half expecting something explosive to happen, although a gun was the last thing on his list of possible weapons. 'I knew it might erupt into something. She might have stuck a knife into him. She probably would if that bastard Cussen hadn't given her the gun.'

He spoke warmly about the police efforts after the shooting to try and find something sympathetic in Ruth's case, so there might be a stay of execution. The police talked to Ruth's friends, mostly asking questions about Desmond Cussen, who they believed had a lot more to do with the murder than had originally been thought.

Davis explains: 'Cussen was madly in love with Ruth and hated Blakely's guts. He gave her the gun. Where else would she have got it from? I suppose she could have got it from Conley. No, my assumption could be wrong, but as far as I was concerned, knowing the background of Cussen and Blakely, it's a fair assumption. Cussen was the sort of bloke that wouldn't surprise you with anything he had. He was one of those types. Anyway it was a *crime passionel* and she wouldn't have hanged anywhere else in the world.'

If Cussen was unpopular and had to persuade people to talk to him at the Steering Wheel, what about David Blakely? 'He wasn't too popular, either, but for different reasons. I even had a punch-up with Mike Hawthorne over him one night. We used to lark around, putting the soda syphon on each other, the sort of things you do in high spirits. I went in one night and by all accounts Blakely had put the syphon on Hawthorne. Mike was absolutely raving.

'I went to the bar and there, right at the end, crouched down, was Blakely. He said to me: "Shhh!!! Don't let the bastard know I'm here, he's going to kill me!" Well, Blakely couldn't get out, so I went over to Hawthorne and asked Mike what was going on. He said: "That bastard Blakely. I'll fucking kill him if I get my hands on him!" I told Hawthorne not to be silly, but he was raging. He said: "I will. I'll break his fucking neck!" "No you won't," I said. Hawthorne told me that I wouldn't stop him and then he took a swipe at me. He missed, but just hooked my glasses off, so I just woofed him one. He was a big feller, but it was just one of those things. He didn't really want to hit me, I'm sure. But he took a swipe in anger and knocked my glasses off. I just went red; and bang! Then it was all finished and we had a drink together.'

Cliff Davis presents an accurate picture of the behaviour of the racing crowd in those days, and an accurate picture of the men who inhabited the drinking clubs. He justifies what Ruth Ellis said to her sister Muriel when describing them. 'They were all little boys who needed their mothers to wipe their arses for them. As for the girls at the club, they thought they were doing them a favour. Once one of them told me that screwing the girls was like sticking it into a bowl of rice. That made me laugh, because I'd heard what the girls had to say. None of these brave racing drivers were real men. They had to go to whores because they couldn't satisfy their wives or girl-friends.'

And who would say she was wrong?

7

Ant Findlater is a mechanic. He lived in Tanza Road, Hampstead, and was working with Blakely on a new racing car. Ruth Ellis lost interest in her trial when she realized that the Findlaters would not be shown as the conspirators who had planned to steal her beloved David from her. She had not wanted to live, but she did want the 'round unvarnished tale delivered'. She wanted to point the finger of accusation at them. She wanted her son, Andy, to know when he grew up that his mother was by no means an evil woman, but instead a victim of the Findlaters' intrigue.

Despite the bruises, black eyes, and split lips she suffered at his fists and the scratches and wounds he displayed to his friends the Findlaters, Ruth Ellis still believed David Blakely loved her. Even though it was Desmond Cussen who was paying to keep young Andy at school and was providing her with a roof over her head, Ruth Ellis was prepared to give up all this security to marry the young racing driver, who so far had given her only insults and misery.

On 8 March 1954, she had an abortion. The following day at lunch, David, guilt-ridden, told her: 'I only wish we could have kept little David. If only I'd had enough money.'

'Surely,' Ruth asked herself, 'he would eventually have come to me and married me despite all the wounding words which had passed between us? If it weren't for the Findlaters we would have found happiness together.'

She had few misconceptions as far as David Blakely was concerned. She knew he was weak, ineffectual, and easily led. She had, more or less, been keeping him. She had lost her job as manageress of the Little Club through letting him drink and buy rounds 'on the slate'.

Desmond Cussen was completely infatuated with Ruth Ellis. The company director was not only well-to-do, but also reliable;

probably the most reliable man Ruth Ellis ever had dealings with. He could and would offer her security. Yet she had not hesitated to place her relationship with him in jeopardy by lying to escape from his flat so as to sleep with David Blakely at the Rodney Hotel in Kensington. It was not even as if David Blakely was a good lover. Of recent months he had had to take amyl nitrate capsules before he was able to satisfy Ruth. He would press her lips against his and then break the capsule under their noses. This inhalation resulted in the slowing down of his orgasm and prevented his premature ejaculation. David had nothing to offer except his sexual attraction, which had not recently been supported by performance. But Ruth was prepared to swallow her pride and his insults, solely because she believed she loved him. 'Surely he must reciprocate?' she continually asked herself.

And as she loved David Blakely, so Desmond Cussen loved her. It is ironic that Ruth Ellis, though desperate at David's brutality to her, treated her alternative lover just as thoughtlessly as the younger man treated her. During the last days before shooting David, she had as good as ordered her alternative lover to act as chauffeur as she chased Blakely first to his flat at Penn, then to his friends at Tanza Road, Hampstead, then back again to Penn, and finally via Tanza Road to the Magdala public house where she at last caught up with her quarry. She gave no thought to the dreadful hurt she must have been inflicting on Desmond Cussen, so it is hardly surprising that such a bitter hatred should build up in the businessman's mind against his younger rival. To be forced to drive the woman one loves in pursuit of a young man of little ability and no morals who could and would offer her nothing, must have been humiliating in the extreme. It is not surprising, therefore, that when Ruth was angry enough to kill, it would be Desmond Cussen who would place in her hand the weapon of revenge.

Ruth Ellis, like many others, had to find someone to blame for David Blakely's atrocious treatment of her. As her 'scapegoats' she selected Carole and Anthony Findlater. All the disgust she felt for herself she transferred to the Findlaters. They hated her . . . and she believed she had undeniable evidence of their hatred. Carole Findlater had been one of David's lovers. Naturally, because of this she would take David's side, however badly he behaved. Ant Findlater, though cuckolded by the man he called 'his best friend', had been able to forget the affair, if indeed he had ever known of it. If he did know, then his memory could be conveniently stilled, especially as David was paying him ten pounds a week to build a car they were to call 'The Emperor'.

For David to have kept running to them for comfort and advice was an open insult to Ruth. But why should David have tried to hide from her anyway? After all, she was far more attractive and sensual than the rather austere, bespectacled, intellectual Jewess.

At the outset of the trial Ruth Ellis had wanted to die. She had killed and she believed in retribution. But just the same, she wanted the world to know how the Findlaters had conspired to separate her from the man she had loved. She believed sincerely that the Findlaters had hired an au pair girl to provide David with a sleeping partner now that Carole was no longer available. That the au pair looked after the Findlaters' baby, Francesca, was just camouflage. The girl's real function was to entice David Blakely away from Ruth.

In the last forty-eight hours before the shooting outside the Magdala, Ruth, driven by Desmond Cussen, had gone again and again to Tanza Road. She had telephoned non-stop until the early hours of the morning in the last twenty-four hours. She believed that on at least two occasions she had heard giggling before the receiver was replaced. She attributed the giggling to the Findlaters and David Blakely laughing at her efforts to speak to him.

These were the thoughts which must have been in Ruth Ellis's mind as she stood calmly in the witness box at the Old Bailey giving evidence on her own behalf at the trial which was eventually to take her to the scaffold.

Shortly before his death in May 1977, the judge at her trial, Mr Justice Havers, recalled clearly that the major emotion at the trial was one of immense calmness. Deprived of her prey, the Findlaters, Ruth Ellis took little interest in the rest of the proceedings.

Ant Findlater today lives in Menton on the French–Italian border. He has remarried, for he and Carole separated eighteen months after the killing of Blakely. His home is a boat anchored in the Vieux Port and he is still a mechanic, though today he works on marine engines instead of racing cars.

Visited recently by a researcher for Thames Television, he

strongly rebutted any suggestion that he and his ex-wife had conspired to separate David Blakely from Ruth Ellis. With her mind warped by drink, drugs, and jealousy, Ruth Ellis had believed sincerely that not only were the Findlaters inserting a human screen between her and Blakely, but that their hatred for her was so intense that they had been delighted to see him with the au pair, whilst Carole could no longer provide him with female attraction because of her husband's relationship with him.

Ruth Ellis's charge concerning the girl being hired to look after the infant Francesca, but in reality being taken on to lure David away from Ruth, was put to Ant Findlater. He frankly found the suggestion ridiculous. He said: 'She was the size of a horse. If David had tried it on, she would have probably told him not to be so silly.'

However, Ant Findlater made no effort to deny that he and his wife had disliked Ruth Ellis intensely. He believed that Blakely's family environment and education were alien to her upbringing in poverty and her subsequent life in the shadow world of the drinking clubs. He and Carole, his wife, knew David's family well and were guests on several occasions at their seat in Penn. They got on very well with his mother and stepfather, who was also passionately fond of motor racing.

The mechanic recalls today that Humphrey Cook was not only a man of money, but maintained an almost Edwardian taste for tradition and comfort. Each week at his home, a watchmaker came in to wind his clocks whilst a cobbler visited regularly to go through his shoes and take away those which needed new soles or heels. A family like the Cooks, said Ant Findlater, would never in a hundred years have accepted Ruth Ellis into their home. For good measure, Ant Findlater added: 'David made that patently clear to Ruth so there couldn't possibly be any misunderstanding.'

In Ant Findlater's opinion, Ruth Ellis was a tarty, platinum blonde who had a tough life. She saw in David Blakely her one remaining chance of escaping from a sordid existence to build a better future for herself. David afforded her with the last opportunity of attaining respectability. She was a drinking club manageress. She was no longer young. Soon her looks would be fading. 'When she realized that marriage was not going to be the end result, she killed him. It was an open-and-shut case,' implied Findlater.

His words were echoed by Christmas Humphreys, who prosecuted. He said: 'It was a cold-blooded murder. All I had to ask was whether or not she intended to kill Blakely. She said "yes", and that was all there was to it.'

The giggling which Ruth Ellis believed she had heard over the phone was attributed by Ant Findlater to her fertile imagination: fertilized by her jealousy. Laughing, giggling, and amusement, he said, could not have been further from their minds at the time.

All that Saturday – the penultimate day – they had been working on the Emperor, the car which they believed was going to earn them their fame and fortune. That very morning they had spent their last seven pounds on connecting-rods, only to find the car needed other spares before it could be raced. When David Blakely and he returned to Tanza Road, they were both extremely depressed. They decided they could not sit at home and be miserable, so it was decided to throw a small party. According to Ant Findlater, David Blakely was so down that he said he could not possibly face another scene with Ruth, for he thought he 'would go mad'.

This was the reason David Blakely did not answer the phone when she rang. This was why Ant or the au pair girl picked up the receiver on each occasion. According to Ant Findlater there was no conspiracy, only exhaustion. Muriel Jakubait and other members of Ruth Ellis's family are still not prepared to accept this apologia. They, like Ruth, believed and still believe, that the Findlaters contributed to her final breakdown. They consider the Findlaters as much the authors of the murder as the woman who pulled the trigger. It is only too easy to theorize after the event. Emotions at the time make one behave in a manner which in retrospect appears irresponsible or unfeeling.

The Findlaters met during the war at Sawbridgeworth in Hertfordshire, whilst Carole was in the WRAF driving a radio truck and Ant was a sergeant in the RAF. Carole, short and slim, dark haired, wearing horn-rimmed spectacles, with a wide full-lipped mouth which she painted vivid scarlet when she went out, was of Jewish–Russian parentage. Her family had come to England at the turn of the century to escape persecution. They had prospered as merchants and she had received a reasonable education. Having a good brain but no particular qualifications, she had decided to become a journalist. Though very young, even before the war she had earned a salary writing articles and sub-editing for small local newspapers.

Carole Sonin grew up to be a woman of considerable drive and enthusiasm. She had an easy turn of phrase and the ability to see beyond the surface of a story. Yet she was no bluestocking. She enjoyed life and like many intelligent people she did not usually suffer fools gladly. This makes David Blakely's attraction for her even more difficult to understand. The two had very few, if any, subjects of interest in common – except sex.

Ant Findlater also came from a middle-class family. His father, Seaton Findlater, was sent to Harrow before returning to his native Dublin as an undergraduate. In Dublin the family had run a successful grocery business for many years, so Ant Findlater had experienced no financial hardship in his youth. Everything had been easy and comfortable. But times change. The family's prospering was no meagre achievement, as they were Presbyterians working in a predominantly Roman Catholic area.

After university, Seaton Findlater had returned to England where he settled at Lower Wick in Worcestershire. He became a well-known racing driver, winning numerous events without ever suggesting that he would become world famous. Like so many fathers, having spent a lifetime in the sport, he became disillusioned with the efforts of the new generation and did everything in his power to discourage his son from following in his tyre-marks. Indeed, he considered his son to be of very limited intelligence and when he met Carole he suggested to her that she was throwing herself away on Ant.

During the months they were both at Sawbridgeworth, they spent every off-duty moment together. This relationship was severed when Ant was posted to Italy. As a young man he was extremely shy and diffident and he had never steeled himself to tell Carole of his feelings for her. But distance lends courage as well as enchantment. He wrote regularly to her and his letters became increasingly passionate. Any fears which Carole might have nursed as to his finding an olive-skinned Italian girl to usurp her place in his affections proved groundless.

Immediately upon his return to London at the end of the war, they met and declared their love. Within days of their reunion they were married at Kensington Register Office, then a white-tiled public lavatory of a building opposite St Mary Abbots Hospital in Marloes Road. At the time Ant was twenty-four, his new wife, twenty-two.

Neither of them had money and they were faced with setting up a home. Unlike those who had been in regular employment prior to the war and so were guaranteed their jobs back by governmental decree, there were few openings in the capital for a man of no qualifications but with a taste for 'tinkering about with engines', and a girl who had been a cub reporter on obscure provincial journals.

Looking back on those early days, Ant Findlater recalls that they were too much in love to be afraid or unhappy at their situation. Today, he states frankly that Carole was always to be the breadwinner in the family, and he remembers with an openly admitted sense of shame that after the trial and execution of Ruth Ellis, when they were being hounded by the Press, Carole wrote an article which earned them a much-needed sixty pounds. 'That allowed us to go on holiday away from all the fuss.'

It was essential that both of them found work. It was, however, clearly unlikely that they would find occupations which would allow them to be together in the same town let alone with the same company. They accepted that they would probably have to face long periods of separation and, indeed, this proved to be the case. Eventually Ant found work as a salesman for a neon-sign manufacturer and Carole went to work on local newspapers in Kent and Nottinghamshire. Her pay was higher than her husband's, a condition which was to continue throughout their married life, except when she was pregnant and unable to work.

Carole Findlater was as ambitious as her husband was easy-going. She did not find living in the provinces provided her with the social stimuli her keen intelligence deserved. Through a friend she heard of an opening as an assistant press officer at the Royal Society for the Prevention of Accidents. She applied and was duly accepted. This brought her to London but provided little scope for her undoubted talents. So even while she was learning what was involved, she was looking around for more congenial and promising work.

Eventually *Woman* magazine offered her a post of sub-editor.

She was paid a very respectable twenty pounds a week. Soon she earned promotion and was writing articles. With this financial backing she took a flat at Colet Gardens, between Talgarth Road and Hammersmith Road in west London. There she was at last joined by Ant.

Though money was short, they were still very much in love. With her meagre savings she bought him an aged Alfa Romeo. This present was not perhaps very wise, for it was this car that was to affect their lives and their future. Firstly, Ant became so immersed in the car, spending every moment he could with his head under the bonnet, that she saw very little of him. This meant that inevitably they grew apart, so that when Blakely appeared on the scene she was mentally and physically ready to take a lover. Secondly, the car was to bring David Blakely into their lives. Ant, though unambitious, must have felt some misgivings over his position as head of the household. His earnings scarcely paid the rent. The gift of the car emphasized the gulf between their earning capacities. It could not have deflated his pride more. He came from a middle-class family and had typical middle-class standards. He knew that traditionally the man is, or at least should be, the chief wage-earner.

When they were together they found themselves bickering. In 1951, the effort of trying to keep the car on the road proved beyond their joint financial capabilities. Resigned to losing his precious car, Ant advertised it for sale. A prospective buyer coming to Colet Gardens to inspect the Alfa Romeo brought with him as his adviser a young man who clearly knew a great deal about cars. Soon Ant Findlater and the youngster were talking cars and racing, excluding from their conversation both Carole and the prospective buyer. This was the first meeting between the Findlaters and David Blakely.

The prospective buyer, perhaps irritated by being ignored, decided not to buy the car. But the meeting had an important outcome on this story. David Blakely had been considerably impressed by Ant's knowledge and enthusiasm for cars. The feeling was mutual, so that it was not surprising that a few weeks later David Blakely telephoned Ant and invited him to come and have a look at an HRG sports car he had been given by his stepfather.

By this time David Blakely was living at 28 Culross Street off

Park Lane in Mayfair, a flat provided by his indulgent stepfather, who lived with his mother across the mews at number 4, which meant they were able to keep an eye on the young would-be racing driver. David shared the flat with his brother and was looked after by his old nanny, who had been brought down from Sheffield.

The HRG, named after its designer H. R. Godfrey, was parked outside the flat. It is likely that as the two men inspected the engine the seed of the idea of building a dream car together was sown. From then onwards David Blakely and Ant Findlater saw much of each other. At first Carole felt left out as the two men talked of little else but cars. Indeed, it is more than possible that she was so incensed at being excluded from their conversation that she decided to have an affair with Blakely, solely to shatter the bond between the two men.

There are stories that David and Carole slept together many times, whilst her husband believed she was attending her National Union of Journalists chapel meetings. It has even been described how on one occasion she actually decided to leave Ant to live with David. But when Ant found her packing her bag he was so upset she changed her mind. It has also been said that David Blakely and she had a terrific row when he discovered she had told Ant that he was the 'other man' in her life. Certainly, David Blakely was such a coward that he could well have feared to face a friend who knew that he had seduced his wife. Whatever the truth, any cracks were patched up and soon David Blakely was once again a welcome visitor to Colet Gardens.

Ant Findlater says that at the time of Ruth Ellis's execution it was suggested to him that Carole had been having an affair with David Blakely. He claims he does not know whether or not it was true. But he recently commented, without any apparent sign of bitterness: 'If the opportunity had been there, David was not the sort of man to pass it up.'

Ruth Ellis had no such doubts. She was certain Carole Findlater had been David's lover. It was this certainty that explains her angry and rude behaviour when the two women first met. They were introduced at a party and according to onlookers, approached each other like skilled boxers sparring for an opening. Afterwards both made catty remarks about the other, Ruth concentrating on what she considered to be Carole's stuck-up manner, whilst Mrs Findlater sweetly exonerated Ruth of rudeness on the grounds of her unfortunate upbringing.

The dislike between the two women was so patent that David Blakely never suggested they should make up a foursome. If he did want to take a girl with him when he was out with the Findlaters, he took his sister, Maureen.

Though Ruth accepted that she would never be welcomed at Colet Gardens, she did not intend to be excluded from any other aspect of her lover's life. He loved motor racing and missed none of the racing events at circuits within touch of London. So she nagged him unmercifully until he agreed to take her with him. When she was with him, the Findlaters stayed away, so strong was their antipathy towards her.

By now Ant was working as a fitter with Aston Martin. The job paid better and was more to his liking than selling signs. To David Blakely the £7000 left him by his father had seemed a fortune. But with drinking and buying rounds for anyone who would listen to his boasts – as well as standing Ant's corner when the mechanic was short of cash – the capital had diminished alarmingly. If he were to save anything, he would have to take immediate action. What could he do with the remaining cash? How could he best invest it and not earn a meagre interest, but instead have a chance of multiplying it many times over? The longer he thought about it, the clearer became the solution. He would build a special car. Ant would help design it and be its mechanic. He himself would drive it to victory. He would call it 'The Emperor'. It would be the prototype for a whole fleet of sports cars which would sell for between £1000 and £1250 each. The royalties on the offspring of the Emperor would make him and Ant a fortune. Of such stuff are dreams made.

Naturally, Ant Findlater was enthusiastic. To work on a car from its very conception! To watch as his best friend drove past the chequered flag in a car he had helped to create! To earn far more money than his wife ever hoped to make from her journalism!

At this moment, when both men were lost in their euphoric dreams, Carole chose to inform them that she was pregnant and would soon have to give up work. The major part of the Findlaters' weekly budget would cease to exist. Ant Findlater would have to stay with Aston Martin, for without Carole's money he could not afford to drop everything to work on the Emperor. It seemed as if their dreams were to shatter around them. But David Blakely, enthusiastic and excited, would not be diverted by the Findlaters' lack of finance. He immediately agreed to pay Ant Findlater ten pounds a week while he worked on the prototype. It was a modest sum, but would at least pay the rent. Carole's warnings as to the extra cost involved when the baby arrived were brushed aside. The future to the two men was golden. When the trade had realized what they had achieved, there would be no difficulty in raising money.

Carole, reluctantly, accepted the situation. It was either that or leave Ant and, with her Jewish upbringing, she had a strong sense of family togetherness. When Ant left Aston Martin it meant that every penny that came into the house was of vital importance. It also meant a change in their life-style. No longer could the Findlaters afford to spend their evenings drinking in pubs or clubs.

By now they had moved to Tanza Road by Parliament Hill, close to Hampstead Heath railway station. Their local pub was a small Charrington's house called the Magdala, just across the road from the station.

Carole Findlater had a daughter, Francesca.

The second meeting between Ruth and Carole took place at a party for David Blakely's birthday. Neither of them was afforded any chance of avoiding each other. Knowing that Carole Findlater had looked down upon her, Ruth Ellis decided to play the part allotted to her. After verbal fencing, she emulated David Blakely's taste for horseplay by squirting Carole with a soda syphon.

The Findlaters, in no uncertain manner, told Blakely what they thought of his lover. Blakely, like many young men, wanted the woman with whom he was living to be accepted by his friends. To try and bring the women together, he told Ruth that unless she apologized, she would never see him again. Ruth, in love, reluctantly agreed and with a gesture typically generous of her, gave Carole a christening robe costing over thirty guineas. Carole accepted the robe with little better grace than she had received the apology.

The infant, Francesca, never wore her expensive present. The robe lay unused in a bottom drawer until Carole gave it away to a casual caller collecting for a white elephant stall.

There was no question as to who would be the godfather of the child. No doubt, David Blakely meant every promise he made on behalf of his god-daughter. He had a sense of the theatrical, which allowed him to play a part which he was unfit to fill temperamentally and which he certainly could not sustain. Had he survived and fallen out with the Findlaters, he would have forgotten Francesca in minutes, let alone days.

The birth of the child meant an added strain on the Findlaters' budget. The only solution was for Carole, who had by far the greater earning capacity, to return to work even though this necessitated employing someone to tend the baby.

In August 1954, David Blakely went to Zandvoort in Holland to drive in an international event. David was never to be lucky on the race track. His Dutch adventure was doomed to failure. The car broke down and instead of celebrating victory, which as a romantic he had already achieved in his dreams, he was faced with having to find the money to cover his expenses, and money was becoming more and more short. The Emperor was always requiring new parts and the cost of spares was constantly rising.

Now, as often as not, Ant had to wait for his weekly salary. The Findlaters would have been in considerable financial difficulty had not Carole by now been earning a substantial salary from *Woman* magazine. She had also been commissioned to write a series of articles on women's subjects in the Soviet Union. She flew out to Moscow for a few days, thus relieving her husband of any sense of guilt over the hours he was spending working in their Islington warehouse, when by rights he should have been with wife and new-born daughter.

Despite his shortage of money, David Blakely could not resist trying to cut a dash at the Crown Hotel at Penn, where he played the successful, well-to-do racing driver. He pressed drinks on casual acquaintances, many of whom would have preferred to be left to drink on their own. He distributed his charms quixotically on all women guests, whatever their age or figure.

Humphrey Cook had by now taken a keen interest in the Emperor. He had, however, begun to know his stepson and he refrained from putting any of his own money into the project. He had decided to wait before tendering help until David Blakely proved beyond all shadow of doubt that he was adult enough to concentrate all his energies and finances on one venture at a time.

This is not to say that Cook was unapproachable. Whenever he and David met, he would ask him about his progress on the car and offer advice on the technical snags they were encountering. Just as he was beginning to believe his stepson had grown up, he learned from local friends that David was spending money ostentatiously in the local establishment. The information made Cook decide that David Blakely, for the first time in his life, would have to dig himself out of the trouble of his own making. When David asked for a loan – odd description for a gift which in the past had never been repaid – for the first time in his life Humphrey Cook gave a definite and decided 'no'.

In his subconscious mind, David Blakely had always felt the reassurance that, if he ran into financial difficulty, his stepfather would come forward to bail him out. Now he was really short of money, with barely enough ready cash to buy his own drinks, let alone to treat his friends to rounds or doubles. The Emperor was a voracious monarch when it came to cash.

It was shortage of money which caused David to spend more and more time in the evenings at the Little Club. Ruth Ellis, passionately in love, could not say no to anything he wanted. She would ply him with drinks, let him put his rounds on the slate, so long as he satisfied her in bed. But this was no longer easy. David Blakely was one of the inadequate young breed who need continual conquests to retain their virility. He had been with Ruth for several months. That he continued to satisfy her made him believe that he was entitled to drink at her – or, more accurate, Maury Conley's – expense.

He did not for a moment give any thought to the fact that it was the club owner who was having to meet the bill for his shortage of cash. Ruth always said: 'Help yourself, David.' And that was enough justification. David Blakely had an easy conscience. If he felt any guilt – which is doubtful – over scrounging off Ruth or of putting her into an invidious position, he could reassure himself that everything would be repaid when the Emperor was completed and the car companies were clamouring to buy.

By now, not even Carole's substantial salary was enough to meet the family's bills, the extra cost of the baby, *and* the wages of the au pair. With the ten pounds a week no longer forthcoming – or only infrequently – Ant Findlater was forced to take a job during the day as a salesman of second-hand cars. This work during the day only allowed him enough spare time to work on the Emperor for three or four hours in the evening.

Thus a descending spiral of failure was forged. The less time spent on the car, the longer the delay in completion. The longer the delay, the less would be the money available. The less the money available, the longer the periods became between his having cash available for buying spare parts, which were vital if the Emperor was ever to be a viable proposition on a track. And the longer the hours Ant spent in the evenings and nights working on the Emperor, the less time he spent with Carole. It is little wonder the marriage did not last long after the spotlight of the Press was focused on the ménage at Tanza Road.

To try to save money, David Blakely closed the Islington warehouse and moved the car to his stepfather's private garage in Culross Street. This may have saved rent, but it also meant that they had to work in a confined space without the facilities they had formerly enjoyed. It also meant risking complaints from the neighbours about noise as Ant Findlater worked long into the night.

Ruth Ellis, no doubt, was flattered at David Blakely becoming more and more dependent on her. There is a will to self-destruction in all of us and, though she must have realized that Maury Conley would eventually find out what was going on and, more importantly, what David Blakely's financial distress was costing him personally, she was prepared to place her job in jeopardy to indulge the man she loved. But even though she might be besotted with him, she was no fool. She knew David Blakely was weak. She knew he had been having an affair with Carole Findlater. She appreciated that he was shallow and selfish. She knew he would always put his own interests before hers, so that it was a waste of time trying to stop him working on his car. She could, however, exact promises from him, whilst he was dependent on her for his drinks. Her generosity with Conley's money could be honed into a weapon which would ensure that never again would he become embroiled with Carole Findlater. Ruth told him, loudly and clearly, that he would no longer be welcome at the Little Club if he continued visiting Tanza Road.

Her threat was effective. With the possibility of losing his source of free drinks, he jettisoned without demur his former mistress. For the time being Tanza Road saw him no longer. In some respects, both the Findlaters were relieved by his absence, even though Carole spoke bitterly of his lack of guts. She had by now recovered from the emotional wounds she had sustained during her affair with Blakely. So David, in his absence, became a suitable whipping-boy to be blamed for her husband being away from home for all hours of the night. She told herself that if it were not for David Blakely and his Emperor, by now her husband would have settled down at Aston Martin and be earning a substantial salary. Then, instead of having to work, she would have been able to stay at home and look after Francesca.

For his part, Ant Findlater could work at night on the car, without having any niggling suspicions that David Blakely was at his home sleeping with his wife. It was no sense of moral outrage that motivated these thoughts, but the hurt to his traditional sense of manhood and the fear of neighbours talking.

But by Christmas, the entire situation had changed. Ruth had been discharged as manageress of the club. She had moved into Goodwood Court with Desmond Cussen, who had invited Andy to spend his Christmas holidays with them there. David, having lost his well of free drink when Ruth was sacked, felt himself no longer bound to keep his promise to her and was once again a regular visitor to Tanza Road.

For Christmas night, Ruth arranged a small party at the flat. She invited Jackie Dyer, the Little Club barmaid, one of Mrs Dyer's many men-friends and two or three other members. She did not invite David Blakely because, it being Christmas, he had gone down to Penn to see his mother and stepfather. The party at Goodwood Court was scheduled to start at nine because Desmond Cussen had to go to his company's cocktail party first. So at seven o'clock in the evening Ruth, Jackie Dyer, and her man-friend decided to go out for a pre-party drink. Having put Andy to bed, they left the flat. However, in case some of their guests turned up early, they left a note pinned to the door with the telephone number of the club they were visiting.

Standing chattering at the bar, Ruth told her two amused friends how she had solved her problem of what Christmas presents to buy for the two men in her life. She had given each of them identical silver cigarette cases!

Meanwhile, down in Buckinghamshire, David Blakely was finding life less entertaining than he had hoped. His mother and stepfather had an invitation to have drinks with a neighbour. He could have gone with them but declined as he did not think he would like the sort of people who would be there. At lunchtime, being alone, he went to the Crown. The bar was almost empty, Christmas being a time for family celebration. He lunched in mid-afternoon at the Old Park, after which the Cooks went to rest, leaving him alone. By six o'clock in the evening he was bored, despite having been drinking most of the afternoon. Making his excuses to his mother and stepfather, he drove to London, taking with him a toy revolver he had bought as a present for Andy.

Arriving at Goodwood Court and finding the message pinned to the door, he lost his temper. Like a spoiled child, he expected Ruth to be waiting for him whenever he wanted her. Going out, he phoned the club from a telephone kiosk and when she was fetched from the bar, he shouted that she should be ashamed of herself and that she was an unnatural mother leaving her son alone. It is always helpful to have a moral hook on which to hang a tantrum.

Like a child scolded by her parents, Ruth apologized to her companions for leaving them and hurried back to Goodwood Court. She found David sulking outside the front door. So neighbours should not hear him shouting at her, she took him into the flat, where they had one of their most violent brawls. Their shouted obscenities woke Andy, who lay frightened in his bed unable to shut out their yells and accusations.

David demanded to know how, if she loved him as she said, she could possibly sleep with Cussen. If it were because the older man paid for the flat or met Andy's school fees, then she was nothing better than a common tart. Ruth, equally viciously, shouted at him that Desmond Cussen was at least a man who could provide for her and did not 'ponce on me like you do'. Then she demanded to know what grounds he had for complaint when he had been 'poking Carole Findlater, though what you can get out of screwing that scarecrow, Christ only knows'. Sneering, she added for good measure: 'Does she pay you for it?'

In his drunken angry mood, the injustice of this accusation sent him berserk. He would prove to her once and for all that her recrimination had no basis in truth. Ruth would go with him that very minute to Tanza Road and would confront Carole. So, still shouting at each other, they slammed the door of the flat behind them and went down to his car. Blakely saw nothing incongruous in taking the mother away from her son – the very offence of which he had been accusing her only half an hour earlier.

Desmond Cussen drove up as the two stood by Blakely's car. Realizing that Blakely was exceedingly drunk, he was considerably alarmed when she got into the car and Blakely drove off. Knowing that Blakely was unfit to drive, he followed in his car. He saw them park outside 29 Tanza Road and David Blakely let them into the house with his own keys. He sat watching the house until it was close to nine, when, with a very sick heart, he returned to Goodwood Court to try to reassure Andy and look after the guests, whose hostess was now missing.

In his fury, David Blakely had entirely forgotten that the Findlaters had gone away to stay with friends at Brighton for the weekend. But long ago, Carole had given him a spare set of keys, so he opened the door and let them in. They continued their squabble into the small hours of the morning, when, their furies having been burnt out, they went to bed and made love.

The next morning when Ruth returned to Goodwood Court, Cussen told her that it was no use her lying because he had followed them and had watched her go into the Findlaters' house. For a moment Ruth ran out of excuses. But she had a fertile imagination and, gathering her wits, explained that David had blackmailed her into staying with him by saying that if she left he would commit suicide. Whether Cussen believed her is doubtful, but at all costs he wanted her to stay with him. So he pretended to accept her story, just as in the weeks ahead he accepted her tales of going north to see Georgina, when she was spending the nights with David Blakely at the Rodney Hotel.

Like a metronome ticking off the seconds before an explosion, so the days were passing before the inevitable crisis.

Blakely and Ruth fought. They squabbled. They spat at each other. He hit her. She scratched him. Row followed row; accusation followed accusation. Ruth Ellis knew about his married woman friend at Penn. Whenever he left her saying he was going down to Silicon Pistons to work, she claimed he was lying and would imagine him sleeping with his mistress. She alternated between love and hate; between passion and loathing.

He, too, was in an extremely emotional state of mind. He told the Findlaters repeatedly that all he wanted was to get away from her. He said he could no longer stand her constant accusations and tearful recriminations. But when away from Tanza Road and with Ruth, he would either reassure her of his love and his intention of marrying her when she was free, or would lose his vicious temper and punch her. The strain of their stormy relationship was telling on both of them.

Under these circumstances, it is not surprising that Ruth went to Dr T. P. Rees, the consultant psychiatrist, whom she had met when she had made a scene at Warlingham Park Hospital, when her husband had been an in-patient there. The psychiatrist prescribed a course of tranquillizers.

On 8 January Ruth and David spent the night together and had an even stormier quarrel than usual. Once again she snarled that he had been sleeping with his Penn mistress. He shouted that she was just a tart for sleeping with Cussen when she said she loved him. Once again they came to blows and there were complaints about the noise at the hotel. The next morning he escaped from her by saying he had to go down to Silicon Pistons for an important meeting. He promised that he would phone her in the afternoon so she would not think he was with the other woman. Ruth waited in for the phone call. But the bell never rang. Blakely did not phone the following morning either. Ruth began telling herself that she was never going to see him again, and that the Penn woman had won an unfair victory.

In despair, she wired him at the company: 'Haven't you got the guts to say goodbye to my face? Ruth.'

David was not only a physical coward but a moral one too. What if Humphrey Cook, already angry over his stepson's behaviour at the Crown, should now hear from his friends at Silicons the story of David receiving wires from women at his work? What if he was to learn of David having a married mistress in the village where he and David's mother had their home? Certainly if anything like that happened, Humphrey Cook would be extremely unlikely to inject any of the vitally needed cash into the Emperor. And as time passed, David Blakely was realizing more and more that he and Ant Findlater had embarked on a venture which was proving far more costly than they had ever anticipated.

After crumpling up the wire and consigning it to the wastepaper basket, he drove to the Crown for a drink to steady his nerves. One did not suffice, nor two. He poured out a garbled and somewhat drunken version of what was happening to the landlord, who advised him that in such circumstances a delay for further thought would be advisable. Needless to say these words of wisdom fell on deaf ears. David Blakely was too weak a man, too craven, to sleep on a problem. He was terrified as to what Ruth might do next. He was afraid of his stepfather's anger; afraid the Emperor would never be completed; afraid to tell his mistress at Penn that he would not be seeing her again; afraid to return to Ruth, yet equally afraid to stay away.

As usual he rushed to his best friends for advice. The Findlaters realized only too well that David was a reed who would sway with the wind. They told him bluntly that he should either stay with Ruth and try to establish a reasonable relationship with her, or leave her once and for all. When pressed, they both admitted they favoured the latter course. 'Could you, with your background, really be happy with this common tart?' they asked. David did not accept their advice. Instead, he crawled back to Ruth, assuring her of his love and that he had every intention of marrying her and providing her with a home. Two nights later, they were again together at the Rodney Hotel where once again the guests were treated to a flaring row. Blakely was so violent, that before they could go to a dance as they had arranged, he had to cover the bruises on her arms and shoulders with make-up.

They could not bear being together, but Ruth could stand even less his being away from her. If he were not with her, she tortured her mind by imagining him with other women. Perhaps he was at Penn with his mistress drinking at the Crown and buying everyone drinks with money which she had provided. Or maybe he was with the Findlaters, sleeping with Carole and laughing with Ant at her discomfiture. Or he may even have returned to his usherette or Mary Newton Dawson or the American model. Or Faith . . . or . . .

By now, David Blakely was one of the semi-professionals of the racing track. Occasionally he was asked to drive in minor events. The Bristol works team had entered for Le Mans. Despite his state of mind, David Blakely was elated to be asked to drive for such a team. In his exuberance, he invited Ruth to join him in France. Naturally, she accepted.

Her reaction was delightfully naïve. She immediately began to take French lessons – paid for, of course, by Desmond Cussen – convinced that by the time she went to France, she would be able to show off by speaking the language, if not fluently, at least eloquently. Like so many romantics, it was just a dream. Her tutor found she took very casual interest in the lessons and made not the slightest effort at preparation.

On 14 January she was granted her decree nisi. In three months there would be no impediment to their marrying. In his more reflective moments, David Blakely must have felt the threats to his freedom were closing in on him remorselessly. Now when he tried to placate Ruth by saying they would marry as soon as possible, she would not be put off, but would look at him levelly and ask: 'When?'

The metronome of destruction was now ticking at a faster rate.

They were fighting more often and violently than ever before. They were hating each other but sleeping together. The classic love-hate relationship. The Steering Wheel Club was one of their favourite arenas of battle. So was the Hyde Park Hotel, which David took a perverse delight in visiting since he had been sacked as a trainee. They met each other there one night in different parties and the guests witnessed another of their fights. Once they started attacking each other they lost all thought of how they might appear to the onlookers.

Having found a Rodney Hotel bill for the two in his wastepaper basket, Desmond Cussen could no longer delude himself about her absences at night.

The completion of the Emperor seemed no nearer. Blakely had shifted the car to a garage where Clive Gunnell, a friend, worked. This enabled Clive Gunnell to help Ant Findlater when he was not working for his employer.

In one particularly unpleasant brawl at Goodwood Court, David Blakely punched Ruth Ellis in the face, blacking her eye. In the scuffle she also twisted her ankle. When he tried to get out of the flat, she snatched the keys of his car from his hand and put them into her bag. Once again, David Blakely turned to the Findlaters to rescue him. He telephoned Tanza Road from Goodwood Court, holding the rampaging Ruth at arms length whilst he did so. But Ant was out. So this time he tried the garage. Finding Ant there, he pleaded like the small boy he was: 'Please come and get me ... come and get me.' Then he added: 'She's taken my keys. Please, please come quickly.'

He then turned all his attention to trying to prevent Ruth's fingernails scoring his cheeks.

Ant Findlater and Clive Gunnell drove to Goodwood Court, not at all sure what they would find on arrival. What they did find was Ruth and David extremely drunk and aggressive. Ruth, quite hysterical, was screeching threats, whilst David was in a corner, snivelling that she had tried to knife him. Perhaps there was truth in his accusation, for a girl who says she slept with Blakely some four to six weeks before the shooting says: 'When he undressed there were livid gashes in his arms and back. I asked him where he'd got them. He said: "It was that bitch. She tried to knife me. And that wasn't the first time."'

Ant Findlater and Clive Gunnell endeavoured to bring some semblance of sanity and dignity to the situation. Gunnell took Ruth into the bathroom to bathe her eye, which was already colouring. In so doing, he provided Blakely with the opportunity to retrieve his car keys from her bag and slip out of the flat door. On returning from the bathroom, Ruth was enraged to find her quarry fled. She hobbled after him as fast as she was able, and the shouting and screaming started up again in the street. To prevent his escaping, she got into the driving seat of his car. Immediately, he got out and sat in Ant's vehicle. Ant followed into the driving seat, whilst Gunnell got into the back. But Ruth was not to be denied. She put her head through the open window and switched off the ignition.

No doubt the scene had its comical aspects for the casual passer-by. But a more sensitive spectator would have realized the elements of tragedy there.

With Ruth holding their keys, they could not drive away. So the three men got out and stood in a half-circle around her, as if subconsciously to shield her from any inquisitive glances which might have resulted in the police being called. To give David Blakely a chance of escaping, Ant Findlater decided to employ similar tactics to those he had used at the flat: to divert Ruth's attention, allowing Blakely to get away. To this end, he and Gunnell made much of Ruth, telling her that they understood her point of view and that Blakely was a swine to touch her. Even as he expressed his contempt for David, Ant gestured his friend to get into his own car.

The ruse worked yet again. David Blakely drove away and Ruth, utterly exhausted by all the quarrelling and shouting, allowed her lover's friend to lead her away to have a coffee at a nearby café in Great Portland Street.

At the Findlaters', Blakely peeled off his shirt. Carole iodined the wounds which were livid on his back. Then she sat him down and told him straight that he was a weak idiot if he went back to Ruth after this clear warning as to how violent she could be when provoked.

That night, Ruth, bruised and with her eye stinging, lay on the couch at Goodwood Court and pictured how her lover would be behaving at Tanza Road. Jealousy was eroding what remained of her sanity. Almost as if she were controlled by some force outside her, she urged Desmond Cussen to drive her to Hampstead. As usual he complied, but it is not too difficult to appreciate his emotions as he was asked to chauffeur the woman he loved to look for his rival.

Parked in Tanza Road, they watched as David Blakely, Clive Gunnell, and the Findlaters came out of number 29 and got into David's car. They followed discreetly and again parked in the shadow of the Hampstead tree-lined streets as the four went into the Magdala. They waited until closing time and then once again drove back behind the four to the Findlater's home. However, after his three friends had got out, David suddenly drove off. Cussen was not prepared for this quick getaway and by the time he and Ruth followed, Blakely was out of sight.

Ruth, now the complete huntress, was exasperated. Where had he gone? No doubt to one of his women. Desmond Cussen drove her back to Goodwood Court, where she made several phone calls without finding any trace of her man. Then she asked herself if he

might not once again have fled to Penn. Once more the com-
plaisant Cussen drove her down to Buckinghamshire.

They reached Blakely's flat at the Old Park in the early hours of
the morning. Ruth hammered on the front door and rang the bell
again and again. After some minutes, Blakely's nanny opened the
door. Ruth barged past her into the small entrance hall at the
bottom of the stairs. A few feet up the stairs she could see David
in his pyjamas and dressing-gown.

She began shouting and raging at him. Terrified, as always, he
ran past her out into the drive. Jumping into his car, he drove off.
By the time Ruth had got back to Desmond Cussen, David had
vanished. He knew the area far better than they did, and had no
difficulty in losing them. By the time they had driven round the
country lanes, then driven back to the Old Park, David's car was
parked outside the front door. Once again Ruth hammered at the
door and rang the bell, but this time there was no answer. Now
lethargic and without spirit, she allowed Cussen to drive her back
to London.

The next morning her eye was almost completely closed, her
ankle extremely painful, and she was suffering from loss of sleep.
But her spirit had reawakened. Once again she was the avenger
and insisted Cussen drive her to Penn. He accepted his role
without demur. *En route* to Penn they saw Blakely's car parked
outside the Bull at Gerrards Cross. Cussen stopped, but for once
asserted himself and insisted she wait in the car whilst he found
where Blakely was drinking.

In the main bar he found his rival and accused him of being a
coward who would only hit women but run away when faced with
a man. Blakely sneered at him, laughing in a cocky manner.
Desmond Cussen, white with fury, shouted at the younger man:
'What about hitting a man instead of a woman for a change?'

'I wouldn't bother hitting *you*!' David sneered.

'Aren't you man enough for that even?'

By now the other customers had stopped talking to concentrate
on the exchange, many of them, no doubt, hoping to see a fight.
David decided like many others before him that discretion is really
the better part of valour and, slipping by Cussen, he made for the
door. But by now, Ruth was standing impatiently in the doorway.
So though denied fisticuffs, the customers were treated to the far

from edifying sight of Blakely shoving a blonde woman out through the door as she screamed abuse at him.

By the time Cussen joined her outside, David Blakely had jumped into his car and driven away. He had too good a start for them to waste time following him, so they drove back to London, where Cussen took her to the Middlesex Hospital in Mortimer Street where they dressed her eye and X-rayed her ankle. It was not broken as she had feared, but only badly bruised. Afterwards they went back to Goodwood Court where Cussen did his best to comfort her. Two hours later there was a knock on the door of the flat. Cussen opened the door to find a delivery boy holding a large bunch of red carnations. David Blakely, once more afraid of her reaction to the scene at the Bull, was trying to make his peace with her. Another episode in her life marked by red carnations!

On 8 February Ruth moved into her own flat at 44 Egerton Gardens. 'Her' flat may be a misnomer, because she paid rent in advance with money supplied by Desmond Cussen. Soon she was being visited at Egerton Gardens by both her lovers, David Blakely always telephoning first lest he should meet Cussen and again be threatened with a fight.

Up until the row at Gerrards Cross, the two men, despite their intense rivalry over Ruth, had tried to keep their relationship on a civilized basis. Indeed, on one occasion, David Blakely had actually invited Desmond Cussen to act as his co-driver in a rally to Brighton.

Mrs Joan Winstanley, a former club owner and now the house-keeper at Egerton Gardens, has recently said: 'I never liked anything about Mr Cussen. He was a surly beast, who never spoke to me or passed the time of day unless I spoke to him first. But I liked David Blakely, though I only saw him a few times. He always arrived and left as though he was in a tearing hurry. But all the same he never failed to call out to me if I was about.'

Considering the sensation the murder was to cause, Mrs Winstanley remembers very little about the woman who was to become notorious: 'I really didn't see much of her, but I liked what I saw. I was amazed when only a few weeks after she had taken the flat, I was woken up in the early hours by the police and told she'd shot her young man.'

It was in this atmosphere of jealousy, hatred, and intense passion that Ruth conceived a child. How she could know which of the two men was the father it is impossible to say. Nevertheless, despite Carole Findlater telling him he was being blackmailed, David Blakely accepted the unborn child as his. Perhaps he felt some pride in siring a child, abating his inner sense of inadequacy. Her pregnancy did not, however, prevent their fighting, and the battles were as violent as ever. After one scene he again sought refuge at Penn. Again she persuaded Cussen to act as her chauffeur. The advertising agents, stockbrokers, and businessmen who make up the main personnel of the Crown were entertained to a battle royal, which David knew could not be kept secret from his stepfather. At least he might keep one aspect concealed from his family and to pacify Ruth he swore to her that he would never again see his mistress in the village. He also promised that as soon as the Emperor was racing, he would marry Ruth.

During her trial, Ruth Ellis was asked by her counsel why she had lost her child. She explained that David Blakely had punched her in the stomach, which she believed had caused her to miscarry. Subsequently, she claimed that far from miscarrying, she had had an abortion, knowing there could be little future for a child brought up in such circumstances. There is evidence that the second version is likely to have been more accurate than her first assertion.

Whichever it was, David Blakely, as usual, was full of remorse afterwards and reassured Ruth as to his love, telling her that he 'wished I had had enough money to keep little David. But I haven't'. This seems to bear out the theory that she had her pregnancy intentionally terminated. Mr Justice Havers has since said that had he and the jury known of her abortion and that she had been taking tranquillizers before drinking Pernod, she would never have hanged.

The Emperor was now almost completed, though Ant Findlater and Clive Gunnell had reservations as to whether it was really ready for the track. David Blakely, however, was becoming more and more desperate as time and money were running out. His life was in shreds. Desperately he wanted to compensate for all the past failures in his private life by winning fame and admiration in his wonder car. So, ignoring the Cassandra warnings of his two friends, he entered the car for a race on 2 April at Oulton Park, in the north of England.

As a result of entering the car for a fixed date, he had little time to spend with Ruth Ellis, who, feeling ill after her abortion, resented playing second fiddle to a car almost as much as to another woman. Ruth, still bleeding, was not prepared to fade conveniently into the background until David had won his race and deigned to notice her again. She was continually telephoning him at the garage, refusing to believe either of his friends whenever they told her he was not there. Eventually David, extremely distracted and feeling as if a female sword of Damocles was hovering over the Emperor's bonnet, silenced her in the only way he knew – by promising once again to marry her as soon as the car was ready. This provided her with a reason to leave him to work on the car in peace.

Considering his past promises it is odd that she was prepared to believe his protestation; but she did. In the few days remaining before leaving for Chester and the race, Ruth Ellis passed the time ringing up all her friends from her club days, telling them the news of the impending ceremony. She drove down to Chester with David and Ant, where they were joined by Carole Findlater, who, as woman's editor of the *Daily Mail* by now, had a justifiable excuse for attending the meeting. She would afterwards write an article on women's fashions at the track.

Despite the friction between the two women, the four of them were excited and confident – or at least pretended to be – as to the outcome of the race. Even Ant Findlater put his reservations behind him.

Often a fraction of a second is all that is needed to transform hope into failure and euphoric dreams into nightmares. So it was with the Emperor. The car was never to be driven before the racing public. It broke down in practice and was out of the race. Blakely, unmindful of Oscar Wilde's words: 'Yet each man kills the thing he loves. Some do it with a bitter look and some men with a flattering word', was not content with a bitter look, but verbally and publicly vented his spleen on the woman who loved him most. He blamed Ruth for the car's breaking down. If she had left him in peace to work on the car it would have been ready. All the scenes she had caused had interrupted his concentration. There was a jinx on the car, and in his opinion that jinx was Ruth.

Despite having no car to race, the four decided to stay over for

96

the meeting and to drown their sorrows in the hotel bar. Whilst they were at Chester, Desmond Cussen had been in Wales. Returning to Goodwood Court he found a note from Andy's school, informing Ruth that the school was breaking up that very day. Cussen immediately phoned Ruth expecting to find her at home. Instead he was told by Mrs Winstanley: 'Mrs Ellis has gone away to watch her "husband" drive in a race meeting.' Only after an extremely angry Desmond Cussen had rung off did the housekeeper find a note Ruth had left for her asking her to make an excuse that she was with Georgina if Mr Cussen telephoned. By the time she received the instructions it was too late, and Cussen knew the truth.

Unlike Goodwood Court, there was no spare bedroom at Egerton Gardens so that when Andy came on holiday he had to sleep on a camp bed in the same room as his mother and David Blakely . . . or Desmond Cussen. It is perhaps fortunate in these circumstances that David Blakely, pleading that he must now sell the Emperor, did not get back to the flat on the Tuesday until the early hours of the morning. No longer having the Emperor's success to dream about, David Blakely was in a mean, surly mood. He no longer mentioned marriage. Soon they were again wrangling acrimoniously.

On the Wednesday, he was in a far better temper. His vanity had been flattered by having his photograph taken as a member of the Bristol team at Le Mans. Ruth immediately told herself that after all everything would be well between them and that once married there would be no tensions and no rows.

She was delighted when he presented her with a copy of the photograph and signed it: 'To Ruth with all my love, David.' She told herself that she had been unfair to him. That his black moods had been solely through his disappointment over the failure of the Emperor. She even thought that her interference in the days before the disastrous experience at Chester might conceivably have prevented his working on the car. Now she urged him not to sell the car. 'Surely,' she asked, 'we can raise the money somehow?'

David was surprised at her volte-face, because as they wrangled throughout the weekend she had denigrated the Emperor and had continually told him to sell the car and cut his losses. She had even told him, despite the honour of his being asked to drive for the Bristol team, that he should give up any idea of becoming a professional racing driver. However, David Blakely was not the man to miss any chance of saving the Emperor and he suggested, quite shamelessly, that she should ask his rival Desmond Cussen to advance the £400 needed if it were to be repaired.

On Good Friday, 8 April 1955, at ten in the morning, David Blakely left Egerton Gardens in an apparently excellent mood. He told Ruth he was going to talk to Ant Findlater about saving the car, but that he would return that evening so that on Saturday he could take Andy out. At least that was the train of intended events according to what Ruth Ellis told the jury at her trial.

Her version did not, however, correspond with the Findlaters' recollections. They said that at the Magdala that lunchtime David told them that Ruth had been pestering him to take her out that evening, but that he could not put up with her tantrums any longer. He said he was desperate, unhappy, and frightened at her increasing violence. At all costs, he believed, he had to get away from her.

Normally he would have gone down to Penn to escape from her. But what of that last scene at the Crown? She would be certain to guess where he had fled and would follow him. He could not cause his mother and her husband any further embarrassment. At this excuse Carole Findlater had snapped at him: 'For God's sake! Don't be so bloody spineless and silly. Any man can leave any woman. What can she do about it?'

David, like a small boy resenting being rebuked, grumbled something to the effect: 'It's easy for you to talk like that. But you don't know her. You don't know what she can get up to!' Carole Findlater shrugged with exasperation. She had said her piece. She must have asked herself what on earth she could have seen in a man so pitifully weak.

Her husband felt extremely sorry for David. He, perhaps, was the only one who could sense what the Emperor's failure had meant to him. It was Ant who suggested that David should stay with them at Tanza Road over the Easter weekend. He reassured David: 'If Ruth comes round and kicks up a scene, Carole and I will deal with her.' David Blakely grasped at the chance to hide behind his friends and accepted the invitation gratefully.

Meanwhile, Desmond Cussen had fetched Ruth and Andy from Egerton Gardens and taken them back to Goodwood Court for lunch. In the afternoon they went to the cinema. Afterwards, Ruth took Andy home and put him to bed, then she made herself up to go out with David Blakely. She sat down, poured herself a drink and waited for him to fetch her. She waited in vain.

By 9.30, suspecting he might have drunk too much and stayed with the Findlaters, she rang 29 Tanza Road. The au pair girl answered and told her the Findlaters were out. Ruth demanded to know if David Blakely was with them. The girl did not know, and said that as far as she was concerned she was alone in the house with Francesca.

Ruth waited another hour. Then she telephoned again. This time Ant Findlater answered. He assured her that Blakely was not there. Ruth told him that she had been waiting for David since 7.30. She asked him to promise her he did not know Blakely's whereabouts. Ant Findlater admitted he had seen David Blakely, but that afterwards his friend had driven off without saying where he was going.

At the Old Bailey, Mr Melford Stevenson asked her: 'When you were told he had left, did you believe it?'

Ruth Ellis replied from the witness box: 'Not the way he said it. He said it rather cocky . . .'

There is no doubt that Ant Findlater had failed to convince her. Again and again she rang Tanza Road. Sometimes Ant Findlater answered and sometimes he hung up the receiver as soon as he heard her voice. She became more and more exasperated, more and more frustrated. David had promised to marry her. She told herself that he must be staying away on purpose, and that could only mean that the Findlaters – and especially Carole – had persuaded him he was making a mistake.

Between phoning the Findlaters, she rang Desmond Cussen, but he did not return to Goodwood Court until after midnight.

At Tanza Road, the repeated telephone calls had scared David Blakely, not knowing what Ruth might do next. He was by now so frightened of what she might do that he sat trembling on the couch. Seeing him look like a very young and scared schoolboy struck a chord of sympathy in Carole's mind. She put her arms round him and reassured him that if Ruth came after him, she and her husband would take care of her. Then she kissed him, took a sleeping pill, and went to bed.

8

Ruth meanwhile, frustrated and furious at her lack of success at trying to communicate with David, had Desmond Cussen drive her to Tanza Road. Her anger was exacerbated when she spied David's grey-green Vanguard outside the house next door to the Findlaters'.

By now she really did not care what the Findlaters – or for that matter anyone else – thought of her or her actions. She had little vestige of reticence left; no pride remaining. For a moment she stood outside the house where the people she believed to be her enemies lived. Then she almost *ran* up the ten stone steps. She rang the Findlaters' bell. There was no response. She rang again . . . and again . . . and again. There was still no answer, so she kept her finger pressed on the button.

Still no reply. It is not surprising that none of the inhabitants of the flat opened the door. By now Carole was probably asleep, having taken her pill. David was too frightened anyway, whilst Ant Findlater could have seen no advantage to be gained in opening the door and confronting an irate Ruth. Why should he have to brawl with her and probably be faced with having to evict her forcibly from the premises? The au pair girl had probably already gone to bed. Besides, if she roused the whole street with her caterwauling, he would, in all likelihood, have to deal with a batch of complaints.

So Ant was the only one who took any action. He went downstairs into the hallway and stood listening, hoping that Ruth would come to her senses and go home. He must have sighed with relief when he heard her high heels tapping down the steps. But his relief was short-lived. Ruth had not departed for the night. Far from it. She had merely gone to the nearest telephone kiosk and once again dialled the Findlaters' number.

The receiver was lifted off the hook and then replaced without a word. Ruth was still determined that nothing would keep her from a show-down with the apology for a man who was hiding from her behind his friends. Once more, she walked back up Parliament Hill to Tanza Road. She tip-tapped up the stone steps again and rang the bell repeatedly. The house remained silent. There were no voices. No sounds of movement. No female giggles.

Here there is some confusion in the story Ruth Ellis told the court at her trial. She said she heard a woman giggling. She thought it *had* to be the au pair, of whom she was already suspicious. Carole Findlater subsequently said she thought it was more likely to be herself.

Memory can often be fallible about such details. It appears a little unlikely that Carole was giggling and joking considering she had only a short time before swallowed a sleeping pill and kissed David goodnight to reassure him. On the other hand, the discrepancy might have been in Ruth's memory and she may well have been confusing two different episodes and been referring to another occasion. Then the Findlaters, as will be recounted, were to give a small party. Ruth had been eavesdropping outside; thus the confusion would not be at all surprising. Although outwardly calm when giving a statement to the police soon after the shooting, the events of the last forty-eight hours before she shot Blakely may well have kaleidoscoped in her mind and the chronological order of events become so enmeshed in a fog of uncertainty that day was unrecognizable from night, let alone minute from minute.

Men suffering intense frustration have been known to punch a brick wall until their knuckles are broken and the skin bleeding. Ruth's reaction to being deprived of confronting the human object of her venom and hatred was to vent her feelings on the Vanguard parked outside. If she could not strike David Blakely personally, she would take out her anger on his car.

She ran across to Desmond Cussen's car and took a heavy rubber torch out of the glove compartment. Then she ran back to the Vanguard and battered in three windows. Desmond Cussen remained seated in his car, making no effort to restrain or quieten her. No doubt, as he watched the woman he loved making an exhibition of herself over his rival, he must have been sucking threads of jealousy between his teeth. It is not impossible that he might have derived a sense of perverse pleasure watching the other man's prized possession being demolished.

At her trial Ruth was to explain: 'I knew the windows were only stuck in with rubber. So I pushed at one of them. It came clean out of the rubber. It didn't break, just made a lot of noise. Then I did the same with the two other windows.' She was also to describe her emotions, saying: 'I was in a rather nasty mood.'

Using her feelings as an excuse for her actions may well have been a subconscious sophistry; justifying the wanton damage because of the hurts she herself had suffered at his fists. The true reason for her behaviour over the car may well have been that pushing in the car windows would probably make a dreadful noise. This would attract the attention of the Findlaters, who surely would not be able to resist watching her from the blackness of their upstairs room. If so, they would be afraid of her causing a disturbance and their neighbours becoming involved. In which case, Ant might well come downstairs to pacify her. If the latter were the truth, then her ruse was to prove successful.

Ant flung open the door and strode down the steps into the street. He did not have time to try to quieten her with understanding words. A flashing-eyed Ruth confronted him, demanding that he should either fetch David Blakely or else she would go in and fetch him out herself. Ant Findlater, already having taken the wise precaution of telephoning the police, told her flatly that David was nowhere in the neighbourhood as far as he knew, let alone in their flat. But he kept Ruth talking and arguing until the squad car drove up.

The police officer in charge was bombarded by Ruth with justifications and complaints as to how she had been treated. Ant tried to explain quietly what it was all about, but Ruth gave him little or no chance to utter more than a couple of words. Ruth claimed that this was nothing to do with the police. She had helped pay for the Vanguard – part of it belonged to her. If she had bashed in the windows, then they were hers to do with as she liked.

The officer tried to persuade her to go home and sleep on it. She refused unless 'her man' came out and spoke to her. The policeman then shushed her into silence to allow Ant to explain that, firstly, David was not there and, secondly, he did not wish to see Ruth or even speak to her ever again.

The arguments and patent friction between the man and the

blonde woman must have convinced the policeman that he was dealing with a commonplace, everyday squabble between, if not husband and wife, then lover and mistress. He believed that by the morning they would both have forgotten the fight. In such circumstances the police usually try to remain cool and as little involved as possible. Years of experience have shown that the result of trying to bring the warring individuals together more often than not results in both the combatants turning on the police. One wonders what that police officer's reactions were when he heard that the outcome of this 'commonplace, everyday squabble' ended in the blonde shooting her lover?

So, the policeman once again advised her to go home before she caused a breach of the peace, when he would have to take action. He thereupon got back into his car and drove off as Ant Findlater closed his front door behind him.

Ruth took no notice of the policeman's warning. Distraught, she was shouting at the top of her voice. Cussen, having watched the entire scene, sat unmoving in his car. By now it was half past two in the morning and to avoid her waking the neighbourhood, Ant again rang the police. The officer of the law this time spoke words of stronger warning, and must have breathed a sigh of relief when she rejoined Desmond Cussen in his car and drove off up the road.

Cussen delivered Ruth to Egerton Gardens where Andy was sleeping. For the remaining hours of the night, Ruth sat smoking incessantly and thinking. She must have relived the events at Hampstead again and again in her imagination. Her mind in a turmoil, her love had by now been transformed into something akin to hate. To her it all seemed so grossly unjust. She had loved David Blakely with all her heart, not with a blind love, because she was well aware of his weakness and faults. Indeed, she loved him so deeply, partly *because* of his insecurity. Despite his bragging and scrounging on her, she had always given herself to him generously. She had given him money so he could show off and play the little man-of-the-world in front of his racing friends. She had allowed him to drink free at the Little Club and to put large rounds of drinks for his friends on the slate. She had cleaned up the club floor and bar after his bouts of horseplay, wiping everything dry after the soda-syphon battles. She had lost the one job in which she had taken pride, solely through him. She had moved from Goodwood Court and the security it represented because David could not sleep with her there. She had lied – and been found out by Cussen – so she could spend nights with Blakely at the Rodney Hotel.

And all the time whilst she had been doing everything he wanted, *he* had been sleeping and playing about with other women. There had been the usherette; the girl to whom he had become engaged; the American model; several hostesses who were friends of Ruth, and when he had proposed marriage, he had only been acting out a farce without any intention of keeping his promises. She wryly asked herself if he had laughed at her naïvety in believing everything he had told her.

There are few stronger emotions than those aroused from a sense of injustice. To be treated unfairly can occasion resentment which may rankle for years. Ruth's anger was so fierce that it would not allow her the indulgence of waiting days, let alone years.

The dawn of Saturday found her in no more settled state of mind. Her fury was as undeviating as it had been in the early hours. She still sat smoking when it struck eight o'clock. Then she picked up the telephone and again dialled the Findlaters' number. Once more someone took off the receiver and hung up without speaking.

Thwarted, she dressed and took a taxi to Tanza Road. Concealing herself in a doorway a few houses along from number 29, she maintained her vigil, shivering as much from exhaustion as from the cold. Close to ten o'clock, she saw Ant emerge and walk down the steps on to the pavement, where he halted, looking up and down the road. Not seeing Ruth, he made a beckoning motion with his hand. Immediately David Blakely appeared in the open doorway.

Ruth felt herself vindicated. She had known from the start that Blakely was there. She had known all along that the Findlaters had been lying to her. Now she had her quarry in her sights again. David joined Ant in the road and they began inspecting the Vanguard, testing the rubber in the windows, clearly trying to see if it would have to be replaced or whether the glass could be put back in without too much cost. Having done this they got into the car and drove away.

Ruth asked herself where they could be going. Certainly they would not wish to drive all day with the wind whistling through the windows, for the weather was by no means warm. Refitting the windows would surely be their priority. This would not take long, as it was not a big job. Neither would it cost much, but it would probably be beyond their capabilities in the middle of the Easter holiday and after everything the Emperor had cost them. So they would have to go to a garage where they were known, and where they would be able to put the charge on account. This meant Clive Gunnell's garage in Mayfair.

Having given them enough time to reach the garage, Ruth went to the kiosk and telephoned. She was careful not to ask for Blakely; instead, giving a false name, she asked for Ant Findlater. As soon as she heard him say: 'Ant Findlater here', she thanked him sneeringly for sending for the police to protect David from her. All but her first few words were wasted. Ant, with what by now must have become a reflex action, rang off the moment he recognized her voice.

Frustrated again, she took a taxi to Goodwood Court where she prevailed on the faithful Cussen to telephone the garage, hoping to catch the two men before the work on the Vanguard had been completed. Cussen phoned asking for Ant and also taking the precaution of giving the name of a racing man he knew to be friendly with Ant and David. He was equally unsuccessful. Ant was becoming a past master at recognizing unwelcome visitors and hung up immediately. Cussen turned to Ruth and shrugged his shoulders.

There was nothing more she could do for the moment. By the time Cussen had dressed and driven her to Clive Gunnell's garage at Rex Place, the work on the car would be finished and the two men gone. Indeed, after the two telephone calls it was probable that they had driven away if the work was not completed to prevent her arriving in person at the garage.

Desmond Cussen could see from Ruth's expression that she was lost in the labyrinth of her mind and was not thinking about practical matters. So he reminded her that her son was alone at the flat and must surely be wondering where his mother had gone. Furthermore he would be hungry and perhaps even frightened at being left alone for so long. So they drove to her flat and gave Andy his lunch. Then they took the boy to the zoo in Regent's

Park, where Cussen gave him enough money to enjoy himself and get home afterwards. They then left him to his own devices.

If Desmond Cussen hoped that by now Ruth would be too exhausted to resume her hunt for Blakely, he was to be sorely disappointed. With Andy off her hands, she felt free to return to Hampstead, and, as she pointed out to him, that was only ten minutes away by car. Ruth was impervious to his feelings and profligate of his time. So Cussen, no doubt again tasting the bitterness of jealousy on his tongue, drove his mistress to look for his rival.

They found the Vanguard, its windows once again in place, parked outside the Magdala public house. It was well after two in the afternoon and the bar would be emptying within the hour. Ruth decided to anticipate Blakely returning to Tanza Road.

Across the road from the Findlaters' was a house which was in the process of being decorated. Ruth stopped one of the plasterers and asked: 'Why are you having to work on Easter Saturday?' On learning that it was a rushed job as the house had been put on the market only the week before, she inquired as to the identity of the owner. Fortunately for her the owner was on the premises and, hearing that the blonde visitor was interested in acquiring a home in Hampstead, invited her in for a cup of tea. It would be interesting to know if the vendor found anything strange or remote about the woman who sipped a cup of tea whilst gazing out through the bay window of her front room at the house opposite.

Ruth, while pretending to take an interest in the owner's eulogies of the structure of the premises and the social advantages of living in Tanza Road, kept a keen observation on the door of number 29. From this vantage point she saw David and Ant return and go into the house.

Excusing herself and saying that she would let her hostess know her decision, Ruth returned to the doorway in which she had hidden the previous evening. From this concealment she watched the two men emerge accompanied by Carole Findlater and the au pair, who was carrying the infant Francesca. The five got into the Vanguard and drove away, turning left down Parliament Hill towards the Magdala.

Ruth, on foot, was unable to follow them. A few minutes later she was picked up by Desmond Cussen who had been driving around the local streets looking for her, having lost her when she went into the house across the road from the Findlaters'. They drove first to the Magdala. There was no sign of the Vanguard. There was little point in their driving off after Blakely for by now they had absolutely no idea where they might have gone. Besides, Andy would now be returning to Egerton Gardens. Arriving at Ruth's flat, they gave Andy his supper and put him to bed.

With mounting bitterness, Desmond Cussen then drove her back once again to Hampstead. It was late evening. The Magdala was full and noisy. But there was no sign of the Vanguard, so they drove to Tanza Road where they found the car parked outside number 29. Ruth stood on the pavement looking up at the second floor flat windows. As she watched, one of the windows was opened; probably to let out the smoke, for Carole was seldom without a cigarette between her lips. Ruth could hear laughter and voices. She could identify David's voice, though, perhaps through nerves, he was talking somewhat frenetically. When he stopped speaking, a woman giggled loudly at whatever he had said. In Ruth's mind it was the young au pair.

From subsequent police inquiries it appears far more likely that it was Charlotte, a psychologist friend of the Findlaters who was a dedicated giggler with an extremely loud laugh. The small party which the Findlaters were giving was intended to help the two men to drown their disappointment at the Emperor's demise and to reassure David that, at least for this one night, surrounded by his friends, he had nothing to fear from Ruth.

Cussen, finding it embarrassing to stand in a street eavesdropping on a private party and fast becoming an attraction for inquisitive passers-by, returned to his car where he sat drumming his fingers on the steering wheel.

At her trial, Ruth Ellis was to describe how, close to ten o'clock, David and Ant had come down the steps with a woman. She had been near enough to them to hear David say: 'Let me put my arm around you for support.' Ruth had presumed this woman to be the au pair and, remembering the giggle earlier, felt confirmed in her opinion that the Findlaters were using their employee to lure David away from her. She would have agreed with what Cliff Davis had said so recently: 'David was not the sort of man to pass up an opportunity.'

Ruth would also give evidence that although she did not see the three return, this was probably because she had to go away for some minutes. This was, no doubt, to deal with the demands of nature. Back in Tanza Road watching, Ruth saw the blinds of the front room, directly under the Findlaters' living room, pulled down. Immediately Ruth assumed this to be the bedroom of the au pair. Following the line of Ruth's distorted thought pattern at this time, she must have wondered: 'Why should the girl be pulling the blinds down? Why? Because they are screwing!' Then, although the party was still going on upstairs, someone switched off the light in the hall.

For her replies at the Old Bailey to the prompting of Melford Stevenson, she had clearly convinced herself that not only was David Blakely having an affair with the au pair, but was that very evening in bed with her. Her belief seemed to be borne out because although she stayed outside the house listening for a further half an hour, she never again heard her lover's voice. Eventually, she gave up and Desmond Cussen drove her back to Egerton Gardens.

Imagination can weave intricate webs, confusing the memory of both time and place. Ruth's account of that evening had many anomalies. She seems to have recalled events out of order and sited people at certain times in places where they could not possibly have been. Certainly, her conviction that the Findlaters were conspiring to use the au pair against her had led her to accept that the room in which she had watched the blinds drawn was in fact the girl's bedroom. Perhaps in jealousy she wanted to believe it; wanted to hurt herself as much as she was already being hurt by him. In fact, the girl's bedroom was at the rear of the house and could not be seen from Tanza Road.

During Ruth's absence at Tanza Road, Mrs Joan Winstanley, the housekeeper at Egerton Gardens, had gone into Ruth's flat to see if Andy was alright. Recently, she has recalled how, as she went into the living room, she had noticed something different. For a moment she could not analyse what it was. Then she realized that the photograph of David in his overalls had either been destroyed or put away in a drawer.

What she felt during the hours that remained of Saturday night, Ruth described succinctly at her trial, when Melford Stevenson asked: 'And what state of mind were you in?' She replied: 'I was very upset.' Succinct, yes, but what an understatement! For two nights running she had not slept. She was crazy with jealousy. Whilst she sat smoking on the Saturday night, she must have kept picturing David in bed with the au pair, his lean hard body contrasting with the rather full body of the eighteen-year-old girl who had not entirely lost her puppy-fat. The impression was cruel and vivid. It would be surprising if she had not turned to relief in her tranquillizers.

So to Easter Sunday, the day which was to be the last day in the life of David Blakely; the day which would lead Ruth Ellis to the scaffold and her meeting with Albert Pierrepoint.

At nine o'clock, she picked up the phone and dialled the Findlaters. There was a long wait before the ringing was answered. David Blakely and the Findlaters were by now so irritated and even unnerved, that when the phone rang they would look at each other without speaking, before Ant would drag himself up to go and answer it. They had long before decided that there was no point in speaking once Ruth's voice had been identified, but that Ant should make one last effort to make her see sense.

Ruth described in court how she had made that first call on the last day. 'I waited a long time before it was answered. Then Ant answered the phone.' Mr Stevenson interposed: 'That is Findlater?' 'Yes,' replied Ruth. 'And what did you say?' In a small voice Ruth answered: 'I said, I hope you are having an enjoyable holiday, because you have ruined mine.' Ant rang off without speaking further.

According to Ruth, she spent the rest of the morning at the flat until just before lunch, when Desmond Cussen arrived to collect her and Andy. The three ate together at Goodwood Court. At her trial Ruth gave evidence that she had no clear memory of what she did during the morning or the afternoon of her 'last day in the free world'. 'I have completely forgotten what I did. My son was with us and we amused him in some way.'

She then told her counsel that at about 7.30 she returned to Egerton Gardens to put Andy to bed. Asked about her feelings towards David Blakely during this period, she replied: 'I was very upset. I had a peculiar feeling I wanted to kill him.'

And when pressed: 'You had what?' She reiterated unemotionally: 'I had an idea I wanted to kill him.'

110

This was almost exactly the same response that she made to the counsel for the prosecution, Mr Christmas Humphreys, when he asked her his one, all-important, question.

Desmond Cussen swore on oath that he had not seen Ruth Ellis after he drove her home to put the boy to bed. This was subsequently to be contradicted by Ruth in statements made after the trial, in which she alleged that Cussen was not only with her on that last evening, but that he, in fact, drove her to the Magdala to find David Blakely. According to a letter from her father, describing what she told him in the condemned cell, hidden in the spine of her family Bible, and the statement made to Victor Mishcon, her solicitor, who took over in the last hours from John Bickford, in whom she had lost all confidence, Desmond Cussen had not only been with her, but had given her the weapon of death. He had handed her the revolver, having oiled it and then taught her how to press the trigger.

There is corroborative evidence that her version of Cussen's part in the crime is justified. If this evidence of the past is true, then there is no doubt that Desmond Cussen committed perjury at the trial.

Muriel Jakubait, Ruth's sister, looked after Andy in the days immediately following the shooting. She remembers on the very first day she was responsible for the boy, asking him what he remembered of that last afternoon at Goodwood Court. He told her that he had seen 'Uncle Desmond give her a revolver, and having oiled it showed her how to work it . . .'

At midday on the Sunday, David Blakely had gone to the Magdala with the Findlaters to meet Clive Gunnell. The landlord of the public house, Mr Colson, remembered the occasion especially well as on that morning he had cashed a cheque for five pounds for Blakely. This cheque was to be the first the landlord had ever received marked, instead of the commonplace 'RD' (return to drawer), with the words: 'Drawer deceased'. He had no reservations in cashing David Blakely's cheques. Blakely was a regular customer at the Magdala and was well-liked by staff and customers.

In the afternoon the Findlaters took their daughter, Francesca, to Hampstead Heath to enjoy the traditional Fair. David had felt safe in the holiday crowd and had wandered from stall to stall with the child perched on his shoulders. That evening, Clive had promised to bring his gramophone and records to Tanza Road for a small intimate party.

So David, with Carole as company, had driven to Clive's house to fetch him and his equipment. Afterwards, the three returned to Tanza Road to join Ant Findlater, who was waiting for them. Soon the soirée was under way. They relaxed and sat talking, drinking, and playing the gramophone. At nine o'clock, Carole ran out of cigarettes. She asked David to buy her some from the Magdala. By this time they were almost out of alcohol, and she dispatched Clive, not only to keep David company, but also to help carry the replacements of beer.

Although it was only a short distance from the Findlaters' home to the Magdala, David and Clive chose to take the car. If they had walked, the events of that tragic night might never have occurred. Ruth, arriving at Tanza Road, found no sign of David's Vanguard. This led her – or Cussen! – to presume the young racing driver might have gone to the Magdala. Sure enough, outside the hostelry she – or they – saw the grey-green Vanguard. The car was the magnet which linked the woman with the gun and the man, of whom she would say: 'I wanted to kill him.'

Through the Magdala's stained glass window, Ruth Ellis watched David Blakely and Clive Gunnell order their drinks. She saw, as David Blakely bought at the off-licence, three quarts of light ale and cigarettes. When they had emptied their glasses, the two men picked up the bottles and carrying them under their arms strolled out into the street.

Clive Gunnell walked around the car to get into the passenger's seat. David had locked the passenger door as they had parked, so Gunnell had to wait by the car door until David unlatched it from the inside.

Ruth watched almost like a snake mesmerizing its prey. David Blakely, holding a quart of beer under his arm, fumbled in his pocket for the car keys. Then, as he extracted them, she hissed: 'David!'

Blakely took no notice of her cry. Either he had not heard her – which is extremely unlikely – or he was determined to ignore her come what may.

Ruth Ellis took the revolver from her bag. She pointed it at

Above: A crowd gathers outside Holloway prison on the morning of 13 July 1955, to stand in silent protest at 9.00 a.m.

Below: The simple headstone in Amersham churchyard which marks the grave of Ruth Ellis, buried under her maiden name of Hornby. Her sister Muriel still brings flowers.

Number 29 Tanza Road, Hampstead, where Blakely was staying with the Findlaters at the time of his death.

Desmond Cussen sitting on Ruth Ellis's right during a party at the Dorchester in 1954.

Ruth's husband, George Ellis, the alcoholic dentist who later committed lonely suicide in a Channel Islands hotel.

Ruth Ellis and David Blakely pictured during a peaceful interlude in their stormy relationship.

Ruth and David pictured with Carole and Ant Findlater.

A postcard from Blakely to Ruth in 1954, as Blakely was trying his luck at Le Mans. 'Darling, have arrived safely and am having quite a good time. The cars are going very well. Looking forward to seeing you. David. P.S. Love to Desmond!!!' The postscript is particularly significant.

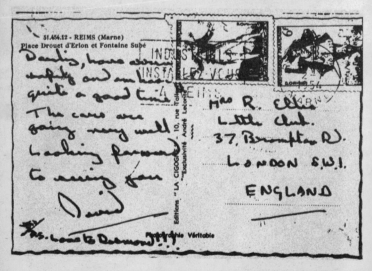

The Magdala public house in Hampstead. The shooting took place on the pavement at the spot where the woman can be seen in this picture.

Mrs Gladys Yule, the passer-by who was accidentally shot in the hand when the last bullet ricocheted off the pavement near the body of David Blakely.

CERTIFICATE OF SURGEON

(31 Vict. Cap. 24)

I, _____ the Surgeon of Her Majesty's Prison of _Holloway_ hereby certify that I this day examined the Body of _Ruth Ellis_, on whom Judgment of Death was this day executed in the said Prison; and that on that Examination I found that the said _Ruth Ellis_ was dead.

Dated this 13th day of July 1955

(Signature) _____

No. 279

At eighteen minutes past nine, 13 July 1955, this notice was posted outside Holloway prison.

Ant Findlater (right) and Clive Gunnell, who was with Blakely when he was shot, on their way to the Old Bailey for Ruth Ellis's trial.

This is the photo of David Blakely that was passed to Ruth Ellis while under questioning at her trial. It prompted her only show of emotion during her two days at the Old Bailey.

Dr T. P. Rees, who was treating Ruth Ellis for depression at the time of the shooting.

David Blakely pictured with Cliff Davis during the 1954 *Daily Express* Motor Rally.

Blakely and spat between her teeth: 'David!' Blakely had always fled from violence. He did not change character – and why should he? – in these last seconds of his life.

He swung around, and on seeing Ruth, the avenging spirit, with the revolver pointing directly at him, ran to seek protection from his friend. There were two shots.

David screamed one word: 'Clive!' Ruth, the avenging angel still, followed him around the car until her aim was screened by his friend. Then she spat at Gunnell: 'Get out of the way, Clive!'

By now Blakely was dithering behind the car and Gunnell. But this time there was no escape. Blakely realized that Clive was no defence against bullets, and turned away again to run past the bonnet of the car and down the hill to safety. There was another shot. Blakely fell. Then another. Ruth, almost as if she was a robot, ran to the twitching body whose blood, by this time, was smeared all over the Vanguard, and fired the fifth shot from point-blank range.

Five shots had been fired, four of them into the body of David Blakely and one which had gone, in the words of prosecuting counsel Christmas Humphreys: 'We know not where.'

During the case, no one described the last seconds before the last shot was fired. Now we know, through other onlookers, that Ruth raised the revolver to her temple and tried to press the trigger, an action which, if the gun had worked, would have blown out her brains. A ballistics expert has said since that after handling the gun – a Smith and Wesson – he is certain that the last shot fired would have jammed. Nevertheless, fire it she did. Slowly, almost as if she were hypnotized, she took the gun from her head and lowered it towards the pavement. Ruth had lost her nerve and could not end her own life. As if in two minds as to whether to put the last bullet into Blakely's twitching body or just into the paving stone, she fired again. This time the bullet ricocheted off the road and into the thumb of a passer-by who was making her way to the Magdala for a quiet Sunday evening drink.

Then shaking, almost as if she were herself dying, she turned slowly towards Clive Gunnell and peering at him through myopic eyes said: 'Go and call the police.'

9

While Ruth was pumping David's body with bullets, many of the customers inside the Magdala were unaware of anything untoward happening outside in the street. At the bar was an off-duty policeman who had arranged a meeting with his girl-friend in the saloon. She had not yet arrived. Mr Colson, the landlord, was rushing between the two bars serving drinks, and he remembers with clarity the noise of gunshots being fired.

'We were very busy, it being Easter Sunday, and suddenly I heard this noise going on outside – shots. Nobody seemed to think it was shots, we all thought it was a car back-firing, and nobody took a lot of notice of it. Then somebody came rushing in and said: 'A bloke's been shot outside', and as far as I remember people went out and saw this bloke lying on the ground outside. There was a bit of a kerfuffle, and then we realized they were revolver shots that we'd heard.'

PC Alan Thompson put down his drink and calmly walked outside. Here was an opportunity for the young policeman to make a name for himself, though this thought was far from his mind. As he walked through the door he saw the blonde young woman with the gun clenched tightly in her hands. People were screaming at her: 'Look what you've done!' but Ruth was well aware. The policeman, not fearing that she would open fire on him, moved slowly towards her. She whispered to him: 'Will you call the police?' With tragic irony he removed the gun from her shaking hands and told her: 'I *am* the police.'

Unconcerned that he may have removed whosoever's fingerprints were daubed on the gun, PC Thompson put the gun away in his pocket. As far as he was concerned, Ruth had pulled the trigger and so she was the murderess. Perhaps a more experienced police officer would have handled the gun with greater care, for had he done so Scotland Yard's fingerprint department *might* have been surprised to have found dabs that belonged neither to PC Thompson nor Ruth Ellis!

Somebody, who rushed into the Magdala during the general mêlée, had called the police and within minutes squad cars from nearby Hampstead police station converged on the pub, as did an ambulance which took David Blakely to New End Hospital. He was DOA – dead on arrival.

Mrs Gladys Yule, her hand spouting blood, did not get the privilege of being taken to hospital by ambulance. In a state of panic, she and her husband hailed a taxi that happened to be touting for business in the Hampstead area. The cab driver stopped and, seeing blood dripping from her wound, refused the fare. Mrs Yule, however, was made of gritty stuff and *demanded* that she be taken immediately to New End Hospital. The cab driver agreed on the condition that Mrs Yule let her blood-dripping hand rest outside the window. The scene would have been comic had it not been for such tragic overtones. The taxi disappeared through the streets of Hampstead leaving a blood-stained trail behind it.

Ruth arrived at Hampstead police station at the corner of Rosslyn Hill and Downshire Hill. There she was offered the customary cup of tea, the panacea for all emotional moments. She was then told to wait. An hour and a half later, three CID officers, Detective Superintendent Leonard Crawford, Detective Chief Inspector Leslie Davies, and Detective Inspector Peter Gill, all of 'S' division – the Hampstead manor – came to her and with an 'I proceeded' voice Crawford announced: 'I have seen the dead body of David Blakely at Hampstead mortuary and I understand you know something about it.'

Ruth was given her third caution of the evening. She was told that she did not have to say anything, but anything she did say would be taken down and might be used in evidence.

The policemen looked at each other, no doubt a little mystified as to how such a fragile young woman, apparently harmless, could have committed such a violent crime. They did not yet know the circumstances which led Ruth to shoot her lover.

They asked her if she had anything to say. She muttered: 'I am guilty.' Although this was what they wanted to hear, for it would make their jobs much simpler, they had to be seen to be doing their work correctly. They asked her whether that was *all* she wanted to say.

Ruth thought for a few seconds and then told the policemen that she would like to make a full statement. The plain-clothes officers were joined by a uniformed policeman. The necessary forms were produced.

It all started about two years ago. When I met David. At the Little Club. In Knightsbridge. I understand what has been said. I am guilty. I am rather confused.

About two years ago I met David Blakely when I was manageress of the Little Club, Knightsbridge. My flat was above that. I had known him for about a fortnight when he started to live with me and has done so continuously until last year, when he went away to Le Mans for about three weeks, motor racing. He came back to me and remained living with me until Good Friday morning.

He left me about ten o'clock a.m. and promised to be back by 8 p.m. to take me out. I waited until half past nine and he had not phoned, although he always had done in the past. I was rather worried at that stage as he had had trouble with his racing car and had been drinking.

I rang some friends of his named Findlater at Hampstead, but they told me he was not there. I was speaking to Findlater, and I asked if David was all right. He laughed and said: 'Oh yes, he's all right.' I did not believe he was not there, and I took a taxi to Hampstead, where I saw David's car outside Findlater's flat at 28 (*sic*) Tanza Road. I then telephoned from nearby, and when my voice was recognized they hung up on me.

I went to the flat and continually rang the door bell, but they would not answer. I became very furious and went to David's car, which was still standing there, and pushed in three of the side windows. The noise I made must have aroused the Findlaters, as the police came along and spoke to me. Mr Findlater came out of his flat, and the police also spoke to him.

David did not come home on Saturday, and at nine o'clock this morning (Sunday) I phoned the Findlaters again, and Mr Findlater answered. I said to him: 'I hope you are having an enjoyable holiday' and was about to say: 'because you have ruined mine', and he banged the receiver down.

I waited all day today (Sunday) for David to phone, but he did not do so. About eight o'clock this evening (Sunday) I put my son Andrea to bed. I then took a gun which was given to me about three years ago in the club by a man whose name I do not remember. It was security for money, but I accepted it as curiosity. I did not know it was loaded when it was given to me, but I knew next morning when I looked at it. When I put the gun in my bag I intended to find David and shoot him.

I took a taxi to Tanza Road, and as I arrived, David's car drove away from the Findlaters' address. I dismissed the taxi and walked back down the road to the nearest pub, where I saw David's car outside. I waited outside until he came out with a friend I know as Clive. David went to his door to open it. I was a little way away from him. He turned and saw me and then turned away from me, and I took the gun from my bag and I shot him. He turned around and ran a few steps around the car. I thought I had missed him, so I fired again. He was still running, and I fired the third shot. I don't remember firing any more, but I must have done. I remember he was lying on the footway and I was standing beside him. He was bleeding badly, and it seemed ages before an ambulance came.

I remember a man came up, and I said: 'Will you call the police and an ambulance?' He said: 'I am a policeman.' I said: 'Please take this gun and arrest me.'

This statement has been read over to me, and it is true.

Ruth put her signature to the statement and was put in a cell for the night. The policemen discussed the statement with each other and could not believe how much this young, frail, blonde night-club hostess had condemned herself out of her own mouth.

The statement warrants close scrutiny. Although she was crucifying her chance of survival, she was also making sure that nobody else was taking the blame.

For a start, she recognized the fact that she was *guilty* of murder: and this was prior to her being charged. Moreover, by admitting her guilt she believed that she would receive the maximum penalty. She had already, some three hours after the shooting, resigned herself to the fact that she wanted to die.

In her statement she mentioned several people: Ant and Carole Findlater, David Blakely, Clive Gunnell. She even remembered the policeman to whom she handed the gun. But nowhere throughout the statement does she mention Desmond Cussen. She gave her means of transport as a taxi. The police made a mental note of this. It is the easiest task in the world for a policeman to check up with the taxi-drivers' headquarters in Islington as to whether anyone delivered an attractive blonde from Kensington to Hampstead – a considerable fare – on Easter Sunday evening.

Taxi drivers are notorious gossips when amongst themselves. The police know this. It would not be too long before the driver of that taxi, which carried a murderess, would come forward and notify the police. But the police did not check this line of inquiry. Perhaps they did not believe Ruth's story about taking a taxi.

All the way through her statement, she laid much of the blame on the Findlaters. She mentioned them more times in her statement than anyone or anything else. Already she had a knife dug in their backs. She truly believed that they were to blame for David's disappearance and she wanted the world to know it.

The most important section of her statement deals with the acquisition of the gun. No doubt it was this aspect that the police considered the most significant. Ruth said: 'I then took a gun which I had hidden, and put it in my handbag. *This gun was given to me about three years ago in the club by a man whose name I do not remember. It was security for money . . .*'

The police were not being fooled by statements of this kind. Although just after the war, guns were in easy supply, people did not accept them in exchange for loans. To take the point a step further, why should Ruth accept a *gun* for a loan, anyway? What use would a gun have been to a girl in Ruth's position?

Everybody who knew Ruth, whether or not they liked her, jumped to her defence when asked about the gun. They categorically agreed that she was not the kind of person to own a gun, let alone use one. Furthermore, if what she says was true, and it had been given to her *three years earlier*, why had not anyone seen it?

Ruth Ellis moved from her flat above the Little Club to Desmond Cussen's flat at Goodwood Court to Egerton Gardens. On each occasion somebody had helped her pack her belongings. Yet *nobody* had ever seen any sign of a gun. If Ruth genuinely believed that this story would be accepted she obviously knew little about the training of the Criminal Investigation Department.

Though at this time the police did not know of the existence of Desmond Cussen and were not concerned about his possible involvement with the crime, routine investigation would inevitably point in his direction. It has since been suggested that Ruth and Cussen struck a deal prior to the killing. It may have been that Ruth would not incriminate Cussen if he, in turn, would provide financially for young Andy after his mother's execution.

Others believe, and are more probably correct, that Ruth agreed to remain silent about Desmond if he would supply her with a weapon and transportation. If either of these theories were substantiated then Ruth was keeping her part of the bargain.

While Ruth was in Hampstead police station, many miles away her sister, Muriel, was preparing the evening meal. 'I was preparing Sunday dinner when my mother came in and said that Ruth was in prison because she had shot David Blakely. I said: "Shot David Blakely? She couldn't have!" My mother said: "She has," and my first reaction to that was who the hell had given her the gun? I believe Cussen telephoned mother to break the news.'

The post-mortem on David Blakely was carried out early on Easter Monday by Dr Albert Hunt, a pathologist at the London Hospital Medical College, with Inspector Davies and Constable George Claiden present. Dr Hunt recorded that there was an entry wound of a bullet in the lower part of Blakely's back to the right and there was a track leading from this through the abdominal cavity perforating the intestine and liver and ending in an exit wound below the left shoulder blade. Another track ran upwards through the chest perforating the left lung, the aorta, and the windpipe, and the bullet was lying in the deep muscles to the right of the tongue.

There was another wound just above the outer part of the left hip-bone penetrating the skin and underlying fat only. There was an exit wound quite close to that. He added that there was also a shallow mark on the inner side of the left forearm. Dr Hunt was not positive whether the latter two wounds were caused by one or two bullets. David Blakely died as the result of shock and haemorrhage due to gunshot wounds.

Immediately following the post-mortem, the detectives were given the bullets, blood specimens, samples of the stomach contents, tablets which Blakely had been carrying, and four items of clothing. These they took, together with the murder weapon, to the Metropolitan Police Laboratory, Scotland Yard.

The return of Detective Chief Inspector Davies to Hampstead police station was short-lived relief to Ruth. She was unaware of what was going on and wondered why nobody had anything to say to her of any importance. Her uncertainty came to an end when the Chief Inspector said: 'As a result of a post-mortem examination conducted on the body of David Blakely, you will be charged with murdering him.' She was duly cautioned twice more. Replying to the final charge, she said: 'Thanks.'

Already the burning jealousy and hatred was transforming into a transcendental calmness. At last Ruth now knew where she stood. This privilege did not extend to Desmond Cussen. He was in limbo. Had Ruth involved him in the murder? Had she kept his name out of the case? Had she said where she got the gun? He could wait no longer: his dilemma was agonizing.

Often we act unwisely to kill the agony of uncertainty. So it was with Desmond Cussen. He presented himself at the police station and made a voluntary statement concerning his relationship with Ruth. He told the station officer that the blonde woman downstairs in the cell had not taken a taxi on Good Friday evening, as she had said (one wonders how he *knew* she had said this as her statement had at no time left the detectives' office) but that he had driven her to Hampstead and waited while she destroyed Blakely's Vanguard.

It is a great pity that, while charity was so dear to his heart, he did not mention that she did not take a taxi on the night of the murder either. He did mention to the station officer that he had been with Ruth on Easter Sunday, *but only until 7.30.* Why, the detectives must have wondered, did Ruth Ellis not mention the name of Cussen in her statement? It was a question that they pursued.

At the time Cussen was doing his 'good deed', the detectives were collecting statements from anyone who fitted into the Ruth Ellis story. High on their lists were the injured Mrs Yule, and Clive Gunnell. They then went to Tanza Road and invited Ant Findlater to accompany them to Hampstead mortuary to identify the body of his 'best friend'.

Ruth was given her second cell-room meal of the day and then was taken to Hampstead magistrates' court, where the bench had been specially convened, being a bank holiday. Detective Chief Inspector Davies gave evidence of her arrest, and the short hearing ended with Ruth being remanded in custody to appear in the same court on 20 April. She was driven to Holloway prison, which was to become her 'home' for the rest of her life. She asked for a Bible and a photograph of David Blakely to be sent in to her.

At first the shooting did not make the headlines. This was because the nation's journalists were on strike, or were at least being affected by an industrial dispute in Fleet Street. Even so, the reporters of the dailies had heard about the murder and were already digging into the background of the leading characters so that they would at least have material for use when the newspaper industry was back to normal.

Among those delving slightly deeper than others into the private lives of Ruth and her associates were Duncan Webb, the star crime reporter of the *Sunday People*, and Duggie Howell, Webb's rival on the *Daily Mirror*. It was these two gentlemen who led the field in the purchase of the 'Ruth Ellis Story', each being told by his editor that money would be no object. Howell was in front by a short head. He had established that Ruth was living at Egerton Gardens and made his way there as fast as the taxi would carry him.

Upon arrival he met head housekeeper Mrs Joan Winstanley, and Mrs Kerr, who owned the block of flats. Although the latter had instructed Mrs Winstanley not to speak to anyone, the housekeeper was won over by Howell's charm and told him what little she knew about 'Mr and Mrs Ellis', believing Blakely to be Ruth's husband.

Then Howell played an ace card. He asked Mrs Winstanley whether or not Ruth had money. He learned that she did not. Whereupon, he made Mrs Winstanley an offer. The housekeeper was bewildered. Howell told her that the Mirror Group of newspapers would be prepared to buy Ruth's life story and the payment would cover *all* Ruth's legal expenses, which, Howell explained, would be very high indeed.

Mrs Winstanley, correctly, replied that she was in no position to sell Ruth's life away to a newspaper. Howell was persistent. He told the housekeeper that her signature on a pre-drafted letter to a solicitor friend of his would at least set the wheels in motion. It was either that or Ruth would have to make do with legal aid and, as Howell explained, her chances of survival with a 'dock brief' would be extremely limited.

Mrs Winstanley appended her signature to the letter which gave Howell formal consent to appoint a solicitor. John Bickford was his choice. That Howell was an old friend of Bickford's was not explained to the housekeeper. Mr Bickford had, however, had experience in another murder case, so the choice was not entirely biased.

Whether the choice, having regard to the nature of the case, was a particularly happy one is purely a matter for conjecture. Bickford's firm, Messrs Cardew Smith and Ross, were not criminal solicitors in the strict sense of the word. But what was being seen to be done was that although solicitors are forbidden to advertise their services, a link with an eminent member of the Press can achieve much the same result.

Bickford's account of how he was introduced to the case was somewhat different. He remembers: 'I received, on a bank holiday, a telephone call from a friend of mine who told me that a Mrs Winstanley had told him about the murder and said that she was Ruth Ellis's landlady, who was very worried indeed, and wanted to find out if there was anything that Mrs Ellis wanted. I was asked to go to Holloway to see her, but it was Bank Holiday Monday and I'm afraid I refused at first. But apparently, as it was a bank holiday, they tried a number of other glorious homes and they couldn't find any. I said, well if Mrs Winstanley liked to give me written instructions, I would go to the prison only for the purpose of finding out whether there was anything Mrs Winstanley could do about it.

'I got those written instructions that day [presumably from Duggie Howell] and went down to the prison in the evening. When I arrived I was told Mrs Ellis was under sedation, so I left a note for her and arranged to call the following morning, which I did. Mrs Ellis had said she would like to see me and I was taken in and I met her for the first time then.'

While Ruth was giving audience to John Bickford in her cell at Holloway, her 'civil' solicitor, Mr Victor Mishcon – who obviously had not heard the news of the murder – was wondering why Ruth had not kept her 2.15 appointment.

She had made this appointment four days before the murder to discuss the welfare of Georgina. Mishcon's curiosity was not long-lasting since, during that very afternoon, Leon Simmons, senior legal executive for Mishcon, received a telephone call from a Mr John Bickford asking him if either he or Mr Mishcon would mind him handling Ruth's case. Bickford then went on to explain about the events of Easter Sunday, much to the surprise of Simmons. The latter raised no objections as Victor Mishcon was primarily a civil solicitor and murder was hardly a common occurrence in their practice.

One of the first things Ruth did after she had settled down in Holloway, was to write a letter to Blakely's mother. On Holloway prison headed letter paper, prisoner 9656 Ellis, wrote:

Dear Mrs Cook,
No dought these last few days have been a shock to you.
Please try to believe me, when I say, how deeply sorry I am to have caused you this unpleasantness. No dought you will hear all kinds of stories, regarding David and I. Please do forgive him for decieving you, has regarding myself. David and I have spent many happy times together.
Thursday 7th April, David arrived home at 7.15. p.m., he gave me the latest photograph he had, a few days hence had taken, he told me he had given you one.
Friday morning at 10 o'clock he left and promised to return at 8 o'clock, but never did. The two people I blame for David's death, and my own, are the Finlayters. No dought you will not understand this but *perhaps* before I hang you will know what I mean. Please excuse my writing, but the pen is shocking. I implore you to try to forgive David for living with me, but we were very much in love with one and other unfortunately David was not satisfied with one woman in his life.

123

I have forgiven David, I only wish I could have found it in
my heart to have forgiven when he was alive.
Once again, I say I am very sorry to have caused you this
misery and heartache. I shall die loving your son. And you
should feel content that his death has been repaid.
Goodbye.
Ruth Ellis.

It is patently clear from reading this letter that Ruth sincerely
believed and hoped that she was going to die. Although there was
never any argument that she committed the murder, murder and
execution did not always go hand in hand.

As Jonathan Goodman and Patrick Pringle point out in their
book *The Trial of Ruth Ellis* (published by David & Charles): 'In
England and Wales there was an annual average of about 150
murders known to the police. Of the 100 or so murderers who did
not commit suicide, only about twelve were hanged; and the quota
of females was much smaller than that of males.

'Of those who were not hanged, a few either escaped arrest
entirely or were tried but acquitted because of insufficient evidence.
Many more were beneficiaries of perverse jury verdicts, the propor-
tion of acquittals to convictions in some years being as high as one
to four, a higher ratio than for almost any other crime. It seems
evident that juries managed to find reasonable doubt where it did
not exist in cases where they considered the death penalty too
severe, and in many other cases returned verdicts of "guilty but
insane" or "guilty of manslaughter" that could not possibly be
justified in law. Of those who were unqualifiedly convicted of
murder and sentenced to death, an additional few were reprieved
on the advice of the Home Secretary, who did not have to justify
his decision. Thus mercy was shown, in one way or another, to all
but a handful of people who had committed the capital crime of
murder.'

But Ruth was not only unaware, but also unconcerned with
statistics, and, as she sat alone in her cell reading her Bible, her
thoughts were with David Blakely – the man she *still* loved.
Wherever he was, she wanted to be with him.

The meeting between Ruth and John Bickford was an uneventful
one. Bickford told her that Mrs Winstanley had asked if there was

anything either he or she could do for her. Ruth expressed her gratitude and asked the solicitor to go to her mother and collect all her belongings and hold them. Then Ruth did an extraordinary thing. She told Bickford to pass a message on to Mr Desmond Cussen to the effect that she had told the police that she had received it as a security for a loan at the club. Bickford smelt a rat.

Instead of Cussen, it was Bickford who was now playing the role of Ruth's courier. He duly did as he was told and then returned to Ruth to report that the mission had been accomplished. He then asked her, for the first time, what she intended to do to get herself out of the mess. Her answer astonished the solicitor. She simply replied that she intended to plead guilty because she had nothing more to live for and that she wanted to join David.

Today, John Bickford reflects upon the occasion which cast a shadow on his self-respect. 'I was rather perturbed about this attitude, and I tried to persuade her to think differently. She said: "But it's no good, I did it and I'm guilty." I told her that even so, it's important for her to try and preserve her life because she had two children for whom she was responsible, as well as a family. She should do everything she could to stay alive. She then asked what she could do. I felt very sorry for her and I said that the first thing to do was for me to find out all the details of this case and then we could look at it and see what we could do. She told me that Victor Mishcon had acted for her in connection with other matters. It was her divorce.

'I got in touch with Mishcon, and he said he was only too happy if I would take the case because I had a certain amount of experience in this type of work and he didn't.

'After I got the go-ahead, I started taking detailed instructions. And, acting upon what she had told me, I went and saw a very great number of people whom she had mentioned. After I had completed those investigations, it was then necessary to make up our minds how the case should be presented.

'At this stage it wasn't for me to decide really how the case should be presented. It was as a result of a very detailed history that I had obtained from Mrs Ellis that she had said that she still didn't really want to live, but she was much more anxious that everybody should know why she had done this peculiar thing. In fact she wanted her story published. And my feeling was that there was just a remote possibility of getting a verdict of manslaughter, and apart from that, if sufficient sympathy could be aroused for her, I should get a recommendation to mercy, which, in those days inevitably led to a reprieve . . .'

Ruth remained composed in Holloway and was slowly settling into the prison way of life. Most of her day was spent reading the Bible or several novels which had been sent in for her. She had regular visitors and an amplitude of letters from friends and acquaintances who had heard, with surprise and shock, about the débâcle outside the Hampstead pub.

Ruth's second appearance in the magistrates' court was a replica of her first. She was remanded in custody for a further week. Seven days later she was represented by Mr Sebag Shaw. It was at this hearing that Desmond Cussen was called to appear as a police witness – much to Ruth's amazement. Mrs Winstanley remembers vividly his lack of composure in the waiting room. In a recent interview with the authors, she said: 'He just couldn't sit still. He was sweating like a pig. I asked him if he was well, but he just ignored me, like he had other things on his mind. He kept pacing up and down the floor. You could sense that he knew much more than he was ever going to say.'

Another surprising visitor in court on that occasion – but for different reasons – was dear old Maury Conley. He had heard about Ruth's outburst of violence 'through the trade', and although not in the least surprised, he was both bewildered and annoyed that she had not requested him to come and see her. Mrs Winstanley remembers how much of a temper he was in over the fact that Ruth had not asked *him* to finance her defence.

Ruth came into the magistrates' court looking resplendent in an off-white tweed suit with black velvet piping. She was still enacting the role of the 'belle of the ball'. She sat in an iron-railed dock, flanked by two prison wardresses.

Evidence about the murder came into the open for all in attendance to hear. She had been through it all in her mind hundreds of times as she sat alone in her cell. Now she was hearing it yet again. The only time she showed any signs of injustice was when Ant Findlater's evidence was over and unchallenged. Why, she asked herself, was there no mention of the Findlaters' part in the tragedy?

It was when Desmond Cussen was called that Ruth looked up and donned her black-rimmed spectacles. If she were expecting any favours from his evidence, she was to be bitterly disappointed. Facts which she intentionally left out of her statement to the police were filled in by Cussen.

He explained to the magistrate that he had been Ruth's 'chauffeur' on her hunts for Blakely and that he had sat and waited while she broke the windows of Blakely's car. Ruth, taking off her spectacles, was visibly fuming. 'Why is he saying these things?' she might have been asking herself.

The journalists in the press box were having a field day. Taking shorthand at tremendous speed, they quickly realized that this was not 'any old story'. For many of them it was the biggest story they had ever been fortunate to cover. But if the reporters were having a rare old time, their news editors were about to have the time of their lives.

At breakfast tables the length and breadth of the country the following morning, businessmen, factory workers, housewives, and schoolchildren read headlines like: COURT HEARS OF THE LOVES OF 'LITTLE CLUB' GIRL (*Daily Express*); and MODEL SHOT LOVER – COURT TOLD (*Daily Mirror*). The *Daily Mail*, which was not going to be outdone, provided the morning's biggest splash with: MODEL SHOT CAR ACE IN THE BACK. They followed on with WITNESS SAYS HER LOVE HAD COOLED, and rounded it off nicely with FOUR BULLETS AS HE LAY DYING.

That Ruth was no more a 'model' than Blakely was a 'car ace' was yet another exemplification that one should not believe all one reads in newspapers. But the old adage bandied about in news offices up and down Fleet Street, that 'you must not let the truth spoil a good story', was certainly the order of the morning.

What the daily newspapers did omit from their descriptive courtroom accounts, was the fact that while proceedings were taking place, Ruth's husband, George Ellis, in his usual drunken stupor, burst into the foyer of the magistrates' court and, at the top of his voice, yelled: 'Stop the trial, stop the trial. I want to see my wife's lawyers.'

He was restrained and taken into a nearby waiting room, where it was established that because of his 'drunken state', it would be better for his wife's case if he were to take a walk and return when he had sobered up. His walk took him to the nearest pub where he was soon met by a reporter from the *Sunday Pictorial*.

The reporter bought Ellis more whisky and then struck up a deal with him. The *Pictorial* would purchase Ellis's life story for a handsome price as long as Ellis did not speak to any other newspaper. It would not have mattered if he had, for the *Pictorial* never used the story, although extracts were taken from it when, several years later, Ellis hanged himself in a Jersey hotel when, a ruined man, he was unable to meet the bill.

The magistrates' hearing was over and Ruth was taken back to Holloway. Now her chauffeur was a member of Her Majesty's prison service. On her return she was told that her life story had been bought by the *Women's Sunday Mirror*, one of the many IPC-owned publications. She would, at last, be able to tell her own unadulterated side of the story. She was delighted!

Bickford's visits to her became more and more regular as he was interviewing her associates about the murder. Despite Ruth sticking to her story about where she had acquired the gun, Bickford was following various different avenues of exploration. He believed, as did the police, the magistrate, and anybody else who had taken more than an academic interest in her case, that the gun was given to her by somebody closer to her than a passing stranger. Cussen, maybe?

On 11 May, Ruth made yet another appearance in court. This time it was in the Central Criminal Court at the Old Bailey. The object of this appearance was so that Mr Melford Stevenson, to be her counsel, could apply to Mr Justice Barrie for the case to be put over to the next session which was to begin on 14 June. His grounds were that many inquiries had still to be made by the defence.

Much of the defence's groundwork had been completed, but the outstanding factor was the search for a precedent. Mr Stevenson was preparing his case on the assumption that he would ask for the charge to be reduced from murder to manslaughter on the grounds that the accused had been so provoked by jealousy that she had lost all self-control. Unfortunately, the all-important precedent was not forthcoming in the books of English law.

Mr Justice Barrie approved of Mr Stevenson's application that the case be postponed until the next session. Ruth Ellis did not know it, but Mr Stevenson had won her an extra forty days. It was one of the very few battles the learned counsel was to win.

While the legal technicalities were being followed, the police were busy trying to tie up all the loose ends. They were far from satisfied with Ruth's explanation about the gun. They were leaving no stone unturned in *trying* to establish the origin.

One of the people to give them their first lead was a Mrs Marie-Thérèse Harris. She was the French teacher who had taught Ruth for a short period while she was living with Cussen at his flat in Goodwood Court. She told the police officer that she *thought* she had seen *a* gun in Cussen's home, but she could by no means be certain whether it was the one they showed her. She had telephoned the police after reading about her ex-pupil's arrest.

Mrs Harris gave the police a statement relating to an occasion when she had come to Goodwood Court to give Ruth a French lesson. Andy opened the door. She told the police:

> I asked him (Andy) for Mrs Ellis's copy book which I marked for her next lesson, and dated the book. I chatted with the little boy and mentioned that we were troubled by pigeons. He said: 'What you want is a gun', and with that he opened the drawer of the table on which I was writing. In the drawer I noticed, among other things, two guns, which at first I thought were his toys. He handled one, the larger one, then said: 'It's all right, it's not loaded', then put it back and closed the drawer and I left.

Upon this information, the police went straight to Goodwood Court to question Cussen. He was asked directly if he had ever given a gun to Ruth Ellis. Naturally he denied it. The police pressed him. They told him that two guns had been seen in his flat in a drawer of a table. Cussen, who must have been inwardly quaking, calmly asked one of the policemen to look in the drawer for himself. In it were an air gun and a starting pistol which, explained Cussen, only fired blanks. The police took the guns and departed.

Returning to Mrs Harris, the police produced the two guns they had brought from Cussen and asked her if either was the one she had seen at his flat. Mrs Harris, unfortunately, knew too little about guns to be able to commit herself as to whether they were or not.

Had police technology been as advanced then as it is today, it would have been possible for the forensic laboratory to have matched oil samples from the murder weapon with any oil that may have been in Cussen's flat at the time the police visited him.

Following the hearing at Hampstead magistrates' court, Detective Chief Inspector Davies completed his report on his investigations. He submitted it, along with twenty-six witness statements, to the Director of Public Prosecutions.

Any personal opinions that Davies had made were included at the end of the report. He said: 'This is clearly a case of jealousy on the part of Ellis, coupled with the fear that Blakely was leaving her. In spite of what Cussen says, that Ellis wanted to be rid of Blakely and he would not leave, the weight of evidence points quite clearly to the position being completely reversed. The two people, Blakely and Ellis, are of completely different stations in life.'

Davies went on, making observations on Ruth's early life. 'The girl is considered by her parents to have done well for herself. However, they both agree that their daughter has always had a violent temper. On meeting Blakely and realizing that his class was much above her own, and finding he was sufficiently interested to live with her and, if we are to believe Cussen, to promise her marriage, it seems she was prepared to go to any length to keep him. Finding this impossible, she appears to have decided to wreak her vengeance on him.'

The only mention Davies made of the all-important question of the gun and its whereabouts was included in an almost throwaway paragraph. 'Efforts have been made to trace from whom Mrs Ellis obtained the revolver used by her in this offence, but so far without success. Inquiries are being continued with this end in view because I find it difficult to believe her story that she received it as security for money she had loaned to a man and because it was a curiosity.'

While the defence were preparing their case, Dr Duncan Whittaker, a psychiatrist, paid Ruth a visit at Holloway. In a two-hour examination on 4 June, Dr Whittaker was satisfied that she was mentally stable, although he adds that an emotionally mature woman would have been prevented from this action by thoughts of her children. When Dr Whittaker put the question of her children to Ruth, her reply was that when she had the gun in her hand she had no thought at all for them.

The doctor also went into as much depth as one can in two hours about female behaviour patterns, including jealousy and hysteria. Ruth was adamant that her behaviour on the weekend of the murder was not 'hysterical'. She felt completely justified.

Dr Whittaker made out his report and handed it to the defence counsel. Most of what the report contained was given in evidence by the doctor at the Old Bailey.

John Bickford, Melford Stevenson, and Sebag Shaw were quite clearly unaware of Dr T. P. Rees's connection with Ruth Ellis. Dr Rees would have given them more than enough details of her mental history had he been asked so to do. But that was one corner of her past life that Ruth was not telling anybody. It was to be her loss.

Mr Stevenson's continual hunt for a precedent was getting nowhere. It appeared that never before had there been a case quite like this. It seemed that a jury had never been asked to consider a case in which the defence had been 'provocation by jealousy'. This did not deter Ruth's counsel. Mr Stevenson was confident. He did not believe that any jury in the land would allow a jealous woman, provoked by her lover, to be a victim of capital punishment. How wrong he was!

Ruth, apparently not interested in her counsel's problems, was more concerned that her hair was losing its peroxide colouring. She made a formal request to the Governor, Dr Charity Taylor, whether it would be possible to have her hair 'touched up' by a hairdresser. The Governor, known to be a kind and understanding woman, checked with the Home Office and was able to notify Ruth, the next day, that it was permissible.

The 'touching up' turned out to be a full peroxide rinse. Shack's of Shaftesbury Avenue were contacted and they supplied all the provisions and instructions for a wardress to transform a mousy grey into a platinum blonde. Although the results of her new-found colouring delighted Ruth, her lawyers were startled. How, they asked her, were they supposed to win the sympathy of the court by presenting her as a down-trodden young lady who had been mistreated at the hands of the man she had murdered, when she was going into the dock looking 'like a million dollars'?

Was, one wonders, Dr Taylor a little surprised at Ruth's 'unusual' request? Did she, perhaps, believe that she was doing Ruth a favour by restoring her to her brittle club-girl image?

Whatever anyone was thinking, Ruth was resigned. The case was to be heard on 20 June and already letters of 'good luck' were arriving for the attention of prisoner 9656 R. Ellis. Ruth read them all with a wry pleasure. The authors were not to know that, far from wanting 'good luck', she only wanted to die. She would be quite satisfied just to have the whole story presented to all those in attendance at the Old Bailey. She was to be denied this satisfaction.

The case about to take place was to be one of the most one-sided legal battles ever to be heard in the famous Number One Court. Had it been fought under the Marquis of Queensberry Rules, it would have been stopped during the first exchange of legal blows.

Although there was a national newspaper strike at the time Ruth Ellis committed her murder, the British public were well aware of what had happened outside the Magdala public house by the time she appeared in the Number One Court of the Old Bailey. Already many people were labelling the case as the most interesting murder of the century, even though from a legal point of view it was nothing more than a mere formality.

The queues outside the Central Criminal Court on the morning of Monday 20 June were vast. Along with the Cup Final, Wimbledon and other major sporting events, there had built up an ever increasing trade for courtroom tickets with as much as thirty pounds changing hands on the black market for a ringside seat in the public gallery. The ticket touts were active. Buyers, willing to pay ridiculous prices for the privilege of seeing a young attractive woman being sent to her death, were little problem. The fifties had already seen the touts in action outside the Old Bailey on two similar occasions: those of John Christie, the necrophile, who accumulated bodies in his terraced house at 10 Rillington Place, and the Christopher Craig and Derek Bentley farce that had taken place two years earlier.

Within minutes of the doors to the public gallery opening, the court was full and buzzing with expectancy. For those that have never been to the Old Bailey, Number One Court resembles a television set with a fourth wall. The judge's bench dominates the setting. To the right of this is the witness box and the jury and Press boxes. To the left sit counsel. Above them, in the gods as it were, is the public gallery. Directly beneath are the 'City Lands', a collection of green leather upholstered benches to which admission is by ticket only. These are usually reserved for relatives of counsel – both prosecuting and defending. Opposite the judge's bench is the vast dock in which the defendant is placed, and it is reached by stairs connecting the cells below.

Mr Justice Havers, who had been a High Court judge since 1951 and all-told presided over some twenty murder trials, quietly entered with his officers and retinue. The court rose and a hum of excitement permeated the arena.

Slowly the judge formally bowed to the barristers. Politely and without over-much emphasis they returned the gesture. Everyone sat down and the star of the show, Ruth Ellis, was brought from the cells. All eyes turned to the wooden dock as she entered. Many of the public were surprised at what they saw. Instead of a dejected young woman, tired-looking, sombre, and about to stand trial for her life, she looked like she was attending the première of a West End show. She was dressed in a two-piece suit with an astrakhan collar, and a white blouse. Her hair was immaculate and dazzling blonde. What impression this must have had on those in attendance at the Old Bailey that morning can only be guessed. It may be interesting, over twenty years after the event, to ask ourselves why her counsel didn't request that she look a little more sober on this, the most important morning of her life. An impression of dejection might – but only might – win some sympathy from the jury. That Ruth Ellis did not want their sympathy had not yet emerged.

That her hair looked brassy in its platinum sheen certainly was a mistake as far as the defence was concerned. Jean Harlow and other film stars had equated ultra-blonde hair with a leaning towards 'tartiness'. Ruth Ellis was to admit to living with two men at the same time, a confession which was hardly likely to endear her with the more strait-laced members of the jury. It would, perhaps, have been better if the dye had been allowed to grow out and she had looked more mousy.

But it had been Ruth's vanity which had prompted her to ask the Governor of Holloway, Charity Taylor, if she might have her hair re-dyed before she appeared at her trial. The Governor from the outset had been sympathetic, and agreed to the accused's wishes.

So now all eyes were on this woman. This blonde tart, as somebody in the public gallery whispered too loudly, focused around the 'theatre'. This was to be her stage and nobody was going to take that away from her.

The Press were extraordinarily interested in the case, so much so that extra seats had to be laid on for reporters from other parts of the globe who were covering the event for their respective newspapers. America, France, Italy, and Germany were just a few of the countries that had taken more than an academic interest in this lady. The fact that they could not understand how a woman could possibly be hanged for shooting her lover in a mad moment of jealousy was by the way. They were anxious, none the less, to see British justice in motion.

The clerk of the court, seated in front of the judge's bench, rose to his feet and read the charge. 'Ruth Ellis, you are charged that on the 10th of April last you murdered David Moffat Drummond Blakely. How say you, are you guilty or not guilty?'

The accused, in a voice not befitting the leading lady and just loud enough to be heard across the well of the court, replied: 'Not guilty.'

Ten men and two women were sworn in to observe and eventually decide this woman's fate. With this ritual completed and the defence counsel not objecting to these twelve people good and true, the show was about to get on the road.

The clerk, still on his feet, continued: 'Members of the jury, the prisoner at the bar, Ruth Ellis, is charged with the murder of David Blakely on the 10th April last. To this indictment she has pleaded not guilty, and it is your charge to say, having heard the evidence, whether she be guilty or not.' The olde worlde vocabulary of the clerk must have fascinated the foreign contingent in the audience.

The prosecution was led by Mr Christmas Humphreys, a brilliant orator who had the gift of winning juries over with his precise and underplayed use of the English language. Son of a judge, Sir Travers Humphreys, Toby – as he was known to his friends – had already been largely responsible for securing the fates of Timothy Evans, and the already mentioned Craig and Bentley. If Ruth Ellis was not to be another of Humphreys' 'successes', she would need everything her defence had hidden up its sleeves.

Assisting Mr Humphreys was Mr Mervyn Griffith-Jones and Miss Jean Southworth. Acting on behalf of Mrs Ellis was Mr Melford Stevenson QC, Mr Sebag Shaw, and the up and coming Mr Peter Rawlinson. Ruth could count her lucky stars that these eloquent gentlemen were representing her.

Mr Humphreys opened on behalf of the Crown. In case the jury were unfamiliar with the events that had brought this dazzling blonde into the outsized dock, Mr Humphreys explained: 'Mrs Ellis is a woman of twenty-eight, divorced, and the story which you are going to hear outlined is this: that in 1954 and 1955 she was having simultaneous love affairs with two men, one of whom was the deceased and the other a man called Cussen, whom I shall call before you.

'It would seem that lately Blakely, the deceased man, was trying to break off the connection, and that the accused woman was angry at the thought that he should leave her, even though she had another lover at the time. She therefore took a gun which she knew to be loaded, which she put in her bag. She says in a statement which she signed: "When I put the gun in my bag, I intended to find David and shoot him." She found David and she shot him dead by emptying the revolver at him, four bullets going into his body, one hitting a bystander in the hand, and the sixth going we know not where.

'That, in a very few words, is the case for the Crown, and nothing else I say to you, in however much detail, will add to the stark simplicity of the story.'

Nevertheless just in case the jury had not taken in what Mr Humphreys had put to them, extracts from Ruth Ellis's statement were read over. If the jury had been unsure as to whether they would be swayed by the prosecutor's eloquence, the statement must have made up their minds for them. And, as if to hammer the final nail into Ruth's coffin, Mr Humphreys went on: 'In 1953 Mrs Ellis was a hostess at the Little Club in Knightsbridge. She lived in a flat over it. There she met Blakely, and at the end of 1953 she began to live with him.'

Not even the painstaking police work guarantees that every detail presented by the prosecution is correct. Ruth Ellis did *not* meet David Blakely at the Little Club but at Carroll's. No doubt the confusion arose from the fact that at the time they met she was hostess at the Little Club.

Mr Humphreys went on to say: 'In the summer of 1954 she began to have an affair at the same time with a man called Cussen. In December 1954 she left the Little Club and went to live with Cussen in his flat in Goodwood Court, Devonshire Street. She continued, however, to see Blakely. It would seem therefore, that for the remaining few months of the story, she was living in that sense with both men.

'Early this year she telephoned a man called Findlater, a friend of Blakely's who had a flat in Tanza Road, Hampstead. As a consequence, Findlater and a man called Gunnell went to Cussen's flat where Ellis was living. It would seem that she was complaining that Blakely was trying to leave her, and she was trying to stop him going.

'On 9 February she went to live in a bed-sitting-room at 44 Egerton Gardens, South Kensington. She lived there with Blakely, who was known as Mr Ellis. While there, she was visited by Cussen.

'But let me tell you at once, as no doubt his Lordship will echo, that you are not here in the least concerned with adultery or any sexual misconduct. You are not trying for immorality but for murder, and the only importance of these movements between her and these various men is that it will help you to see the frame of mind she was in when she did what it cannot be denied in fact she did.'

It was a pity that while Mr Humphreys was about it he did not explain where she got the gun from and that pastis and pills had brought her to the state of mind in which it is doubtful if she knew what she was doing.

Mr Humphreys went on to explain to the jury what exactly went on from Good Friday until Ruth was arrested outside the Magdala public house on Easter Sunday evening.

The jury were intently interested and by the time the prosecutor called his first witness, they must have already made up their minds as to their verdict. Melford Stevenson QC was going to have to be at his best to utilize any flexibility the jury may have had left.

Police Constable Philip Banyard, who had prepared a plan of the area where the shooting took place; Detective Constable Thomas Macmacken, of the photographic department at New Scotland Yard; and Mrs Joan Winstanley, the chief housekeeper at Egerton Gardens were all called upon to tell their small parts of the story. None was cross-examined.

Then, the man who should have been in the dock rather than

being the chief witness for the prosecution, Desmond Cussen, was called. How interesting it would be in retrospect to know the feelings of Cussen as he walked from the waiting room into the witness box. Did he, one wonders, feel *any* pangs of conscience that perhaps it was he, as well as Ruth, that should have arrived at the Old Bailey via the back staircase of the cells rather than by car from London W1?

Even though he was far more composed than when he appeared at Hampstead magistrates' court, he was nevertheless pale, and casual observers noticed small beads of sweat trickling down his forehead. Cussen was to be the ideal chief prosecuting witness. He began: 'I knew Blakely for about three years. I first met Mrs Ellis about two years ago, when she was manageress of the Little Club, Knightsbridge, of which Blakely was a member. She became a close friend of Blakely's and lived with him. In October 1953, I too, became a close friend of hers.'

Humphreys, not standing on ceremony, asked: 'You will not mind if we use plain words. Were you her lover at some time?'

Cussen rightly replied. 'For a short time.'

'When was that?'

'About June 1954.'

'What was Blakely's position? Had he broken with her? Was he still seeing her?'

'He was away for about a week.'

'When he came back, what was the position?'

'He carried on seeing her and being very friendly.'

'Did she,' Humphreys went on, 'at some time live with you?'

'She left the Little Club at the end of December 1954 and came to stay at my flat.'

'And what was her attitude to Blakely?'

'It had not changed.'

'How long did she live at your flat?'

'About two months. Then she went to Egerton Gardens.'

'Do you know in what circumstances she was living there?'

'I understand that Blakely stayed there with her.'

'Did you see her at Egerton Gardens?'

Cussen paused. He thought hard. 'Yes.'

'Did she continue to see you at your flat?'

Again, Cussen thought carefully before committing himself. 'Yes.'

Mr Humphreys continued his examination of Cussen. The witness was leaving a good impression with the jury and more than once he glanced in their direction to see all was well. Humphreys then moved on to the night of the murder. Cussen looked uneasy.

'On Sunday 10 April did she and her son spend most of the day with you at your flat?'

'Yes,' replied Cussen truthfully.

'How old was the boy?'

'Ten.'

'That evening, did you drive her back to Egerton Gardens?'

'Yes.'

'About what time?'

'About 7.30.'

'At 7.30 on the Sunday night: and that is the last you saw of her?'

Committing perjury, Cussen answered: 'Yes.'

Indeed, he did drive her back to Egerton Gardens at about this time, but only so that she could put young Andy to bed. What might have raised Mr Justice Havers' eyebrows would have been Cussen's answer to the question, albeit hypothetical: 'And then what did you do?' Perhaps the reply, 'I drove her back to my flat in Devonshire Street and then on to Hampstead', might have thrown the jury and Mr Humphreys into a state of confusion. But it was not to be. Mr Humphreys sat down and allowed the stage to be dominated by Melford Stevenson.

Desmond Cussen was by far the most important witness that the defence would cross-examine. It is easy, twenty-two years after the event, to record the questions the distinguished counsel should have asked Cussen, but on that Monday morning Mr Stevenson was only prepared to stick closely to the brief prepared by Ruth's solicitor, John Bickford. Stevenson began: 'You have told the jury that you and this young woman were lovers for a short time in June 1954. Is that right?'

'Yes.'

'Were you very much in love with this young woman?'

'I was terribly fond of her at the time, yes.'

'Did she tell you from time to time that she would like to get away from Blakely, but could not, or words to that effect?'

'Yes.'

'And at that time did she repeatedly go back to him?'

'Yes.'

'At a time when you were begging her to marry you if she could?'

'Yes.'

'Have you ever seen any marks or bruises on her?'

'Yes.' Cussen's monosyllables were becoming tiring.

'How often?'

'On several occasions.'

'How recently before Easter had you seen marks of that kind?'

'On one occasion when I was taking her to a dance.'

'When was that?'

'25th February.'

Mr Justice Havers interrupted. 'Of this year?'

'Yes, my Lord,' replied Cussen.

The judge, confirming what had just been said, repeated: 'When I was taking her to a dance?'

Cussen, ever ready to please, replied: 'Yes.'

The defence counsel continued: 'Did you help to disguise bruises on her shoulders?'

'Yes.'

'Were they bad bruises?'

'Yes, and they required heavy make-up too.'

'I do not want to press you for details,' (the greatest understatement Melford Stevenson was to make throughout the all-too-short trial) 'but how often have you seen that sort of mark on her?'

'It must be on half a dozen occasions.'

Perhaps had Mr Stevenson asked the ever-willing Cussen if she ever told him where the bruises had originated from, it might have painted a clearer picture in the minds of the jury of how Blakely had been torturing her body as well as her mind. But it was not to be. More concerned with her treatment at the hospital rather than her treatment at the hands of Blakely, the defence counsel inquired: 'Did you on one occasion take her to the Middlesex Hospital?'

'Yes, I did.'

'Why was that?'

'She came back when she was staying at my flat, and when I arrived back, I found her in a very bad condition.'

'In what respect?'

'She had definitely been very badly bruised all over her body.'

'Did she receive treatment for that condition at Middlesex Hospital?'

'Yes.'

And with that, and perhaps to the considerable surprise of Ruth Ellis, Melford Stevenson sat down. The cross-examination of Cussen was finished. Cussen could hardly believe it. Where, he must have wondered, were the tricky questions. He was not asked when he *really* last saw Ruth. Whether she had acquired the murder weapon from *him*. Whether it was *he* that taught her to fire it. Whether it was *he* who drove her to the scene of the crime. None of it! Instead, peripheral questions about her bruising, her relationship with him and the origins of their meeting. For someone who was later to be described by the Press as 'the real murderer, although he never pulled the trigger', Desmond Cussen came off amazingly lightly. He was now free to stand down and take no further part in the life of Ruth Ellis. He glanced over at her, as well he might, for it was the last time he was ever to see her. No longer did he have to send her flowers and make-up in prison to ensure she did not involve him in the case. He could now pull down the shutters on this sad episode of his life with confidence.

In a recent interview, the judge, Mr Justice Havers, told the authors that he never believed the accused's account of where she acquired the gun and he could not possibly rule out the possibility of her having received it from Cussen. With more than a tone of irony, he simply said: 'But the defence counsel never mentioned it and I can only act on the evidence put before me.'

Mr Bickford, her solicitor during the trial, explained some years later his reasons for recommending to Melford Stevenson that they should not pursue the matter of the gun. He said to the authors: 'One of the reasons for reticence about it was because it was very akin to the Thompson and Bywaters affair. In those days, the moment you had two murderers or people charged with murder, then the whole atmosphere changed until it would have looked like a conspiracy to murder, which was one thing which would have been completely fatal, not only to her chances of an alternative verdict, but equally fatal to any chance of reprieve.'

Anthony Seaton Findlater, Blakely's best friend and mechanic, was called next. His evidence concentrated largely on the night of the murder and the phone calls Ruth had put through to Tanza Road. Findlater related for all in Number One Court how on the night before the tragic event, Ruth had pushed in the windows of Blakely's car. Then Mr Stevenson asked him: 'Was it quite plain when you spoke to her on the telephone that she was in a desperate state of emotion?'

'No,' said Findlater.

Stevenson, not really believing the reply, repeated: 'What?'

Findlater stood his ground. 'I said, no.'

Pursuing the point. Stevenson added: 'Do you mean she was quite calm? Do you really mean that?'

Findlater, not realizing what the counsel was striving at, answered: 'It was just a telephone conversation. She rang me up, as she had done hundreds of times, and asked if I knew where David was. It was just a telephone conversation.'

Melford Stevenson, retaining the usual courtroom courtesies, but by now becoming more direct, said: 'I know it was just a telephone conversation. Just bear in mind what she said and the way she said it and the fact that she afterwards pushed out those windows. Did you observe no indication of her being a very desperate woman at the time?'

Findlater, not giving an inch, said: 'No.'

Stevenson diverted his tactics. 'Never mind the word "desperate". Was it obvious to you that she was in a state of considerable emotional disturbance?'

But Findlater was not going to be swayed by the demanding Queen's Counsel. 'Well I did not get that impression over the phone. She might have been.'

'Perhaps you are not very good at judging that sort of thing on the telephone. Are you?'

Determined not to be made a fool of, Findlater replied: 'I think so.'

Stevenson must have decided he was fighting a losing battle on that line of inquiry, so he moved on. 'At the time of these events, did you have in your household a young woman of eighteen or nineteen who looked after your child?'

'Yes.'

'On the evening of Easter Sunday, was there a Rolls-Royce outside your house?'

'Yes.'

'Did you and Blakely go out with this young woman and get into the car?'

Even though Findlater's job brought him into direct contact with motor cars, he could not possibly have forgotten being a passenger in a Rolls-Royce. In most people's lifetimes there cannot be many occasions when they are the privileged passengers in the most luxurious car in the world. But Findlater, the man who could remember with clarity the tone of Ruth's voice some three months earlier, was at pains to recall whether or not he travelled in a Rolls-Royce. He answered: 'I can't remember.'

Mr Stevenson, working on the lines that have been mentioned, repeated: 'You cannot remember?'

'No,' replied Findlater.

'As you were walking down the steps of 29 Tanza Road, did not Blakely say to the young woman: "Let me put my arm around you for support"?'

But again Findlater could not remember. At last, it seemed Mr Stevenson had done some good for the accused's case. He had shown that perhaps Findlater was not as good a witness as was first believed. Christmas Humphreys had damage to repair and wasted little time getting to his feet.

'You will appreciate what is being suggested,' he reminded Findlater. 'That there is some reason for Ruth Ellis being jealous of some new woman being on the stage?'

Findlater, as if by some miraculous act of God, regained his memory and said: 'I did not even know that Mrs Ellis knew we had a nanny. She knew we had one, but this was quite a new one.'

Christmas Humphreys reassured him. 'What my learned friend is suggesting is that Ruth Ellis, in hanging about, might have seen Blakely in the presence of an entirely new young woman. I am sure you will help us if you can, if you were fooling about or anything of that sort. Was there any incident with a young woman outside that you can remember?'

Again, as if in a blinding flash, Findlater's memory returned. 'No,' he said most definitely.

There was no love lost between Findlater and Ruth Ellis. Up until the moment Ant Findlater stepped down from the witness box, Ruth Ellis must have hoped the full story – as she interpreted it – of the Findlaters' conspiracy to separate David from her would come to light. At this time she wanted to die, but also wanted the truth to be known.

Mr Justice Havers recently described her behaviour in court saying that he was surprised at her outward calmness. He concluded that she was certain that she was bound to be convicted, that she had made up her mind. 'She had got to face it.'

Perhaps she was calm as she entered the dock because she looked upon the prosecution as a foregone conclusion and that she did not want to live having shot the man she loved. But from the moment she realized her defenders were going to let, if not dogs, then sleeping Findlaters lie, she became resigned and spiritless. She took no further real interest in the charade being played out in the Number One Court of the Old Bailey.

Mr Bickford gives his explanation of this. 'On the morning at the Old Bailey when the trial was just about to take place, not to cross-examine the witness for the prosecution in a derogatory manner was the counsel's decision. It was thought it would be interpreted as mud-slinging on the part of Ruth Ellis and might not create a good impression.

'There is absolutely no criticism of the counsel in this. And it is only my personal opinion, of course – and it is very nice to have hindsight – if they had been cross-examined that would have caused Ruth Ellis to give her evidence in a very, very different way indeed, and created, I think, an exceptionally good impression. But in point of fact, she was so upset that the witness for the prosecution had not been cross-examined that she virtually threw her life away and as a result the counsel, Mr Melford Stevenson, was deprived of his right to address the jury after the evidence for the defence. And this, of course, was disastrous. The only possible verdict of course was guilty and such was the atmosphere then created by Mrs Ellis's callous indifference that the jury made no recommendation whatsoever.

Clive Gunnell, who by the mere fact that he was invited to the Findlaters' party was now giving evidence at the Old Bailey, was next in the witness box. He told the story as he had seen it. No new light was shed as far as Mr Gunnell's answers were concerned.

Because there was never any doubt as to what gun was fired and who pulled the trigger, the evidence of the next witness, Lewis

Nickolls, director of the Metropolitan Police laboratory, New Scotland Yard, was merely perfunctory. He explained, for the sake of the jury, about the six items that were handed over to him by Chief Inspector Davies and Detective Constable Claiden.

Police Constable Alan Thompson told how, whilst off-duty, he had been taking a quiet drink in the Magdala when he heard a commotion taking place outside and his police instincts took him away from his pint. There he saw Mrs Ellis standing with the gun in her hand and calmly asking the approaching PC Thompson to call a policeman. He didn't need to.

A woman with the ornate name of Gladys Kensington Yule gave a description of how a Sunday evening stroll along Parliament Hill and the edges of Hampstead Heath culminated in severe injury as a bullet ricocheted off the pavement and through the base of her thumb. It is possible that her evidence damaged Ruth Ellis's case more than any other.

Major Gwilym Lloyd George, the Home Secretary and supporter of capital punishment, subsequently pointed out that not only had Ruth Ellis pumped four shots into her lover, but she had wounded a casual passer-by with a ricochet. His inference was that unless murderers and murderesses were deterred by the fear of the rope, the general public were in danger of being wounded or killed by some anonymous felon.

The pathologist who performed the post-mortem on David Blakely told the jury of the cause of death. The police evidence followed. First, Detective Constable Claiden and then Detective Chief Inspector Davies gave evidence as to what happened from the time Ruth was brought into Hampstead police station until the moment she put her signature to a statement.

As the Chief Inspector stepped from the witness box, Mr Humphreys remained standing and said: 'That is the case for the prosecution.' It was all too painfully short. Now Melford Stevenson had the near-impossible task of winning the hearts of the jury with an opening speech for the defence. Onlookers in the Public Gallery and the City Lands must have regarded it as a classic 'open-and-shut case'. It might not have been quite so had any of the three defence counsels asked Mr Cussen more pungent questions. But it was not so. It would undoubtedly have helped had Ruth Ellis told the entire story from the beginning: had she only wanted to live.

But she knew that to have told the truth, the whole truth, and nothing but the truth would have meant possibly getting off on a manslaughter charge and spending many long years in Holloway prison and that she did not want.

In his opening speech Mr Stevenson slowly and concisely relayed: 'It cannot happen often in this court that in a case of this importance, fraught with such deep significance for the accused, the whole of the prosecution's story passes without any challenge from those concerned to advance the defence.

'Let me make this abundantly plain: there is no question here but that this woman shot the man. No one is going to raise any sort of doubt in your mind about that. You will not hear one word from me – or from the lady herself – questioning that.

'She is charged with murder, and one of the ingredients in that offence is what lawyers call malice; and the law of England, in its mercy, provided that if a person finding themselves in the position in which this unhappy young woman now is, has been the subject of such emotional disturbance operating upon her mind so as for the time being to unseat her judgement, to inhibit and cut off those censors which ordinarily control our conduct, then it is open to you, the jury who are charged with the dreadful duty of trying her, to say that the offence of which she is guilty is not the offence of murder, but the offence of manslaughter; and that, members of the jury, is what we, on her behalf, ask you to do in this case.

'You have nothing to do with morals. The question you have to decide, yea or nay, is whether or not this woman is guilty of brutal murder. You will hear the sad story of her association with the young man who is now dead. It is always an unpleasant thing to say anything disagreeable about someone who is dead, but I venture to think the story she will unfold to you can leave no doubt in your minds that he was a most unpleasant man.

'The facts stand out like a beacon that this young man became an absolute necessity to this young woman. However brutally he behaved and however much he spent of her money on various entertainments of his own, and however much he consorted with other people, he ultimately came back to her, and always she forgave him. She found herself in something like an emotional prison guarded by this young man, from which there seemed to be no escape.

146

'There is not in this any question of "unwritten law", as it is called in some other countries. But when you have heard her in the witness box, you may take the view that there is really no doubt that this young woman was driven by the suffering she endured at the hands of this man to do what she did, and it so operated her mind that her judgement for the time being was unseated and her understanding was gone, and that malice, which is the essential ingredient in the offence of murder, was absent in this case, so that you can perfectly properly return a verdict of manslaughter rather than a verdict of wilful murder.

'Members of the jury, that will depend upon the view you take of this girl when you see her here in the witness box. You will observe that she is now a calm and undisturbed person. You have got to try and put yourselves in the situation in which she found herself during that Easter weekend, when this man, whom she needed as one of the fundamental requirements of her existence, having, as you will hear, shortly before amended his conduct and behaved towards her in a way that gave her every hope for the future and bestowed on her all the marks of attention as before, went away and chose to consort with these rather odd people in Hampstead, in whose flat he spent the whole weekend. It was in those circumstances, and driven to a frenzy which for the time being unseated her understanding, that she committed the crime about which you have heard this morning.

'You will hear – and I am going to call a very eminent psychiatrist who will tell you – that the effect of jealousy upon that feminine mind can so work as to unseat the reason and can operate to a degree in which a male mind is quite incapable of operating.

'Now, members of the jury, there are dozens and dozens of cases in which the courts have considered this matter which is called provocation. It always has to be considered on the facts which arise in the individual case; but never before, as far I know, and as far as all the industry of those associated with me can reveal, has any court had to consider a case in which the defence relies upon jealousy, and the state of mind in which a woman gets when a man to whom she is devoted behaves as this one did, as constituting this defence of provocation.'

Eloquent as was his speech, one could not help finding that

Melford Stevenson's voice fell upon deaf ears. By this time the jury had heard as much as they wanted to hear. By most juries, untrained in the art of examination and cross-examination – and most of them never having been in a courtroom in their lives – events and people are seen in stark black and white; never a shade of grey. They had heard that Ruth Ellis took a gun and killed her lover, so therefore she had committed murder, not manslaughter. What mattered was the impression she was *now* going to put across. If anyone was going to save Ruth Ellis from the death penalty, it was she.

All eyes focused upon her as she calmly, calculatedly walked across from the dock to the witness box. The courtroom was silent. Her stiletto-heeled shoes clicked in time to her heartbeat. A member of the public gallery remembers her as being a 'typical West End tart'. If that was the impression she left on the jury then the case was lost before she had said a word in her defence.

Ruth Ellis took the oath that everything she was about to say was to be the truth, the whole truth, and nothing but the truth. It was. However, she might, too, have committed perjury had Melford Stevenson asked her questions that required direct answers about the all-important gun. She answered questions, put to her about her career in clubland, about her domestic life, and about the man she was soon to join in death.

'Did he come and live with you in a flat which you occupied above the club?'

'Yes.'

'At that time, how did he behave towards you?'

'He was very concerned about me. He seemed very devoted.'

'At that time, were you still married?'

'Yes.'

'And he was engaged to another woman?'

'Yes.'

Her voice was so quiet that everyone in the courtroom was finding it very difficult to believe that this quietly spoken young woman was the vicious criminal who had pumped four bullets into her lover: one at a distance of less than three inches.

'Did he,' asked Mr Stevenson, 'come to sleep with you at your flat nearly every night, and did you spend the weekends at Penn?'

'He stayed there from Monday to Friday, and spent the weekends in Penn.'

'And at that time were you very much in love with him?'

'Not really.' What prompted Ruth to deny her love for Blakely when she wanted to die for having killed the man she loved we shall never know.

The defence counsel moved on in haste. 'As time went on, how did he show his feelings for you?'

'In the December of that year I had an abortion by him, and he was very concerned about my welfare. Although he was engaged to another girl, he offered to marry me, and he said it seemed unnecessary for me to get rid of the child, but I did not want to take advantage of him.'

'When he offered to marry you, what did you say to that? How did you take it?'

'I was not really in love with him at the time, and it was quite unnecessary to marry me. I thought I could get out of the mess quite easily.'

'What mess?'

'I decided I could get out of the mess quite easily.'

In the eyes of twelve good, respectable, jurors, Ruth had undoubtedly damaged the picture that Melford Stevenson had tried so hard to paint of her. Did they ask themselves, one wonders: 'How could a woman sleep with a man she didn't love, fall pregnant by him, and then get out of the mess without a thought for the foetus in her womb?'

Mr Justice Havers wanted to clarify what Ruth meant by 'mess'. 'You mean the child?' he asked.

'Yes.'

In an even more inquisitive tone, he asked: 'Without his marrying you?'

Matter-of-factly, she replied: 'Yes.'

The judge raised his eyebrows and noted down her reply. Mr Stevenson, realizing the damage done, went on: 'Did you in fact get out of trouble in the way you have described in February 1954?'

'That is quite correct.'

The judge, still uncertain of what he had heard, said: 'You had an abortion?'

'Yes,' was the reply.

Mr Stevenson, who was politely giving way to the interruptions, continued. 'You knew that Blakely was engaged to be married?'

'Yes. I didn't take our affair seriously until he had broken it off. I tried to tell him that our association was not good for club business, and we should stop living together. Mr Blakely didn't like the idea of ending our affair at all.'

'And so the association continued until the summer of last year?'

'Yes. David then went away to the Le Mans motor race, and he stayed away longer than he should have done. That was when my affair with Mr Cussen began.'

'When you had an affair with Cussen, what did you hope or think might happen as far as Blakely and you were concerned?'

'I thought it might finish it. I thought that Desmond would tell David we had been intimate, and I thought that would finish it.'

'But what actually happened?'

'As soon as Blakely got back, he came straight to see me at the club. I didn't tell him of my affair with Desmond.'

'But what happened as far as you and Blakely were concerned?'

'At that time he was getting – David was getting – rather jealous. He asked me what I had been doing, and all kinds of things like that, and, of course, I did not tell him.'

'Did your association with Blakely in fact end there?'

'It began again.'

'At whose insistence? His or yours?'

'David's.'

'Did you try to avoid this happening?'

'It was very difficult. I was running a business, and he was there all the time. He was entitled to walk in. He was a customer, and he was hanging around the bar all the time. He was spending money in my bar. I could not tell him to go away.'

'Do you remember one night when you were at the flat with him, the question of marriage cropping up between you?'

'Yes. He asked me to marry him.'

Mr Justice Havers asked Ruth when this was, but Ruth appeared to be oblivious to anyone around her to anything but the memory of David. The examination of her relationship with Blakely continued, but none of her answers was winning the sympathy of the jury, and that, after all, was the order of the day. Melford Stevenson must have realized this when he focused the attention of his questions upon the violence that Blakely had inflicted upon her.

'By October 1954, was there a further change in his behaviour towards you? How did he treat you physically?'

'He was violent on occasions.'

'What sort of violence?'

'It was always because of jealousy in the bar. At the end of the evening when he got upstairs, it was always about the things he had been seeing me do, and so on and so forth.'

'How did this violence manifest itself?'

'He only used to hit me with his fists and his hands, but I bruise very easily, and I was full of bruises on many occasions.'

'When he complained about your working in the club, and exhibiting his jealousy, how did you take it?'

'I often told him to go and not come back, sort of thing, but whether I meant it or not, I said it anyway.'

'When you said that, did he ever go?'

'No.'

At this juncture the judge felt it was time to adjourn for lunch. It was an apt time in many ways for the question of violence would, with any luck, remain in the minds of the jury.

When all returned after luncheons taken in restaurants, pubs, and clubs, the accused, Ruth Ellis, came up from her cell and returned to the witness box. She then told the jury that during the latter part of 1954 she decided to leave the employ of the Little Club because she believed it was a way of breaking up her relationship with Blakely. To pass her time she took a modelling course and French lessons with the intentions of these serving her well should she wish to pursue an alternative career.

Melford Stevenson continued his examination by asking her where she went after she had left the Little Club. Ruth told him that she moved into the Devonshire Street flat of Desmond Cussen.

'And what,' asked the learned counsel, 'was Blakely's attitude to your doing that?'

'He did not like me going to live with Desmond at the flat. Last Christmas night he arrived at the flat and there was a scene.'

'Did you often see him at Goodwood Court?'

'When Mr Cussen was away, David and I used the flat.'

'In February of this year, was there another scene?'

'Yes. We had been drinking quite a lot.'

'And did you sustain injuries?'

'I sprained my ankle, got lots of bruises and a black eye. But I think David realized he had gone too far, for I was really hurt.'

'The next day, did Mr Cussen take you to the Middlesex Hospital to have the injuries treated?'

'Yes.'

'After this scene, Blakely sent you carnations?'

'Yes.'

And handing Ruth an exhibit, Mr Stevenson asked: 'And was this card enclosed?'

'Yes.'

'Please read it.'

'Sorry, darling, I love you. David.'

'After this, you made up your quarrel?'

'Yes. I took the flat in Egerton Gardens, and David came to live with me.'

'I do not want to mention any names, but after you had been there a short while, was there some trouble about a young woman?'

'Yes.'

And, again without mentioning names: 'Was that woman down at Penn or Beaconsfield?'

'In Penn.'

'And did you on one occasion remain all night outside the house where that other woman was living?'

'Yes.'

'And did you see Blakely come out in the morning?'

'He came out at nine o'clock in the morning. He had hidden his car at the back of the Crown public house, which is just down the road.'

'What were your feelings at that time?'

'I was obviously jealous of him now. I mean the tables had turned. I was jealous of him whereas he, before, had been jealous of me. I had now given up my business – what he had wanted me to do – left all my friends connected with the clubs and things behind, and it was my turn to be jealous of him.'

'How did you react?'

'I told him we were finished and it was all done with. I asked him for the key to the flat back, but he would not give it to me. He returned to the flat after an absence of about a week.'

'Why did you take him back?'

'For the same reason: because I was in love with him.'

'Were you anxious to take him back?'

'Oh, yes.'

'In March, did you find that you were pregnant?'

'Yes.'

'At the end of March, did you do anything about that pregnancy? What happened about it?'

'Well, we had a fight a few days previously – I forget the exact time – and David got very, very violent. I do not know whether that caused the miscarriage or not, but he did thump me in the tummy.'

'And that was followed by a miscarriage?'

'Yes.'

It might have been helpful for the jury, had her solicitor, John Bickford, found the doctor or doctors that had examined her following this miscarriage. Their evidence would have cast aside any doubts anyone in the courtroom may have had that it *was* through Blakely's fists that Ruth lost their child. The doctor was never traced. He joined the long line of potential witnesses who might have helped Ruth had they been brought into the limelight.

Mr Stevenson's examination continued with Ruth showing no signs of stress as she related for all to hear the stormy relationship she had had with the man she had shot. However, this hard exterior was broken for one solitary moment when she was handed the photograph of David which he had signed 'To Ruth with all my love, David'. She looked at it nervously and then, almost out of character, began to cry. The court was shocked. If they had felt that this woman was devoid of any feelings, they were now seeing the other side of her. She held on to the photograph that obviously meant so much to her – even now. Mr Stevenson, believing that he might now be winning some sympathy from the jury, asked the judge if she could sit down. This ploy had worked effectively when five years earlier the chief witness for the prosecution at the trial of Timothy Evans was asked the selfsame question. He accepted and immediately won the sympathy of the entire courtroom. He was John Christie. But Ruth was made of grittier stuff. Christie did not want to be implicated. Ruth was, and did not feel she ought to escape the noose that was drawing tighter around her neck as the minutes ticked on. She politely declined the judge's kind offer.

Events leading up to the Sunday of the murder were gone over, but little new light was shed on the canvas. She admitted phoning the Findlaters and asking to speak to Blakely. She explained how Cussen drove her to Tanza Road and how, after she had heard female giggles coming from within, she had pushed the windows of Blakely's car out of their rubber seating. Mr Stevenson moved on to the all-important day: Easter Sunday.

'The next morning, which was Easter Sunday, did you telephone the flat again?'

'Yes. I thought if David was sleeping in the lounge, and the divan is next to the phone, he would be the first to pick it up.'

'Was it in the lounge he used to sleep when he went there?'

'Yes. There is no other room – only one bedroom and a small room.'

'You telephoned?'

'Yes, just before nine.'

'What happened?'

'What I thought would happen: the phone would either be answered by David, or picked up immediately and taken off to stop it from ringing. I waited a long time before it was answered, and then Anthony answered the phone.'

'This is Findlater?'

'Yes.'

'What did you say?'

'I think I said: "I hope you are having an enjoyable holiday, because you have ruined mine."'

'Did you remain in your flat until lunchtime?'

'Just before lunch, yes.'

'What did you do then?'

'Mr Cussen picked me up with my son, and we went over, and I took something to eat at Mr Cussen's flat, and we spent some time at his flat.'

'As far as the morning is concerned, were you waiting for a telephone call?'

'Yes, I thought David would still phone.'

'And did he not?'

'No.'

'How did you spend the afternoon?'

Ruth thought. She answered slowly: 'I have completely forgotten what I did now. My son was with us, and we amused him in some way. I do not know what I did.'

Ruth was changing from 'I' to 'we', but Melford Stevenson didn't pursue the point as to who 'we' meant. Perhaps this could have been a good time to have put to the jury that Desmond Cussen made up the partnership. It was possible, indeed very probable, that they had forgotten Cussen's role in the drama by this time. Would it not be a good idea to jog their memory? But Mr Stevenson did no such thing. He was not implicating Cussen. He asked instead:

'At what time did you put the child to bed?'

'About 7.30.'

'There was still no message from Blakely?'

'No.'

Ruth explained that she was very upset and that she had a peculiar idea that she wanted to kill Blakely. If ever there was any doubt as to whether the executioner's rope would be placed around her neck, that voluntary statement certainly eradicated it. Whether or not Mr Stevenson believed what he had just heard, one can only speculate, but in an inquisitive tone he asked:

'You had what?'

Ruth, not steering from the path she had chosen, replied coldly: 'I had an idea I wanted to kill him (Blakely).'

'And we have had the evidence about your taking a revolver up to Hampstead and shooting him. Is that right?'

'Quite correct.'

Whether counsel was expecting a logical answer to his next question, only he can say, but upon asking: 'Why did you do it?' the answer: 'I do not really know, quite seriously. I was just very upset', must have knocked Mr Stevenson's sense of logic out the window and all the way to St Paul's. The judge, who must have been equally mystified, repeated Ruth's answer, to which she replied again in the affirmative. Mr Stevenson, trying to prove the then non-existent law of diminished responsibility, asked: 'When you say you had a peculiar idea that you wanted to kill him, were you able to control it?'

'No.'

'And then you went up, in fact, and shot him. Is that right?'

'Yes.'

If not totally bewildered, then somewhat baffled at what he had just heard, the defence counsel sat down and Christmas Humphreys rose slowly to his feet. Ruth Ellis had just done the major part of the prosecution's work. Nobody in court that afternoon, least of all the jury, could have expected what was to be the shortest cross-examination on record. Mr Humphreys asked one question and one question only:

'Mrs Ellis, when you fired that revolver at close range into the body of David Blakely, what did you intend to do?'

Without thinking, and matter-of-factly, Ruth signed her own death warrant. 'It is obvious,' she answered, as if nobody in the court was quite sure why she had committed the act, 'that when I shot him I intended to kill him.'

Any question of a defence on the grounds of insanity had just vanished into thin air. Mr Humphreys added a polite 'thank you' and sat down.

Today Mr Christmas Humphreys has not changed his opinion of Ruth Ellis and her behaviour at her trial. He believed she was a cold-blooded murderess and there were no palpable excuses for her crime. From the moment her reply to his one important question was spoken, any suggestion of manslaughter was silenced and any doubt as to her sanity was dispelled.

Melford Stevenson, who could not have been expecting such a short pause in his questioning, was now on his feet once more and calling his next witness, Dr Duncan Whittaker, who proudly announced himself as a Master of Arts, a Member of the Royal College of Surgeons, and a Licentiate of the Royal College of Physicians. His titles may have impressed the lay members in attendance, but it did not take too long before Mr Justice Havers could gather the relevance of his evidence.

Dr Whittaker, far from being familiar with Mrs Ellis, discussed how a woman's jealousy is a great deal more far-reaching than a man's. Indeed, to the question put to him by Mr Stevenson: 'You mean that a man's love is a man's boast, a woman's is her whole existence?' Dr Whittaker replied: 'They are more prone to hysterical reactions than men.'

The straw which broke the judge's back, metaphorically speaking, was the answer given to Mr Stevenson's question: 'And under the influence of these hysterical reactions, what becomes of the standards of conduct and control?'

The doctor replied: 'They are inclined to lose some of their inhibitory capacity and solve their problems on a more primitive level. This is not applying to women in general, but if they do have hysterical reactions, they are more prone to hysterical reactions than men. A man in the firing line in a war sometimes gets a paralysis that ensures his removal from the front . . .'

If the jury were able to follow the doctor's arguments, the judge certainly was not. He duly interrupted: 'I thought we were talking about women. What has the firing line got to do with a woman? If you want to talk about men, very well, but I thought we were talking about this woman.'

Melford Stevenson took the point, even if the doctor did not, and he continued by asking: 'Did you interview Mrs Ellis at Holloway prison on 4 June?'

'Yes.'

'How long were you with her?'

'Two hours.'

More acute observers in Number One Court that day might have been asking themselves why a doctor who had only known the accused for two hours should be called upon to give evidence about women's behaviour patterns in general. Those more familiar with the case could be excused for wondering why Dr T. P. Rees was not standing in the witness box shedding light on the behaviour of Ruth Ellis, whom he knew and had treated for several months. It would have carried a good deal more weight. It would have established that Ruth Ellis had created such a scene at Warlingham Park Mental Hospital, whilst her husband was being treated there for alcoholism, that she had to be given tranquillizers. She had not only shouted for anyone to hear at the hospital that her husband had been having an affair with a woman doctor, but had gone up and down the bus queue outside demanding to know if anyone had seen him misconducting himself at the hospital with the doctors or nurses. Ever since, she had taken the pills when suffering from intense emotional distress.

It was Christmas Humphreys who again poured cold water on any line of inquiry that Melford Stevenson was trying to pursue when he asked the doctor: 'In your view, was she at the time, within the meaning of English law, sane or insane?'

The answer, 'sane', ruined Mr Stevenson's case and certainly made up the minds of the jury: assuming there remained any lingering doubt.

Mr Stevenson, defeated and dejected, added: 'That is my case, my Lord.'

Why did the defence put this psychiatrist into the box, when far from helping Ruth's case his evidence was deleterious to it?

Mr Bickford, years later, explained: 'I was endeavouring to get all the sympathy I could, and there was just a possibility of a verdict of manslaughter on the grounds of lack of premeditation. This was an extremely weak case. You see, the laws then relating to the state of mind of an accused person were very different from what they are today. It was a case in which one could not plead insanity in accordance with the McNaghten Rules. It was a case where Ruth Ellis had gone through all the transports of rage and jealousy until I am quite convinced she had got into a very calm state of mind where she was in a sort of stratosphere of emotion, in which she thought everything she did was right and justified. Furthermore she even thought there was no other course open to her. Of course we consulted the psychiatrist. We went through every possible examination on that. I'm convinced that what we did eventually led to this new law of diminished responsibility.'

Mr Justice Havers, looking at his watch, released the jury and there followed a discussion on a point of law between counsel and judge about the element of jealousy. Mr Humphreys, who by now must have felt another case was over and done, announced: 'I accept my learned friend's propositions that this woman was disgracefully treated by the man who died, and I accept my learned friend's proposition that it would tend to lead her into an intensely emotional condition, even as that hypothetical person "the ordinary, reasonable human being". These conditions may well apply elsewhere. But was she brought more than into a state where it would be reasonable for her to hit and hurt him? One must take into account that the actual crime was planned and prepared. There was some pursuit of that purpose through the streets of London, and during the time of an hour or two; and finally, the man she killed was an unarmed man, and without any semblance of a struggle, she shot him in the back.'

As if to acknowledge 'point taken', the judge adjourned the court until the following morning. It would be overnight that he would decide whether to allow the defence plea for a charge of manslaughter to be considered.

On day two of the trial, before the jury were ushered to their seats, the judge announced: 'I feel constrained to rule that there is not sufficient material, even in view of the evidence most favourable to the accused, for a reasonable jury to form the view that a reasonable person so provoked could be driven, through transport of passion and loss of self-control, to the degree and method and continuance of violence which produced the death, and consequently it is my duty as a judge, and as a matter of law, to direct the jury that the evidence in this case does not support a verdict of manslaughter on the grounds of provocation.'

The end for Ruth Ellis was nigh.

Melford Stevenson conceded defeat at the hands of old-established law and the jury returned to their places. Mr Stevenson then explained to them that he would not proceed with a closing speech for the defence. Ruth Ellis must now have known what was in store for her. The members of the public gallery, again having queued for long hours, certainly had a good idea.

Mr Humphreys, again displaying his courtroom courtesies, added that he, too, had nothing to say. So now the judge had to make his summing-up and direct the jury. It is doubtful if any one of the twelve members of the jury had any doubts about the outcome. For them, tea would be early that evening.

'Mrs Ellis is charged with wilful murder, which in our law is the unlawful killing of one person by another with malice. What is meant by malice is this: the formation of an intention either to kill or to do grievous bodily harm. Long premeditation is unnecessary; the intention either to kill or to do grievous bodily harm can be formed at any moment of time up to the moment when the act is done. But there must be intent, and in considering such a matter you should have regard to the type of weapon used: whether it is a lethal weapon or not.

'In this case, six shots were fired by a Smith and Wesson revolver – a lethal weapon. Three or four were fired into the body of Blakely, and one was fired at extremely close range. In order to fire the revolver, there had to be pressure on the trigger each time.

Having regard to the nature of the weapon, the number of shots fired, and the fact that the gun has to be cocked each time, you will have to ask yourself this very serious question: whether you would not be compelled to the conclusion that there was, in the circumstances of this case, at least the intention to do grievous bodily harm, if not to kill.

'If all the evidence compels you to that conclusion, and you are satisfied that Mrs Ellis intentionally fired the shots, then that would amount to a verdict of guilty of murder.

'You may think it very difficult for a person who fires a revolver of that type six times and hits a person three or four times with shots from it to have any other intention than to do at least bodily harm.

'If a person does an act towards another wilfully which a reasonable person would know can cause death or grievous bodily harm, and death results, that is murder. If the person could not have contemplated either of those circumstances, she would be guilty only of manslaughter, which is the unlawful killing of one person by another without malice – that is to say, without the intention to kill or to do grievous bodily harm.

'You should have regard to the statements Mrs Ellis made after her arrest, and to those which she has given in evidence.

'At first, she made a statement saying that she was guilty, but apparently that was before she was charged with any offence. She then went on to explain how she got the revolver, and later how she took the gun and shot Blakely. She said in her statement: "I thought I had missed him, so I fired again."

'In the witness box, she said she was very upset and wanted to kill Blakely. She said: "I do not know why I shot him – I was just very upset." Replying to Mr Humphreys' question in cross-examination, her answer was: "When I fired the revolver at close range, I intended to kill him."

'Members of the jury, that is the crucial issue for you to decide in this case. Are you satisfied – and it is not challenged by the defence – that she fired those shots deliberately into the body of Blakely?

'It is not a defence to prove that she was a jealous woman, and you may think her evidence strengthens the case for the prosecution, because she said: "I wanted to kill David."

'I am bound to tell you that even if you accept the full evidence of this woman, it does not seem to me that it established any sort of defence to the charge of murder. According to our law, members of the jury, it is no defence for a woman who is charged with the murder of her lover to prove that she was a jealous woman and had been badly treated by her lover and was in ill health, and that, after her lover promised to spend the Easter holidays with her, he left her without any warning and refused to communicate with her, or that he spent the holidays with his friend, or in the company of another woman, or that he was committing misconduct with another woman, and that, as a result of that, she became furious with him and emotionally upset and formed an intention to kill him which she could not control. None of these facts individually affords any defence, nor do they collectively afford any defence.

'There is one other observation which I should like to make, and that is that this court is not a court of morals. You will not, therefore, allow your judgement to be swayed or your minds prejudiced in the least degree because, on her own admission, when Mrs Ellis was a married woman she committed adultery, or because she was having two persons at different times as lovers. Dismiss those questions from your minds.

'There is no evidence whatever that Mrs Ellis was, at the time when she did this act, insane. The defence did not seek to put that forward, and it is a matter which is not open to you to consider in this case.'

No evidence as to her state of mind was given, other than the vapourings of the psychiatrist who had spent a full two hours with her. No evidence of her past mental instability was given. No psychiatrist was asked what would have been the effect of drinking pastis on top of tranquillizers. Dr William Sargant has since said that such a combination would have made her completely without control. Desmond Cussen was never asked if, on the last night before the murder, he had plied her with Pernod.

'If you are satisfied that the accused deliberately fired those shots at Blakely, and as a result he died, it is not open to you to find a verdict of not guilty.

'If, on a review of the whole evidence, you are left in reasonable doubt whether at the time she fired those shots she intended to kill or do grievous bodily harm, you will find her guilty of manslaughter.

'If, on the consideration of the whole evidence, you are satisfied that at the time she fired those shots she had the intention of killing or doing grievous bodily harm, then your duty is to find her guilty of wilful murder.'

The jury returned to discuss what little the judge had left open for discussion. There were ten men and two women. Most of the jurors had already made up their minds – or, if not, would go along with the majority. In a recent interview, a member of the jury explained to the authors what went on during the twenty-three minutes they were out.

'It was a two-way fight really. I was the one pushing for a "guilty" verdict; the one who believed she should hang for murder. Another chap – I can't remember who he was – tried to come to her defence. I remember him saying: "We're all men of the world, aren't we? We know what goes on at these clubs. We can understand how a woman can get jealous and be motivated to kill, can't we?" That wasn't the point, I explained to him. The judge had told us that we had to decide whether or not she had meant to kill him, and in her own words she had admitted this. It was all over as far as I was concerned.

'Actually, while we were discussing this one point, the thing that still sticks out in my mind was that the others were going backwards and forwards to the toilet. I reckon that of the twenty-three minutes we were out, only about thirteen were spent actually discussing the case.

'Anyway, when everyone had relieved themselves we continued the discussion, but really there seemed little to discuss. I said she should be found guilty of murder and this other chap thought we ought to be a bit lenient on her because of all that she had gone through. The fact was the judge didn't direct us towards leniency. Either she meant to kill this lover of hers or she didn't. I said this to the other chap, and after about ten minutes he agreed. The other ten members went with me and that was that. There was really nothing to argue about. I mean, it was Mrs Ellis, herself, who admitted she meant to kill him.'

The jury returned and one of the members who had not been active in the discussion stood forward as foreman. No official foreman had been elected. The clerk rose to his feet.

'Members of the jury, will your foreman please stand? Mr foreman of the jury, are you agreed upon your verdict?'

'We are.'

'Do you find the prisoner at the bar, Ruth Ellis, guilty or not guilty of the murder of David Blakely?'

'Guilty.'

There was no recommendation to mercy. Ruth had asked for none. But then there were so many matters left unsaid at the trial, which if spotlighted might well have influenced the jury to sympathy. Could the judge have suggested to the jury that they might make such a recommendation? No. Mr Justice Havers has recently said: 'A judge has no powers to suggest to a jury that they should do so. That has been decided by the Court of Criminal Appeal. Juries are very unpredictable. Nobody knows why, when they do make such a recommendation. Maybe they do so for some reason which never emerges in court. They never say why, of course.'

But Ruth Ellis's judge believed that if the defence had been allowed to show she was not responsible for her actions through a combination of drink and drugs, that she had had a miscarriage caused by Blakely punching her in the stomach, and that the gun had been put into her hand and she had been driven to the site of the murder, the jury might well have shown compassion.

As the word 'guilty' rang around the court, nobody moved, least of all Ruth Ellis. She had nothing to say when asked and that only left Mr Justice Havers to pass the formal sentence for the crime of murder. One could almost *hear* the silence as he donned his black cap and said in sad monotones:

'Ruth Ellis, the jury have convicted you of murder. In my view, it was the only possible verdict. The sentence of the Court upon you is that you be taken hence to a lawful prison, and thence to a place of execution, and that you there be hanged by the neck until you are dead, and that the body be buried within the precincts of the prison within which you shall last have been confined before your execution, and may the Lord have mercy upon your soul.'

All eyes in the courtroom focused upon the fragile woman in the dock, who was not overtly perturbed. As two warders moved to take her arms, she gently and calmly brushed them aside and made her own way down to the cells below in readiness for her last journey on earth: from London EC4 to N7.

The Press reporters rushed impatiently to the Press room to phone through tomorrow's headlines. The members of the public gallery – having got their money's worth – dispersed to tell their children how they had seen a woman sent to her death. The barristers collected their papers, conferred, and went along to their chambers.

It was all over before lunch on the second day. Desmond Cussen did not stay to hear the passing of the sentence. He had come to his senses long before and realized that he should not have got involved with Ruth in the first place. He was to say shortly afterwards: 'I must sort my life out. This is another episode over.'

What would have been his answer, one wonders, had he been asked by somebody with insight to the true story, whether he felt that it was *he* that should be preparing to meet the executioner? But that question was fantasy. Nobody except Ruth and John Bickford knew the true part that Cussen had played.

Within minutes the courtroom began filling up again. There were new faces to hear a new case. An entirely fresh atmosphere permeated the wooden rectangular room. The trial of Ruth Ellis was now history.

Ruth Ellis had twenty-one days left on earth to tell someone the true story of the happening on that fateful Easter Sunday night. Nobody in court was convinced that her explanation of where she acquired the murder weapon was true. Most believed, particularly the members of the Press, that even if it were given to her in exchange for a debt, somebody, somewhere, must have taught her to fire it. Most believe they knew who the tutor was, but nobody was talking. Least of all Ruth.

11

It was not Ruth Ellis's fate, but all the events leading up to her execution and the ripples which spread in the murky pool of public revulsion, which made her life and death important. As the headlines confronted the public, few of the readers could have had the slightest notion that an accomplice may have played a leading role in the murder of David Blakely. Although the judge, the jury, both prosecuting and defence counsels, her solicitor, her family, and friends did not question that she had committed the murder, none of them believed that the gun had been given to her under the circumstances she described with little conviction before and during the trial.

On her return to Holloway prison, Ruth was housed in the condemned cell, which adjoined the execution chamber. Ruth was, however, unaware of the geographical layout of the prison, and that she was but a few paces from the gallows. Her last days were spent reading the Bible, making stuffed toys from materials brought in by her mother, and – a new interest – whiling away her hours piecing together jigsaw puzzles. Between these activities, she received visitors. All of them to reassure her that a reprieve would be inevitable. Instead of being comforted, Ruth was annoyed. She did not want a reprieve and she made this known.

One of her most regular visitors was her brother, Granville. On one of his visits, she slipped a note into his hand requesting that next time he would bring her a lethal dose of poison. But Granville did not want his sister to die. So he handed the note to his father who read it and tore it up. Ruth was destined to die at the end of a rope.

Every day relatives and friends visited her, mouthing words of comfort, if not joy. She told them in no uncertain terms: 'I have committed this crime. I must die for it.' This was her philosophy; her kismet. But to her parents it seemed ludicrous. Why sacrifice life if it could be saved? Ruth was calm, resigned. She accepted her fate. Not so the Press in newspaper offices up and down Fleet Street; and in the House of Commons campaigners were doing everything in their power to make sure that this young mother of two was not going to become the fifteenth woman in this century to be executed in Great Britain, above all for a crime of passion.

Letters to the Press from Sir Beverley Baxter, Mr Anthony Greenwood M P, and the Methodist Leader, Dr Donald Soper, all emphasized that out of humanity alone Ruth Ellis must not be executed. Throughout the country petitions were being passed around the pubs, clubs, and at sporting events to try to persuade the Home Secretary to show mercy. Eventually, fifty thousand signatures were forwarded to the Home Office. How many actually reached the desk of the Home Secretary is, of course, another matter.

It was not only British journalists who campaigned furiously for action. Many foreign reporters, some of whom had sat through the trial, others who had been revolted by the Press reports, protested vehemently in print. *Le Monde*, for instance, was critical of the British system:

> English law does not at the moment recognize any inter-mediate stage between the rational and balanced being who kills in perfect awareness of what he is doing and the total lunatic who is not conscious of his own acts. As everyone knows, the Englishman is – or believes himself to be – a creature of *sang froid*, and the legal system in force supports this fiction in overruling once and for all any emotional troubles or irresistible impulses. As seen by the upholders of tradition, the place accorded to so degrading a concept as the *crime passionel* seems precisely to be the true measure of 'French decadence'. But the doubts which began increasingly to be felt will certainly be stimulated by yesterday's trial.

The article went further, highlighting the difference between English and French law. As if to prove their argument, a woman in Corsica was tried and convicted for the premeditated murder of her lover. She was sentenced to two years' imprisonment with a suspended sentence, and immediately released on probation.

Ruth Ellis, despite her few French lessons in preparation for Le Mans, would not have been able to translate *Le Monde* if it had been available in her cell. This was a pity. Their argument might have sown a seed of injustice in her mind which would have motivated her to take immediate action to save her life, instead of waiting till the last twenty-four hours.

Crusaders were fighting on her behalf outside the prison long before any practical steps were taken inside the high walls of Holloway to save her. After a meeting with his client, John Bickford – against Ruth's wishes – sent a letter to Major Gwilym Lloyd George stating the reasons the defence believed she should be reprieved. On Bickford's suggestion Leon Simmons also wrote to the Home Secretary, describing the heartbreak and misery Ruth had endured during her marriage to George Ellis. Few barristers and solicitors working in the criminal field believed that the Home Secretary would allow the execution to take place.

During the trial, even the prosecuting counsel, Mr Christmas Humphreys, stated flatly that Ruth had been treated disgracefully, and that it was not surprising that she was in an intensely emotional condition. He added: 'These conditions may apply elsewhere.' Elsewhere, one assumes, was in the good offices of the Home Secretary.

But while others became increasingly inflamed with anger or exasperated in sympathy, Ruth herself remained calm. Her serenity occasioned much comment, not only amongst her friends and visitors, but also with Dr Charity Taylor. It took Jackie Dyer, the club barmaid and her confidante, to cut through the protective layer of Ruth's pretended impassiveness. Jackie Dyer, with the unromantic practicality of her French forebears, did not believe Ruth's explanation as to how she got the gun. She told Ruth this in no uncertain terms. She begged her friend to tell her the *whole* story. But Ruth was not going to be drawn into any explanation. She said she *had* already told the whole story. The barmaid-cum-hostess remained unconvinced.

Her Member of Parliament was Mr George Rogers, who had recently been campaigning to clear the name of Timothy Evans. Indeed, he had managed to persuade the House to support a private inquiry into the Christie–Evans association.

Mr George Rogers, in a recent interview, recalled Mrs Dyer's first visit to him. 'It was a normal day in the House when I received the usual green card from a visitor in the lobby. I went out to the lobby and there was Jacqueline Dyer accompanied by an Arab. She started to tell me the story of Ruth Ellis, and begged me to help her to get a reprieve. At first I was rather reluctant, because I'd been mixed up in a previous murder case which had caused me a great deal of trouble.

'She was so sincere and persuasive about the impending fate of Ruth Ellis and I never like to say no if someone asks me to help. So, I finally agreed to take up the case with the Home Secretary and see what I could do.'

Because of the newspaper strike, Mr Rogers had been one of the many who had read little of what had transpired. Mrs Dyer, however, provided him with all the details and explained that, although she accepted Ruth was guilty of the crime, the extenuating circumstances were such that for Ruth Ellis to die for the shooting would be a travesty of justice.

Mr Rogers explained: 'Mrs Dyer told me that it wasn't really Ruth's fault because somebody made her drunk and took her to the scene of the crime, placed the gun in her hand and when David Blakely came out of the pub, encouraged her to shoot him. Mrs Dyer's deep sincerity, and the fact that she was my constituent, made me agree to take up the case and see if I could get clemency from the Home Secretary.'

Jackie Dyer told Mr George Rogers that Desmond Cussen had given Ruth the gun and that if Ruth were going to die he should not get off scot-free. With these facts brought to his attention, Mr Rogers decided that before he proceeded any further, it was important he should pay Ruth a visit in Holloway. He applied for permission to the Home Office and upon it being granted, he met the condemned woman for the first time.

'It was certainly a very unpleasant experience as far as I was concerned. I had a headache for three days afterwards, I was so moved by the whole business. I was of course seen in the cell and there was an opening between us, with wardresses sitting all around us.

'Apart from my natural depression in being involved in such a visit to such a tragic woman, I was deeply depressed by the whole atmosphere of the prison. Everything was grey. Everything, even

the wardresses, and the whole thing was most depressing altogether.

'I was rather surprised at my first impression of Ruth Ellis. She
was obviously a woman who'd been brought down to the very
edge of truth and there were no longer any signs of the sort of
woman I'd imagined she was before she was charged with murder.

'Here she was facing death and this had stripped her of all
feminine vanity and behaviour in the sort of way that she must
have had it when she was pursuing her normal life in the club. She
was rather thin and very pale. A rather fragile sort of person, with
brassy yellow hair. Her eyes were rather shallow, not much depth
to them.'

Ruth listened with indifference to what the MP had to say to
her. He pleaded with her to tell the truth about all the extenuating
circumstances. Ruth listened intently but would say nothing. She
knew if she told the MP the truth, he would use her words to try
and get her a reprieve. She wanted to die. She said so on many
occasions.

Realizing he was making no impression on her mask of calm,
Mr George Rogers tried another tactic. He raised the subject of
her son, Andy. Immediately she reacted. Nobody, it seemed, had
used this line of argument to persuade her to fight for her life. The
MP asked Ruth whether she was so determined on self-destruction
that she did not care about the effect of her death on her son. Not
only had the boy no father, but soon he would be without a
mother because she would have been hanged. Ruth was visibly
moved. Perhaps death was not a solution to all her problems;
certainly it was not the answer to her son's future. She agreed for
the first time that Mr George Rogers should apply for clemency.
The campaigning Member of Parliament had won the first round
in what was to become a lengthy battle.

If Mr Rogers needed further inspiration, the next morning's
Daily Mirror provided it. The famous columnist William Connor
– better known to the paper's millions of readers as Cassandra –
wrote a leader entitled 'Should Ruth Ellis Hang?' Such was the
power of the article, that it is reproduced here in full:

On July 13th Ruth Ellis is due to be taken to a place of
execution and there to suffer death by hanging and her

body buried in the precincts of the prison where she has been confined.

The jury in this case swiftly pronounced her guilty within twenty-three minutes.

They made no recommendation to mercy.

The judge said that no other verdict was possible.

Her lawyers decided to make no appeal.

Death at the hands of the public hangman is very near and only the Home Secretary, left with the last agonising decision, can save her from the shameful doom in a prison yard.

It is unlikely he will do so.

What sort of killing was this?

It was a fierce, white-hot murder. Ruth Ellis fired six shots at her lover. Four of them hit him. She had to pull the trigger for every shot she aimed at him.

It was not one continuous burst of fire but six separate, deliberate operations. One deadly wound resulted from the muzzle of the gun being held within three inches of the dying man's body. Pity comes hard after such dreadful deeds.

Compassion weeps but is silent.

Yet had I the power I would save her. This was a murder of love and hate. The one as fierce as the other – the storm of tenderness matching the fury of revenge.

In human nature, where passion is involved, love and hate walk hand in hand and side by side. The difference between them is a hair's breadth. The one can change to the other in a trice. Infinite sweetness and affection become infinite wickedness and black insensate cruelty. This was no slow poisoning. But a sudden explosion of the forces of evil that are latent in the hearts of more men and women than would care to admit it – terrible, senseless, evil, and all too human.

There are thirteen more days to go. By the nature of her crime, by the nature of her appearance, by the ingrained horror that most people have at the prospect of a woman shortly to be dragged to the scaffold, it is inevitable that millions of people will be increasingly drawn towards the

170

shortening shadow of the hideous event to come. Some will be fascinated – morbidly so. Others will be horrified and haunted. But there will be an almost tribal unanimity in the interest of the case. It is part of the degrading price that capital punishment demands – and always gets.

Justice not only has to be done, but it also has to be seen to be done. And so have the barbaric penalties of the execution. They, too, have to be seen to be done.

This ghastly business, this obscene ritual which we, who claim to be the most civilised people in the world, have never succeeded in getting rid of, is witnessed by many people – most of whom have the decency to want to vomit.

The sheriff has to be there. The gaoler, the surgeon, the chaplain and the hangman are present, 'and such other persons as the sheriff requires or allows'.

These by law may even include the relatives of the prisoner, and any Justice of the Peace for the country who wants a ghastly day out.

You who read this paper – and millions like you – are the key supporters of this sickening system whereby with panoply and brutality mixed with the very dubious sauce of religion and consolation we bury our worst malefactors in the quick-lime grave.

You may shy away from your terrible responsibility and say that justice has been done.

But justice is not full retribution. Justice is not maximum vengeance, and if it were, the bursting gaols that we now have would be ten times more overcrowded and the gibbets would creak in every county in the land.

The prospect of judicial execution never stopped any murderer. By all the records that have ever been examined, the scaffold does not prevent the use of the gun, the knife, the fatal blow, the strangler's hands or the phial of poison.

Ruth Ellis does not matter any more than her two most recent female predecessors to the hangman's noose – Mrs Merrifield and Mrs Christophi.

But what we do to her – you and I – matters very much. And if we do it, and if we continue to do it to her sad successors, then we all bear the guilt of savagery untinged with mercy.

With the brave and hard-hitting article before the public, Mr Rogers wrote explaining to the Home Secretary that he had come to the conclusion that this was a case for reprieve, especially as new information from Mrs Dyer threw doubt upon the evidence that the crime had been premeditated. The Home Secretary ignored this letter.

Mr George Rogers, MP, and Jackie Dyer, barmaid, were a formidable combination. If one failed, the other would try. Though his letter was lost, if not swept under the carpet, hers was forwarded by the Home Office to New Scotland Yard. After going through the usual bureaucratic channels, it eventually arrived on the desk of Chief Inspector Davies at Hampstead. He made a cursory visit to Mrs Dyer and, after questioning her about her visit to Ruth, asked her to make a formal statement. Jackie Dyer told the policeman that on the two occasions that she had helped Ruth pack her cases – from the club to Goodwood Court, and from Goodwood Court to Egerton Gardens – she had never seen any sign of a gun.

In her statement she said: 'David Blakely seemed to me to be a fool of a man who shouldn't go out with a girl like Ruth. He was very jealous of Ruth and was even jealous of me because she thought a lot of me. They quarrelled frequently, and he beat and kicked her. I saw them fighting in the flat one day, and he pushed her out of the flat and she fell down six stairs. She was frequently bruised about the body.

'I had not seen Ruth for two months before the shooting, but I frequently rang her up, the last occasion being ten days before the affair. On the last occasion she told me that she was very happy and that she and David were going to get married.

'I feel that Ruth shot David because of the way he treated her and in my opinion he asked for what he got. I wrote to the Home Secretary after I had seen Ruth in prison, because I wanted to help my friend, and because she must have been driven to it by the way Blakely treated her.

'During one of my visits to Ruth I gathered from her that Cussen had given her the gun, and that he had driven her to Hampstead on the night of the shooting. She later denied that Cussen had given her the gun, but I cannot see who else could have given it to her. I still press the question every time I see Ruth, because I think she is telling lies when she says he did not give it to her. It is also my opinion that Ruth did not go to Hampstead by taxi, but was taken there in Cussen's car.

'I intend to do everything in my power to save my friend's life because I think it is only justice, and I know the life she had to lead with Blakely.'

Mr George Rogers' words had sown a seed of doubt in Ruth's mind. Perhaps it was not so romantic to talk of an eye for an eye, and a tooth for a tooth, if this meant the sordid charade that authority would bring one to hang by the neck until one be dead. Why had her defence not fought more vigorously to save her life despite her earlier wish to die? Why had they not indicted the Findlaters? Why, despite her wish to keep the source of the gun secret, had her defence not insisted on Cussen coming forward. Yet she liked John Bickford . . . and had had faith in him. Now she wondered and eventually came to believe her faith was misplaced.

6 July was an eventful day for the Home Office. A letter arrived addressed to the Home Secretary, from an Alexander Engleman who explained that he used to be a receptionist at the Little Club and knew Ruth well. The letter explained that too much notice had been taken of the gun and too little had been focused on the taxi that Ruth was supposed to have hired to take her from Kensington to Hampstead. The letter provoked enough interest for the police at Hampstead to pay a visit to Engleman, who, it must be said, was half expecting them.

He related to Detective Constable Claiden how, one night in 1954 when the Little Club had closed, Cussen came up to him and asked him if he could give him a lift home.

'I accepted and went downstairs with him. Outside the club I looked for his car, and he pointed to an old taxi which was parked across the road, and said "This is my car." I asked him where his other car was, and he said: "It's in dock. I've borrowed this. Jump in." He went to the driver's seat and put on a chauffeur's cap, then drove me to his flat, where I went in and had a drink with him. After a while I left him and came home.'

The police decided it might be interesting to visit Desmond Cussen again. Cussen, who had apparently disappeared from the scene since Ruth was sentenced to death, had maybe thought it advisable to keep out of harm's way. He must have known, even at this late stage, that Ruth might implicate him. No one can be tried twice for the same murder; but Desmond Cussen had never been indicted.

The police spent two days unsuccessfully trying to trace the company director. The report read: 'We have made inquiries of a number of friends of both Blakely and Cussen, but none could remember Cussen ever having used an old taxi-cab. It may well be that he did so when driving Engleman home but it would appear that it was an isolated incident. No information could be obtained concerning the possible ownership of the machine.

'Cussen had not been seen, and although intensive inquiries were made to trace him, he could not be found. It is believed that he returned to London during the afternoon of 6 July 1955, but his present whereabouts are unknown. If, within the next few days, Cussen is traced he will be interrogated in respect of the use of the taxi-cab with Engleman, and of the possibility that he drove Ellis to the scene of the murder.

'Even if it is established that Cussen drove her to Hampstead on that evening, it would have little bearing on the culpability of Ellis in this matter, but so far there is not a shred of evidence to show that Cussen did take her to the scene of the crime.'

So, where was Desmond Cussen? It cannot be ruled out that he was being 'hidden' by the national newspaper which had purchased the life story of Ruth Ellis, so that no other paper could anticipate their feature. Only Ruth Ellis and Desmond Cussen knew the sequence of events leading up to the crime. Ruth Ellis was in prison, condemned. This made Desmond Cussen a valuable property. If he were arrested too, the reporters might have no exclusive story. They were taking no chances!

With time running out for Ruth, Cussen was eventually traced to nowhere less than his flat at Goodwood Court. Chief Inspector Davies and Detective Constable Claiden, the hunters, were invited into the flat of their quarry. Any plans they had to surprise Cussen by their knowledge as to his owning a taxi, were fated to failure. Without hesitation he admitted to owning a taxi, but said he had sold it in September 1954 and so, he could not possibly have used it to drive Ruth to Hampstead in April 1955.

A statement to that effect was taken from Cussen, but such are the wheels of governmental bureaucracy that it did not reach the powers that be until after Ruth was dead. But both Engleman's statement and Detective Constable Claiden's subsequent report were passed to the assistant commissioner of 'C' Department, and from there to the Home Office. By the time the Home Secretary sat down to consider the Ruth Ellis case, at the home of his sister, Lady Megan Lloyd George, in Wales, he had Engleman's and Claiden's contributions.

Cassandra's article may well have inspired Mr George Rogers to fight for clemency. It is not impossible that a letter from Mrs Gladys Yule which appeared in the *Evening Standard* on 11 July might have moved the Home Secretary in the opposite direction. The letter contained all the venom of somebody who would sleep easier at night *after* Mrs Ellis was dead:

> Don't let us turn Ruth Ellis into a national heroine. I stood petrified and watched her kill David Blakely in cold blood. These hysterical people, getting up petitions for a reprieve, and those rushing to sign them – do they realise that Ruth Ellis shot Blakely to the danger of an innocent passer-by, a complete stranger? As it is I have a partly crippled right hand for life ... *crime passionel* indeed! What *if* other countries would let her off from her just punishment? When has Britain followed the lead of others? Let us remain a law-abiding country where citizens can live and walk abroad in peace and safety.

Whether he saw the letter or not, Major Lloyd George decided there should be no reprieve. Across Ruth Ellis's file was written THE LAW MUST TAKE ITS COURSE. Ruth Ellis would be executed on the morning of 13 July.

Hundreds of miles away, in the north of England, a publican was notified by the Sheriff of London that he would be required at Holloway prison on the morning after next to perform an act for which he would receive the sum of fifteen guineas and travelling expenses. The publican told his wife that he would not be pulling pints tomorrow night because he had 'a job to do'. His wife did not ask any questions. She knew his mission. The publican's name was Albert Pierrepoint.

It was during mid-afternoon on 11 July that a Home Office

messenger notified the Governor at Holloway that the Home Secretary did not see fit to reprieve Ruth Ellis.

The Governor, Dr Charity Taylor, went personally to the condemned cell to break the news to Ruth Ellis. For the first time since she had pulled the trigger of the gun that killed Blakely, Ruth showed outward signs of deep emotion. She became hysterical; lay on her bed screaming: 'I don't want to die! I don't want to die!' Dr Taylor consoled her, then returned to her other duties.

It was unfortunate for John Bickford, her solicitor, that he should have been the first visitor Ruth received after being told of her impending execution. Not mincing her words she threw at Bickford a Niagara of abuse culminating in the fact that she no longer required his services. As far as *Ruth* was concerned, Bickford had not acted in what she considered her best interests. The fact that she was going to be hanged was purely and simply *his* fault, in her opinion.

The solicitor was staggered. 'This was the thing that absolutely had a tremendously deep effect on me and, in fact, I can't say it ruined my life, but it had such a profound effect as to change my life.

'When I went to tell Mrs Ellis that her reprieve had been refused, something which she already knew, she turned to me and said: "I know what you've been doing. You have been taking a bribe in order that I should be hanged and Cussen should go free."

'Of course, this was a rather devastating thing to be told, and she said she wanted to have Mr Victor Mishcon. Thereupon, I very promptly got in touch with him. He was quite wonderful and took over the best he could.'

Mr George Rogers MP was the next visitor. He asked her an assortment of questions and then brought up the subject of the welfare of Andy. Who, he asked, was going to look after the boy in the difficult days ahead? Ruth was unsure. He offered his services, which she gratefully accepted. Again he asked her where she had got the gun and how she had travelled to Hampstead. But Ruth was saying nothing further. She simply asked a favour. Would he ask Leon Simmons – a man she liked and respected – to come and see her. She explained to Mr Rogers that it was vital that her new solicitors should come immediately. Ruth's wish was Mr Rogers's command.

It was not only Mr Rogers who contacted Victor Mishcon and Leon Simmons. John Bickford felt duty-bound to let the other solicitor know that he had been 'sacked' and that Ruth Ellis wanted Mishcon to represent her. Mr Rogers's call only confirmed what the 'new' solicitors were going to do anyway.

Bickford rendered an account to Mishcon of what Ruth had implied up until the moment she dismissed him. He suggested that Mr Mishcon should pursue the question of the gun. Both Mr Mishcon and Simmons acted on this suggestion and said they would visit her first thing the next morning – 12 July. Time was becoming scarce.

Early on the following morning, Ruth's new legal advisers were shown to the condemned cell where Ruth greeted them with the poise she would have extended to her 'favourite' guests at the Little Club. She first spoke to Leon Simmons about matters appertaining to her will. But Victor Mishcon was more concerned in trying to save her life. Tactfully he asked her if there was anything she would like to tell them about the gun?

Her earlier hysteria behind her, she reiterated: 'I'm not asking for a reprieve. I'm quite composed to the fact that tomorrow is the end.'

Mishcon was now in a dilemma. If he pressed her too hard, she might well break down and then the waiting period for death would be all the more devastating. But if he were to have any chance of saving her, he had to know the truth. So, like Mr Rogers before him, he concentrated on the 'what about Andy' tactic. It worked. He asked Ruth what would become of her young son when for the rest of his life he would be faced with the daunting prospect of being tagged 'the son of a murderess'? Mishcon rammed the shaft home by adding: 'Don't you own it to your son to leave behind you a record of truth? Shouldn't he hear the true story, in *your* own words, and not just read about it in the newspapers?'

Victor Mishcon was aided by Leon Simmons who, knowing her well from the past, was able to prevail on her to tell the truth. Ruth capitulated. She turned to the solicitors and explained: 'You're the only people who have been able to persuade me to do this. I suppose the truth would have been found out anyway after I've gone. I'll tell you what happened if you promise not to use it to try and save me.'

Victor Mishcon was not making any promises. His sole objective was to obtain from Ruth a *true* statement.

Ruth added: 'I don't want to get anyone else into trouble – one life for a life is enough. I didn't say anything about it up to now because it seemed traitorous.'

She then slowly and concisely made the statement she should have made at Hampstead police station; the statement she should have given in the witness box at the Old Bailey: the statement that would *probably* have saved her life.

I, Ruth Ellis, have been advised by Mr Victor Mishcon to tell the whole truth in regard to the circumstances leading up to the killing of David Blakely and it is only with the greatest reluctance that I have decided to tell how it was that I got the gun with which I shot Blakely. I did not do so before because I felt that I was needlessly getting someone into possible trouble.

I had been drinking Pernod (I think that is how it is spelt) in Desmond Cussen's flat and Desmond had been drinking too. This was about 8.30 p.m. We had been drinking for some time. I had been telling Desmond about Blakely's treatment of me. I was in a terribly depressed state. All I remember is that Desmond gave me a loaded gun . . . I was in such a dazed state that I cannot remember what was said. I rushed out as soon as he gave me the gun. He stayed in the flat.

I had never seen the gun before. The only gun I had ever seen there was a small air pistol used as a game with a target.

This was read back to Ruth, but before putting her signature to it, she added:

There's one more thing. You had better know the whole truth. I rushed back after a second or two and said: 'Will you drive me to Hampstead?' He did so, and left me at the top of Tanza Road.

With the statement signed, Mishcon added at the bottom of it: '12.30 p.m. 12th July 1955'. He and Simmons then informed Ruth that it was their duty to notify the authorities of the truth. She listened without comment. Her secret was out. There was nothing further for her to do.

Courteously, Victor Mishcon asked her whether he could have her permission to put this signed statement before the Home Secretary. Reluctantly, she agreed. Then she mentioned, almost in passing, that earlier during Easter Sunday, Cussen had driven her and Andy to Epping Forest for firing practice. Her addendum was not added to the statement.

Immediately on leaving Holloway, Victor Mishcon telephoned the Home Office to request an immediate interview. The Permanent Under-Secretary, Sir Frank Newsam, was otherwise engaged at the Ascot races. His place was being temporarily occupied by Mr Philip Allen, Assistant Under-Secretary of State. Mr Allen surveyed Ruth's 'new' statement with astonishment and assured the solicitors that every inquiry would be made to verify the facts. Now it was a matter of hours not days.

The news of Ruth's statement travelled with speed along Fleet Street, and, by the time Mr Mishcon left the Home Office, he was confronted by a score of eager reporters hoping for a 'last-minute reprieve' story. They were to be disappointed. Victor Mishcon tactfully informed them that as a life was at stake, it would be better if he were to say nothing for the present.

Philip Allen, meanwhile, had instructed one of his secretaries to make two telephone calls: one to Ascot requesting Sir Frank Newsam to return to London immediately; the other to Hampstead police station requesting the presence of Chief Inspector Davies at New Scotland Yard.

Davies unfortunately was unable to go anywhere. He was at home in bed suffering from a bout of flu. Detective Constable Claiden attended in his absence.

Sir Frank, annoyed in the extreme that he had been disturbed at such an important race meeting, reluctantly returned to London.

Instructions had been left at Scotland Yard for Claiden to go straight away to the Home Office. Here he was interviewed by Philip Allen.

The civil servant informed the police officer that there was a last minute inquiry concerning the death sentence imposed on Ellis. He then posed a number of pertinent questions regarding the revolver used by the murderess in the commission of the crime.

The officer replied that it had not been believed that Ellis had had the weapon for three years, but the police could not prove otherwise as they had been unable to trace its origin.

Mr Allen seemed particularly interested in the possibility that it had been given to her by Desmond Cussen. D C Claiden observed that it was possible that Cussen had given her the gun, but the only evidence of his possession of guns, from Mrs Harris, the French teacher, failed to show that he was in possession of a revolver a week or two before the tragedy. Throughout the entire inquiry the police did not obtain any evidence to connect Cussen with the revolver in question.

Mr Allen then moved on to the subject of transportation. Was it possible, he asked, that Cussen could have driven Ellis to Hampstead on the night of the shooting? He was told, yet again, that it was possible but that nothing had arisen to confirm that suspicion.

Why, one may wonder, did Claiden not tell Philip Allen about Cussen once owning a taxi-cab? After all, Ruth did say in her original statement immediately following the shooting, that she arrived at Hampstead in a taxi!

DC Claiden was then asked by Mr Allen *if* Ellis had made a statement to the effect that Cussen had given her the gun and driven her to Hampstead on that night, would it be possible to charge Cussen with having been an accessory to the crime?

Mr Allen was told that, given sufficient evidence, including these two points, it might be possible to charge Cussen. The most important consideration must be that Cussen knew that the gun he had given her was to be used for the purpose of shooting Blakely. This had to be substantiated by evidence other than Ellis's, which would be then that of an accomplice. The discussion was terminated at this point as Mr Allen was due to report to the Home Secretary.

Claiden returned to Scotland Yard to discuss the position with Deputy Commander Rawlings. They were interrupted by a telephone call demanding their presence at the House of Commons. At last the wheels of justice were moving, albeit slowly.

When they arrived a typescript of Ruth's latest statement was handed to them. The implications of the statement were discussed at some length, and as a result D C Claiden and D I Gill were instructed to trace Cussen and interrogate him in the light of the 'new' information. The policemen left the House of Commons at 4.30 and began to search for Cussen.

The police were now aware of Cussen's involvement in the murder. What they had to do was prove it. Even Sherlock Holmes might have been hard pressed to have solved this 'impossible' piece of police work in so short a time.

Cussen had been working in his office all that afternoon and was totally unaware that Ruth had made a statement implicating him. However, the early editions of the evening papers must have put him in the picture. It cannot be ruled out that he might well have been told of events by his friend in the Fleet Street newsroom, prior to the newspapers reaching the vendors.

Whatever happened, it is certain that a telephone call from *somebody* to his office to tell him of the latest development was enough to make him leave work early that evening and make himself very scarce.

The police were to write: 'We first telephoned his office, and were told that twenty minutes earlier he had left and was believed to be returning to his flat. We went straight there but found that he was not at home. Telephone inquiries of a number of his associates and also places known to be frequented by him were made, but without success . . .'

Early evening saw the ever increasing crowds descend upon Parkhurst Road – the street outside Holloway prison. People were prepared to sleep 'rough' all night so as to get a view of the execution notice the following morning. The rush-hour traffic was reduced to a snail's pace.

A little earlier, had anyone been around, they might have noticed a small man, neatly dressed, go through the main gates. He was welcomed by prison officials. He had arrived on time. He was never late. Upon gaining entrance to the prison, he was offered a cup of tea by the Governor. He was then taken to the condemned cell whereupon he peeped through the 'judas-hole' to view Ruth Ellis reading her Bible.

He was then handed a file containing her weight, height, and other relevant details. Using another door, he entered the execution chamber and, using a sandbag – the same weight as Ruth – as his model, tested that the mechanism of the spring-loaded drop was in order and correct. There would be no technical hitch for

Albert Pierrepoint at nine o'clock the next morning. While the equipment was being tested, Ruth Ellis was removed from her cell for a short period of 'exercise' so that she would not hear the crash of the trapdoor in the adjacent execution chamber.

While Pierrepoint was testing the execution equipment, Ruth's brother, Granville, joined the crowd outside and bumped into a newspaper reporter who recognized him. It was suggested that they both go and look for Cussen and try to make him 'confess' to his part in the crime.

'I started by going to Mr Mishcon, but he didn't want to see me. We then went to the Home Secretary's place, but he didn't want to see us either. We then began our search throughout London looking for Cussen. But this resulted in little success.'

Ruth, meanwhile, was writing letters to people who had tried to save her life. She sat, watched by wardresses, as she wrote firstly to Mrs Dyer:

I am quite happy with the verdict, but not the way the story was told. There is so much people don't know about.

To Mr George Rogers:

I am quite well – my family have been wonderful. Once again I thank you and your wife. Goodbye.

Mr George Rogers had by this time taken care of Andy and installed the boy at his home in Sudbury. To Andy it was like a holiday in the country. As far as he was concerned his mother was abroad on a modelling assignment. He liked Mr and Mrs Rogers.

The last night of her life, Ruth was visited by her immediate close family. For them it was an agonizing visit. Ruth, however, reassured them that it would be all right. The goodbyes were brief. Ruth's parents then left and now all they could hope for was a last-minute reprieve that they knew, in their heart of hearts, would not be forthcoming.

Ruth's last letter before she retired for the last time was to Leon Simmons, a man she had immense respect for; one of the few men in her life whom she trusted. To him she wrote:

Just a line to thank you for coming along with Mr Mishcon this morning.

I have given Mr George Rogers authority to take Clare Andrea away for a holiday.

I am now content and satisfied that my affairs will be dealt with satisfactorily. I also ask you to make known the true story regarding Mrs Findlater and her plan to break up David & I – she should feel content, now her plan ended so tragically:

Would you please ask my mother to go to David's grave and put flowers, pink and white carnations. (Ask her to do it for me.)

I would also like to answer David's brothers (newspaper remarks). I admire Derek for defending his brother. I would have been cross with him if he had not. But he said he would have to have more proof than he heard in court before he would believe my story. My reply to Derek is, I am sorry. I cannot give any more proof than I have.

I did not defend myself. I say a life for a life. What more proof can he want? I have spoken the truth, and I want you to make the truth known for my family and son's sake.

Well, Mr Simmons, the time is 9.30. I am quite well and not worrying about anything.

Thanks once again.

Ruth Ellis.

Ruth then retired for the night. Whether she was able to sleep in peace with all the noise from outside penetrating the walls of her cell, one wonders.

Peace was not what the police were experiencing in their search for the missing Cussen. They kept observation on his flat in Devonshire Street until late in the evening. Just before midnight they received radio instructions from Deputy Commander Rawlings to withdraw from their position.

The search for Cussen had ended in failure. Though not for Granville Neilson and his reporter friend. To this day Neilson claims emphatically that he found Cussen in somebody's flat. Cussen, according to Neilson, was in no mood to give himself up: he was in bed with a woman and told the two men to 'get lost'.

This, however, is hotly denied by Duggie Howell, the *Women's Sunday Mirror* reporter, who recently claimed that on the last night of Ruth Ellis's life, Desmond Cussen was sitting drinking coffee and a stronger beverage at his home. Assuming Howell's account to be true, why did the journalist not notify the police?

Any last-minute representations to the Home Secretary fell upon deaf ears. Major Gwilym Lloyd George had made up his mind and nothing short of a full Cussen confession was going to change it.

Ruth rose early on 13 July. At 6.30 a Roman Catholic chaplain entered her cell and administered the Last Sacraments. She made her confession.

With an inhuman disregard for the fate she was about to suffer two hours later, Ruth wrote a postscript to Leon Simmons:

> Dear Mr Simmons,
> Just to let you know I am still feeling alright.
> The time is 7 o'clock a.m. – everyone (staff) is simply wonderful in Holloway. This is just for you to console my family with the thought that I did not change my way of thinking at the last moment.
> Or break my promise to David's mother.
> Well, Mr Simmons, I have told you the truth and that's all I can do.
> Thanks once again.
> Goodbye.
> Ruth Ellis.

While the noise was mounting outside the prison gates, Ruth spent her last hour kneeling before a crucifix, which had been fastened to the wall of her cell at her request, and praying to the Almighty for forgiveness.

Mrs Violet Van der Elst, the foremost campaigner for the abolition of capital punishment, led the chant of 'Evans–Bentley–Ellis'. Hundreds of people joined in.

The faces of David Blakely, Desmond Cussen, and, no doubt, the Findlaters, must have flashed through her mind during this last hour. She may, too, have reflected on the lies she had told. The lies which had encamped her in the condemned cell of Holloway prison.

At a few seconds before nine o'clock, Albert Pierrepoint, his assistant, Dr Charity Taylor, a surgeon, the prison chaplain, and the rest of the entourage entered Ruth's cell. She drank a large tot of brandy, which she welcomed. Her wrists were strapped behind her back and she was quickly ushered to the adjoining execution chamber.

With the same calm exterior with which she committed her crime, she walked upon the scaffold where her ankles were strapped together. Pierrepoint then looked into her eyes and placed a white hood over her head.

Prior to doing this, Pierrepoint could not help noticing Ruth pursing her lips and almost posing in the same manner as she did for gentlemen folk at the Camera Club. It surprised the executioner.

He adjusted the rope in its correct position, walked around her to the lever and, with a sharp jerk, caused the fatal injury to her nervous system which is consequent with judicial hanging.

Ruth Ellis was dead.

Pierrepoint explained, many years later, that Ruth Ellis was 'the bravest woman I ever hanged'. He was the doyen, having hanged some twenty-plus women in one morning many years earlier. He collected his fifteen guineas and, for him, a good morning's work had been completed.

The chanting outside had now become tribal-like and it had completely obliterated the noise of the traffic.

Nine o'clock on the morning of 13 July 1955 will remain in the memory of several people. It is not a time they will ever forget.

Ruth's sister, Muriel, recalls: 'I ran around my house from room to room. I couldn't cry. I really couldn't cry. I was too stunned to cry. I just couldn't believe it. I just went from room to room with my head in my hands saying "no, no, no". It just wasn't real.

'To this very day it isn't real. Nobody could have done such a thing to Ruth. She was not a wicked girl at all. Just a friendly girl who'd help anyone. She'd have given her last penny to anyone.'

Mr George Rogers and his wife were using all their wits keeping young Andy away from the wireless or newspapers. 'We did our best to shield the boy from his mother's tragic death. We thought it best that it should be broken to him gently a while afterwards. But I think he knew what had happened.

'As for my reaction? We were all very silent and conscious of the moment in a way that I'd never been before when someone was hanged, because it was the first personal contact I'd ever had with such a case.

'It hit us rather badly. I had the same sort of feeling when my relatives died. A great feeling of loss. I suppose one takes these things to oneself really. I felt a personal involvement with the whole thing. Especially as I'd seen her only a short time before.

'It's not nice to think of someone being hanged, which in any case is a very barbarous method of disposing of people.'

John Bickford still remembers the morning with clarity. 'If I remember rightly, she was actually hanged at nine o'clock in the morning. I remember walking across Blackheath Common, feeling quite dreadful. I remember she had a powder compact which, when you opened it, it used to play a tune which is well known, *La Vie En Rose*, and I remember that it was this tune that was going through my mind and nothing else. I felt in all that Ruth Ellis should never ever have been hanged, if only for the reason that it did nobody any good.

'It didn't act as a deterrent and it could well have been that after eight to ten years she would have emerged a very responsible citizen and capable mother for her children.'

The last person to see the body of Ruth Ellis – for it was he who had the harrowing task of identifying her – was her brother, Granville. 'At the actual time she was hanged, I was in Fleet Street, in the newspaper office. I was watching the ticker-tape machine. I was actually waiting in anticipation hoping that there would be a last-minute reprieve.

'I watched it come over the ticker-tape and tears were rolling down my face. Big Ben struck nine. The words were coming on to the tape . . . "Ruth Ellis . . . The execution has now been carried out . . ."

'I then left Fleet Street and was driven to Holloway prison to identify my sister's body.

'There were a few people around Ruth at the time. She was laid with a cross at the top of her head and two candles on either side. She was laid out. She did actually look as though she had died *normally*, but it wasn't so. I could see it wasn't so. She was made up, with lipstick and powder. I turned around and said to the governor: "Doesn't she look beautiful?"

'A man came up to me, I don't know who he was – he may have been the executioner – and said: "You're a very brave man." We then went upstairs to a court of inquiry and the coroner kept on repeating that the *murderess* has now been executed. This went on for some considerable time. In the end I just saw red and shouted: "Can't you think of something bloody well else to say, other than *murderess*?"'

'Dr Charity Taylor took me from the room. I looked a bit faint apparently. She gave me a glass of water and sat me down for a little while. Then I went. I'll never forget that morning. How can I . . .?'

And so the life and events of Ruth Ellis had drawn to a close. The police closed their files on the case and people were now able to sleep easier at night knowing that this *murderess* had been executed.

Desmond Cussen returned to his routine way of life, but tried desperately to forget the woman that could have so easily taken him to the gallows with her.

Continuing life in England would be to prolong any risk that still may have existed. He emigrated to Australia to start anew, and closed a chapter of his life he would much rather forget.

Although Ruth Ellis was buried within the walls of Holloway prison, fifteen years later her remains were disinterred and it was left to her son, Andy, to decide where her final resting place should be. She now lies in the small Amersham churchyard of St Mary's, just a few miles away from David Blakely's grave at Penn.

Perhaps they were destined never to be far from each other – even in death.

12

Ruth Ellis shot David Blakely and was hanged by the neck until she was dead. A simple statement of fact. But the drop through the trapdoor did not end the story; rather, it was the beginning of more important events than the sordid entanglement of a club hostess and her two lovers.

Neither Ruth Ellis nor David Blakely had led particularly edifying lives. She was a hostess, promiscuous, and, according to some reports, a peddler of pornography; a madam who could arrange for her club clients to be 'entertained' by her friends if not by herself. David Blakely was a conceited braggart, living off women and afraid of facing up to the scenes his behaviour inevitably provoked. He was brave enough to beat up women, but fled whenever challenged by a man. It is not rare for a man to be brave in sport and cowardly in his life. On his two feet he ran away at the first hint of danger.

The other characters in the Ruth Ellis murder were not very admirable either.

Desmond Cussen was a man with money and influence. He made a fool of himself over a club hostess. He even kept her whilst she bestowed her favours on a younger rival. He was a jealous man who gave his woman a gun rather than an ultimatum. Again and again, he meekly drove her as she sought Blakely. He was totally without pride. He was besotted with Ruth Ellis, but he turned his back on her and dismissed her from his life the moment she was sentenced to death and he knew he had escaped from legal involvement. Until the foreman of the jury said 'guilty', Desmond Cussen had sent in flowers, food, and make-up for his mistress. That one word ended his largesse.

Maury Conley, Ruth's employer and patron, was a pimp who treated girls as commodities to be hired out or used by him and his friends whenever he required. He employed madams to take the risks for him and to safeguard his freedom after police action had made it too hot for him to continue to deal as a wholesaler and retailer in female flesh.

Ant Findlater, David's friend, today claims that he did not know his wife had had an affair with his 'best friend'. He greeted the suggestion recently with equanimity. Clearly he attached no blame to David if it were true. He probably, at the time, put motors before morals. He allowed David Blakely to employ him to work on the Emperor, when he must have been aware, at least, that there was an empathy between his wife and his employer.

Jackie Dyer, still alive, is refreshingly honest and does not aspire to sainthood.

The other 'extras' who played minor roles in the tragedy were the mentally adolescent racing-car drivers, squirting each other with soda-water to try and prove their fragile manhoods, and the club hostesses and whores who surrounded them. The hostesses were generally less honest than the whores who stood in the doorways of Piccadilly and Park Lane openly soliciting clients.

As is so often the case, the innocent suffered the most from the eddies of the crime and its punishment. Few who knew Ruth Ellis and David Blakely away from their professional ambiences, have remained untouched or been able to forget the affair.

Ruth Ellis's family have all had their lives distorted by the shooting of David Blakely. Her father is dead, as is her younger sister, whose death was hastened by her sorrow over her sister's execution. Her mother lives out the remnants of her life in the shadow world of the mentally sick. She talks little, even to Muriel, who, as always, is the anchor of what remains of Ruth's family. Muriel visits her mother every week, even though she can seldom break through the screen of indifference Mrs Hornby has drawn around her consciousness.

Muriel has to content herself with feeding her mother sweets and cakes and talking to her as if she were a child. In 1977 Mrs Hornby disappeared from the hospital where she was being nursed. It was snowing and she was missing all night. She was not located by the police dragnet, but by her two sons, who found her lying unconscious in a disused pigsty in the hospital grounds. It is unnecessary to labour the point that Mrs Hornby's mental deterioration stemmed from the date of her daughter's execution.

Muriel has had to suffer slights and insults, which have not diminished with the years. Two decades after her sister's hanging, she was asked to take her custom elsewhere by the hairdressers she had used for years. They had learned who she was and did not want to tend the hair of a 'murderess's' sister. As was stated at the outset of this book, she has also been blamed – totally irrationally – for the deaths of victims of violence, solely on the grounds that but for Ruth's execution, capital punishment would still be in existence.

Her daughters have also been affected. They have tended their aunt's grave in Amersham church cemetery and, loyally, have never denied their relationship to her.

Granville Neilson saw the body of his sister after she had been hanged. A scarf had been tied around the neck to conceal the ravages of the rope. On the same day he attended the inquest on his sister, and erupted in anger at the constant use of the word 'murderess'. He had to leave the room to recover. The memory will haunt him through the rest of the nights he remains on this earth.

It is impossible to assess the effect of Ruth's death on her son Andy. He was old enough to appreciate what was happening and told his Auntie Muriel that he had seen 'Uncle Desmond' give his mother the gun and teach her how to fire it. He is an intelligent man, but his career, not surprisingly, has so far lacked stability.

Andy's half-sister, Georgina, though only three at the time of the shooting, must also have had her character moulded to some extent by her relationship. How else could she have brought herself to write for the Press about an episode of which she could have no memory whatsoever? She even suggested that, though without acting experience, she should play the part of her mother in a proposed film.

Dr William Sargant, who knew neither of the main characters, has spoken vehemently of his horror at his partner not being called at the trial to give evidence as to Ruth Ellis's state of mind.

The priest who was outvoted at the Home Office inquiry as to whether Ruth Ellis was fit to be hanged has described the experience as one of the most traumatic episodes in his life.

Other friends of Ruth who could have given evidence as to what she suffered from the fists of her lover will never understand why they were not called to give evidence, and so win the jury's sympathy and earn her a recommendation to mercy.

Lord Chief Justice Rayner Goddard, known to many as the 'birch 'em and hang 'em' judge, has been recorded as saying that he regretted the hanging of Ruth Ellis. Not because he thought there was any doubt whatsoever about her guilt or the conduct of her trial, but simply because she was a woman.

Bickford also believed that Ruth Ellis was a victim of undisclosed circumstances, even though she was the author of the secrecy which ensured her conviction and denied her any recommendation to mercy.

In December 1973 the *People* published an article on the Ruth Ellis case. In this article, John Bickford, Ruth Ellis's solicitor at the time of her trial, described how the previous year he had decided he must disclose to Scotland Yard what he knew about certain suggestions made by Ruth Ellis in her death-cell statement. The *People* reporters referred to his words as 'shattering'.

Bickford said that during his first interview with Mrs Ellis, she asked him to convey to a 'Mr X' the information that she had told the police: she had got the gun from a man she had met at the Little Club, who had offered it as security for a loan. Bickford told the reporters that he had done as she requested and that he had met Mr X, at the mystery man's flat.

During the conversation, Mr X had told Mr Bickford that he had given Mrs Ellis the gun. He added that having cleaned it and oiled it, he had shown her how it worked. Mr X said that at the time, Mrs Ellis was 'beside herself' and was so persistent that, because he was deeply in love with her, he gave way and subsequently drove her to a wood where he showed her how to fire the gun into a tree.

On the way back from this firing practice, having reloaded the gun, Mr X had thrown the spare bullets and the cleaning material into the Thames. Mr X also told Bickford that, on the night of the murder, he had driven Mrs Ellis to Tanza Road, near the Magdala.

The day following his interview with Mr X, Bickford again saw Mrs Ellis, who confirmed Mr X's version of events. However, she instructed Bickford to keep his account secret as she wanted to 'get the whole thing over with . . . so I can die and join David Blakely'.

Bickford explained to reporters that though Mrs Ellis had wanted to die, she wished the full story to be told so that her friends and family should know the truth. When her application for a reprieve was denied, Ruth Ellis asked Bickford to invite Victor Mishcon to come and see her. Bickford suggested to Mishcon that he – Mishcon – should ask Ruth Ellis where she had got the gun.

Bickford told the reporters: 'I succumbed to the temptation to let sleeping dogs lie.' It was only recently, when he was older, that he realized what he ought to have done. He went to the police and told them what he knew.

Bickford then commented: 'If she had not been given the gun, there might have been a chance for her passions to cool and the crime might never have been committed.' Bickford believes that the Director of Public Prosecutions was informed of what he had told the police but, evidently, decided not to proceed any further.

Albert Pierrepoint, who augmented his publican's income by efficiently dispatching those found guilty of murder and condemned to death, has said that the hanging of Ruth Ellis turned him against the system.

Ruth Ellis's death *was* important. It convinced many people that the time had come to end the grisly legal killings. Most of the public were disgusted, though no doubt some extracted a surreptitious thrill, from reading the details with their breakfast.

Many men and women had been hanged over the centuries and apart from the abolitionists who waited and prayed outside the gates of Holloway on the last morning of Ruth's life, the crowd must have had much in common with those mobs which thronged to Tyburn to watch the Tobymen turned off. As the notice of execution was posted outside Holloway, a man was seen to hold his small child up so she could see the notice, even though she would have been unable to read it.

Mass hysteria can be frightening. And it is this aspect which alarmed the editor of *The Lancet*, the journal of the medical profession. Shortly after the hanging of Ruth Ellis, on 23 July, under the heading 'The Death Penalty', their leading article dealt with this subject.

The laws against witchcraft were repealed in this country in

1736; but they had been recognised, long before that, as an ugly piece of inhumanity, disgracing the statute book. To many of our countrymen today, and to the whole peoples of some European countries, the death penalty seems as grotesque as did the witchcraft laws to 18th-century Englishmen. The feeling against it has been intensified by three notorious executions within the last few years: that of Evans, who may have been guilty of the crime for which he was hanged; that of Bentley, who was not guilty of killing but of shouting – in a moment of violent agitation – incitement to another to kill; and that of Ruth Ellis, hanged for a murder done in a state of acute jealousy. All these people were executed in accordance with our country's law, after fair trial; but their deaths have excited a great deal of uneasiness, not only among those who, in an emotional frenzy, stood outside Holloway gaol on the eve of 13 July, shouting 'Evans– Bentley–Ellis', but among many whose sober concern it is that the laws of this country should be as worthy as any in the world, and among all who believe that an increasing preoccupation with murder trials and judicial executions is harming us as a people.

Capital punishment was abolished in New Zealand, Queensland, Denmark, Italy, the Netherlands, Norway, Sweden, and Switzerland, at dates ranging between 1870 and 1942; it remains legal in Belgium but (with one exception, in 1918) has not been enforced since 1863. Hence it is hardly surprising that the comment of other countries on the hanging of Mrs Ellis has been adverse and outspoken. To the Swedish people our failure to either abolish the death penalty or allow it to fall into disuse seems barbarous. To the French it seems that we apply it with blind disregard of differences in the circumstances and character of the crime. Tried in other countries, some of the people we hang would suffer only a short term of imprisonment; and though we may condemn such leniency, we can hardly fail to be impressed by the very wide discrepancy in current punishments for identical offences.

Evidence received from Denmark, the Netherlands, Norway, and Sweden by the Royal Commission on Capital

Punishment 1949–53 indicated that murderers who, after their release from imprisonment, commit further crimes of violence are rare, whereas those who become useful citizens are common. Figures published in the White Paper on capital punishment show that the same is true of reprieved murderers in this country. Unlike some other crimes, murder is seldom part of a recognisable life-pattern: it appears unexpectedly, probably taking even the murderer by surprise. The habitual murderers – the Smiths and the Christies, obsessed by some emotional abnormality – are fortunately rare.

The opinion of foreigners on our practice might weigh little with us as a people were we ourselves entirely easy about it. But public protests against the executions of Bentley and Mrs Ellis make it quite clear that we are not. It has often been said, and is transparently true, that the death penalty punishes the innocent with the guilty. Not merely the criminal, but his whole family, endure the alterations of hope and fear which a murder trial imposes – a long-drawn-out anguish far more horrible than all but the worst of murders. Once the sentence is carried out, the punishment of the criminal is complete – but not the punishment of the family, who have to live with the memory and stigma of his execution. Mrs Ellis leaves two young children, as well as her parents, to carry this unmerited burden. Such minorities deserve a voice. The children, who must inevitably be deprived of the 'normal home life' of which we nowadays speak so glibly, have been dealt, in addition, a most shattering psychological blow. Any law which, in its enforcement, does gross injury to innocent people strikes at the whole concept of justice.

And not these children only, but many others have been harmed by the recent emotional orgy. A father at Holloway prison gates lifted up his six-year-old daughter so that she could say she had seen the notice announcing the death of Mrs Ellis. Children in a school near the prison are described by one of their teachers as being in a ferment: 'Some claim to have seen the execution from their windows, others spoke with fascinated horror of the technique of hanging a female.'

Our means of communication are nowadays so efficient that the same unwholesome excitement was shared by children up and down the country. When an incident becomes the news of the day, presented at twenty million breakfast tables, it becomes for the time an important part of our national life. The murderer, instead of quietly and decently receiving whatever deserts are deemed to be just, becomes the star of an immense and often long-remembered drama or even entertainment, quite frankly enjoyed by many people, and none the less because its horrors are true.

It is this aspect of the death penalty which seems to us more dangerous and destructive than any other. As we said at the time of Bentley's hanging: 'Whether an execution is actually seen or imagined the mental effect is qualitatively the same, and in our view the perpetual preoccupation with the condemned cell and the gallows is harmful to the mental health of society.' We gild the worst of crimes with publicity, and associate it with an act of communal violence: small wonder if the youngsters swallowing the poison find the idea of violence dangerously attractive. Used as we use it, the death penalty may well be causing more crime than it prevents. Let us hope that those Members of Parliament who have launched a new attempt to get the law changed will succeed in freeing us from this recurrent demoralisation.

Mr and Mrs Neilson received many hundreds of letters, most expressing repugnance at their daughter's execution. Some, however, wrote that the noose was the just weapon of retribution, not only for the killing but for the sins their daughter had committed in the type of life she had led. The Old Testament belief: 'Life for life, eye for eye, tooth for tooth, hand for hand, foot for foot, burning for burning, wound for wound, stripe for stripe' still persisted. But only among a minority.

The national Press, no doubt delighting in increased circulation, published extracts from many letters they received. Mrs Gladys Yule expressed her opinions in the form of a painting as well as a letter. She stated that as a casual passer-by who had suffered considerably through being hit by a bullet ricocheting off the ground, she had little sympathy with Ruth Ellis. Nevertheless, despite the unjust injury she had suffered, it did not deter Mrs Yule from making sums of money from various newspapers. Her judgement is understandable. Others wrote, more from emotion than logic, that if Ruth Ellis had been reprieved there would have been nothing to deter other murderers.

One of the men who wrote several times to Arthur Neilson was Mr Sydney Silverman MP, a solicitor who fought doggedly for over two decades to get rid of what he considered a hangover from medievalism.

He introduced The Murder (Abolition of Death Penalty) Bill into the House of Commons on 4 December 1964, having previously sponsored the clause in the Criminal Justice Bill of 1947, suspending the death penalty for five years, as well as the Death Penalty (Abolition) Bill of 1956, both of which were passed by the Commons but rejected by the Lords. It was the Bill of 1956 which first used the expression: 'diminished responsibility'.

Eventually, through constant lobbying and continual appeals to the humanitarian emotions, Silverman won the day. In 1965 the death penalty was suspended for an experimental period of five years. Parliament did not, however, wait for the expiry of this period before introducing a Bill to outlaw the noose for good. On 16 December 1969, the Murder (Abolition of Death Penalty) Bill 1965, became law.

While this Bill was being discussed during a lengthy debate in the House, Quintin Hogg (now Lord Hailsham) rose to his feet and said: 'At this point, I digress for a moment to the question of the prerogative of mercy. Whatever the result of the debate today – and certainly if it turned out that the House was not prepared finally to abolish capital punishment – I feel that the Home Secretary (Mr James Callaghan) should, on any view, cease to be solely responsible for the exercise of the prerogative. I say that not only because I myself feel wholly inadequate to face that responsibility, as indeed I should, but because I think that in the past Home Secretaries have proved inadequate. With respect to a distinguished succession of gentlemen of humane and civilized bent, I say that they demonstrably made mistakes. Oddly enough, the mistakes they made have erred occasionally in the direction of severity.'

Mr Hogg went on to give some examples: 'One has only to

mention some of the cases, such as Evans, Bentley, and Ruth Ellis . . .'

It must be appreciated that Britain was not in the forefront of reform, for most European countries had abolished the irreversible punishment decades earlier.

So, hanging came to an end. The rope was coiled up and put away for ever; the gallows were dismantled. No longer would warders have to play endless games of cribbage to divert the condemned man from counting off the remaining seconds of his life. No longer would the prison governor have to break the news of mercy being withheld. No longer would a man of God have to escort a human being to the scaffold, reading the burial ceremony *en route*. No longer would a man be paid to murder legally a fellow human being on our behalf. No longer! No longer?

Evidence from other countries contradicts the theory that capital punishment is the final deterrent. Indeed, some policemen believe that the cornered murderer, who knows that apprehension will result in death, sees no reason why he should not kill again, for he has nothing more to lose. Holland and the Nordic countries have reported that their experience is that murderers who have served their sentences and been released seldom return to crime. Murder is an offence usually of emotion, statistics showing that more often than not the murderer and his victim are related. Thus murder is hardly a crime of habit.

Most sociologists, the religious, and criminologists breathed a heartfelt sigh of relief when they heard the words: 'No person shall suffer death for murder, and a person convicted of murder shall be sentenced to imprisonment for life.'

Yet only in April 1977, the *Daily Express* leader recommended that Mrs Thatcher make the restoration of capital punishment part of the manifesto for the next election. In the paper's opinion, such an act would receive wide public support. They may be right. Opinions are largely moulded by the Press, television, and radio. But if their estimation of public reaction proves to be correct, then the more enlightened can only echo the words of Robert Burns:

> *Man's inhumanity to man*
> *Makes countless thousands mourn!*

─────────────── EPILOGUE ───────────────

This epilogue is based upon the first interview that Desmond Cussen gave after the Old Bailey trial. Peter Williams, a leading television reporter, went to Australia to get it. He was at the time producing a documentary for Thames Television, The Story of Ruth Ellis, *transmitted in June 1977.*

To the lawyer's mind, the Ruth Ellis case was a bore. It was remarkable only in its simplicity.

A 28-year-old woman, Ruth Ellis, took to herself a lover, David Blakely, who was a racing driver. She sensed he was getting tired of her. Rather than lose him, she went to a public house in Hampstead, London, where he was drinking, waited for him to leave the bar, and then emptied a .38 Smith and Wesson revolver into him. If ever there was an open-and-shut murder case, surely this was it.

At the Old Bailey, where she stood trial for her life on 20 and 21 June 1955, Ruth Ellis made the whole affair even simpler. Mr Christmas Humphreys QC led for the prosecution. For the only time in his distinguished career as advocate and judge, he wrote down the question he wanted to ask the accused prisoner in the dock. It was this:

'Mrs Ellis, when you fired that revolver at close range into the body of David Blakely, what did you intend to do?'

Ruth Ellis replied: 'It is obvious that, when I shot him, I intended to kill him.'

The lawyer paused. 'Thank you,' he said, and sat down.

That was the extent of the cross-examination of the accused woman. The trio of defence counsel could hardly have been more formidable. Mr Melford Stevenson QC leading, with Mr Sebag Shaw and Mr Peter Rawlinson. But at that moment, they knew that, legally, the case was as good as over. As Mr Rawlinson (now

Sir Peter) told me: 'Here was a woman admitting, on oath, in front of a judge and jury, that she had committed murder.'

Mrs Ellis was an attractive woman, attractive enough to keep a job as a night club hostess. There were ten men in the jury of twelve. Yet, midway through the second day of this trial, which had become a formality, they took only twenty-three minutes to reach their verdict. Guilty. There was no recommendation to mercy. Ruth Ellis would be hanged by the neck until she was dead. And Mr Justice Havers, black-capped and grave, added this as he sentenced her:

'In my view it was the only verdict possible.'

Ruth Ellis was hanged at Holloway prison, London, on 13 July 1955. She was the last woman to be executed in Britain.

These then are the facts. But the known facts don't spell out the whole story. This book tries to remedy that situation. And, while admiring the authors' grasp of their subject, I don't necessarily agree with all their judgements. Yet we share, I believe, a recognition of the two key questions that lie at the heart of the fascination of the Ruth Ellis case.

The first is: where did Ruth Ellis get the revolver with which she shot David Blakely?

The second is: what part did Desmond Cussen play in the last few months of her life?

For there were two men in Ruth Ellis's life, not one. Blakely, the man she shot. And Desmond Cussen, the man who knew so much more about the background to this case than he was ever asked about in court.

They came into Ellis's life at roughly the same time. It was 1953. Blakely was a fledgling racing driver. He was, at twenty-four, four years younger than Ellis when he died. He was public school educated; commissioned in the army during his national service. He had money – at least during the early part of their relationship. His father had left him £7000 and his stepfather gave him an allowance.

He worked in the office of an engineering factory and, with the help of friends, he financed and built his own racing car. He called it the Emperor. He raced at Oulton Park, Brands Hatch, Silverstone and other British circuits, and he competed on the Continent, too. He lived with his mother and stepfather at Old Park,

199

Penn, Buckinghamshire and he had a flat in the West End, which his former nanny looked after for him.

Blakely relaxed and drank at a few favoured clubs in London's West End. He drank with his close friends in the world of motor racing. It was at Carroll's Club, in Duke Street, that he met Ruth Ellis. That was where Desmond Cussen was also to meet her, casually, over a drink, later that year.

Cussen was thirty-three when Blakely died, five years older than Ruth. His family had a chain of retail tobacconist shops in London and South Wales and he was a director of the company. He joined the RAF at seventeen, trained as a bomber pilot in South Africa, and learned to fly Lancasters. He was demobilized in 1946 and became articled to a firm of chartered accountants. His particular responsibility was a couple of shops in Aberystwyth in Wales. He was comfortably off, with a flat at Goodwood Court, in the West End. Like Blakely, he was a bachelor.

Unlike Blakely, he was not about to marry another woman. In November 1953, Blakely's engagement was announced to the daughter of a Huddersfield woollens manufacturer.

Blakely was apparently unperturbed about dividing either his loyalty or his energy. For, within a couple of weeks, he began to live with Ruth Ellis.

As for Ellis herself, as Mr Christmas Humphreys was to say at the trial, she took 'an alternative lover' in April 1954. Desmond Cussen – for he was that lover – would prefer that I said that he 'struck up a relationship with Ruth. After all, to say that we were lovers, that we were living together, gives the wrong impression. I was simply trying to provide a home for Ruth and the kiddie.'

'You weren't sleeping together?'

'Well, yes, but only when she came home at nights, which wasn't very often. Then, occasionally, intimacy took place.'

Ellis . . . Blakely . . . Cussen. The emotional triangle that was to disintegrate only with Blakely's death, precisely a year after Cussen 'struck up a relationship' with Ellis.

And what of Ellis herself? The witness, the police who saw her after the shooting, and watched her at the trial, thought her, without exception, cold, hard, unemotional. If she was, it's perhaps not so surprising.

She had already built around herself a protective shell against a world she thought harsh and unfair. She was born Ruth Hornby, in Rhyl, North Wales. She was pregnant by the time she was fifteen. The father was a Canadian soldier named Clare. They were going to get married. Then Clare flew home to demobilization – and to his wife and three children. On 15 September 1944, Ruth gave birth to a baby boy. She named him Clare Andrea Neilson, for 'Neilson' was the name that her father, and then the family, had adopted during his professional career as a musician.

Her parents moved to London and Ruth took a job, modelling in a camera club. At nineteen she was working as a hostess in a Mayfair night club. But, though they appreciated the money she brought home, there were fierce rows with her father. This continued until Ruth was presented with an opportunity to escape into what she saw as respectability. One of the customers at the club wanted to marry her. And, after a rapid courtship, in November 1950, she married a dental surgeon named George Ellis, at Tonbridge Register Office.

But the marriage didn't work. Ellis was educated, cultivated, and an alcoholic. Sober, he loved her. Drunk, he often beat her. She became pregnant again, but before her daughter Georgina Ellis was born in October 1951, the marriage was as good as over. Ruth walked out. A year after the wedding, the protracted procedure that would end in divorce four years later began.

This was Ruth Ellis's life; a few words to describe a multitude of experiences. By the time she was twenty-five, she was the mother of two children, had been deserted once, petitioned for divorce once, and beaten many times. She had the bruises to prove it. They were both physical and psychological.

To support herself, she went back to her old haunts and her old job, working for her old boss, Maury Conley. Conley was later to be described in court as one of London's most successful vice bosses. Ruth was his mistress. He made her manageress of the Little Club, an afternoon-and-evening drinking club in Knightsbridge, London.

Blakely was one of her most regular customers. Initially, he chased Ellis. To her, he was a 'poor little rich boy', to be indulged and enjoyed sexually. But, as the months passed, the initiative changed. Now, it was Ellis who was concerned – worried because Blakely's motor-racing friends noted what they saw as a gap in class and either patronized her or were icily indifferent. Worried, too, because this was the world in which she wanted so desperately to be accepted.

And, as if the mould from which this woman was created was never to be broken, Blakely began to beat her. Savagely. Just as George Ellis had done. They fought at the club and at their flat. They fought over money which Ruth Ellis, by this time early in 1954, was supplying to feed Blakely's appetites in drink and motor racing. They fought because Blakely had other women.

And, always in the background, Desmond Cussen. The alternative lover who would be willing to chauffeur her in her pursuit of an errant David Blakely; willing to pay for her to become a model or to learn French; willing to look after her son during the school holiday, to make him breakfast if his mother failed to come home until after he'd gone to school, to hear Ruth's tantrums and maudlin self-pity over the latest slight she felt Blakely had inflicted upon her. Desmond Cussen who was, in short, devoted to her.

In February 1954, Ruth was pregnant again with David Blakely's child. She had an abortion.

In April 1954, Ruth began to sleep with Desmond Cussen. Blakely was furious when he found out after returning from a race meeting at Le Mans. Now, the stage was set. The players were in place. And, as Ruth Ellis was to confide in the death cell of Holloway prison, just before the final curtain:

'Desmond was jealous of Blakely as in fact Blakely was of Desmond. I would say that they hated each other.'

Today, Desmond Cussen keeps a florist shop in Perth, Western Australia. He lives nearby in a neat, first-floor flat, close enough to the Indian Ocean to hear the shouts of the surfers as they ride the great rollers.

It is difficult to imagine Desmond Cussen hating anybody. He's a man who appears so used to the knocks life has inflicted upon him that he's come to expect more. He's been described – and is described in this book – as a solitary man, a loner when he visited the drinking clubs in London's West End during the 1950s. I get the feeling that he hasn't changed in this respect; that he has many acquaintances but, I suspect, few friends.

His handshake is warm and firm. I believe he avoids lying if he can possibly do so. By that, I mean he avoids the actual word of the lie passing his lips. If you have the wrong impression, and it suits him that you should remain in ignorance, he will leave the correction unsaid. It's a sin of omission, rather than commission. Like most of us, if it's easier to keep quiet, he will keep quiet. After all, he's kept quiet for the past twenty-two years.

His morality, like his dress and his language, appears to be of another era. His moustache traces a thin black line above his upper lip. He wears a light jacket with a dark shirt and a tie that's an explosion of colour. His shoes are white and pointed. 'Winkle-pickers.' He speaks of 'being intimate' with Ruth, in a very proper fashion, when he describes his relationship with the woman. Hippies, or 'surfies', may live just next door, but, to Cussen, 'pot' is still something in which he stands the flowers he sells.

He drives a red mini-van, in which he collects the flowers from the wholesalers early every morning. He is punctilious. He arrives early at his shop, however late he may have been drinking a few glasses of beer the previous night. He's proud of the shop itself and of what he's done to it. He's called it Chez Fleur, which is a touch incongruous as it sits among its neighbours in the arcade of the beachside shopping precinct. On one side, a hamburger stand; on the other, a supermarket. He's built the shelves and planned the layout, including the 'cold room', which is a large refrigerator crammed into a corner just out of sight of the customers. The shop is neat, almost painfully neat.

One other observation about Desmond Cussen: I believe he finds it difficult to say 'no'. I first met him beside his red mini-van. I introduced myself and we shook hands. I told him why I'd come – to show him a film, made by director Chris Goddard and myself for Thames Television, on the Ruth Ellis case, in which certain allegations were made. His mouth snapped shut. 'I have nothing to say.' He said it three or four times. But he said it as if he feared that, to enter into *any* form of conversation would mean, almost inevitably, that he would agree to what I had to say.

He rang John Hudson, a colleague from TVW Channel 7, the Perth TV station, the next day. 'If these allegations are so serious, I suppose I ought to see the film.'

He saw the film. 'I have nothing to say.'

We sat and drank three beers together. It was in one of the new generation of Australian pubs where water doesn't run in a channel beside the bar to carry away spittle and cigarette ends. Perth isn't like that. Desmond Cussen talked about life in Australia. He loves the country. He'd sold his share in the family tobacconist business in London in 1964. He'd come to Australia, he said, to start all over again. He had £10,000 and his hopes were high.

First, he joined a trucking company in Sydney to discover how things worked in the business world. He pulled out because he didn't like some of the deals he saw going on.

He sold second-hand cars. He had his business closed down because the local council said he didn't have the right trading licence.

He set out to drive across Australia in 1967. He saw Perth, liked it, and decided to settle for a while. He began to do feasibility studies for a firm of estate agents. After three years, he left. He couldn't make it pay. He'd lost £3500.

He tried speculating on stocks and shares. He lost.

He went into the import–export business and discovered that company money appeared to be going into someone's private account. He left.

Nor has he found being a florist easy. 'There're worms in the carnations this autumn. Now they've sprayed them with a new insecticide and the leaves are turning brown.' Desmond Cussen's business is on the verge of bankruptcy.

He tells all this with only a trace of bitterness. Almost as if he expected it. Only once is he moved. He almost married, once, since he's been in Australia. She died of cancer.

He rang John Hudson at eight the next morning. That evening, in my hotel room in Perth, we discussed the statement Ruth Ellis made in the death cell, at Holloway prison, the day before she was due to be hanged.

. . . it is only with the greatest reluctance that I have decided to tell how it was that I got the gun with which I shot David Blakely. I did not do so before because I felt I was needlessly getting someone into possible trouble.

I had been drinking Pernod (I think that is how it is spelt) in Desmond Cussen's flat and Desmond had been drinking too. This was about 8.30 p.m. We had been drinking for some time. I had been telling Desmond of Blakely's treat-

204

ment of me. I was in a terribly depressed state. All I remember is that Desmond gave me a loaded gun. Desmond was jealous of Blakely as in fact Blakely was of Desmond. I would say that they hated each other. I was in such a dazed state that I cannot remember what was said. I rushed out as soon as he gave me the gun. He stayed in the flat. I rushed back after a second or two and said: 'Will you drive me to Hampstead?' He did so, and left me at the top of Tanza Road.

I had never seen the gun before. The only gun I had ever seen there was a small air pistol used as a game with a target.

signed
Ruth Ellis
12.30 p.m. 12th July 1955.

He knew what he wanted to contribute.

'First, let me say quite clearly that I did not give Ruth the gun. Nor, on that occasion, did I drive her up to Hampstead . . .

'Mr Bickford (Ruth's solicitor) says he doesn't want to hurt me, so why is he saying that I told him the same story, only two days after the murder? The statement that Ruth gave is not true in any way.

'There was no question of us drinking Pernod together. To the best of my recollection, it was a gin and tonic I poured her and she said: "I don't feel like drinking. I'd rather have a cup of tea." And she went off and made one. Besides, the police would have smelled Pernod on her breath, if she'd been drinking so heavily . . .'

That was the easy part.

So, what was he doing that day?

Cussen had made a statement to the police the day after the murder and he'd told them that they'd spent the day in the flat. Now, he added that they'd listened to the radio, played records, entertained the child, Andrea.

How was Ruth?

'She hadn't been her normal sort of cheerful self. In fact, she was exceptionally quiet. She seemed preoccupied, as if she had something on her mind. Didn't really want to talk about anything.'

Then, as he told the police twenty-two years before, he added that he'd driven Ruth and her son, Andrea, to Egerton Gardens, the home they were sharing with David Blakely – and for which Desmond Cussen was helping to pay the rent. That was at 7.30 p.m. – two hours before the murder. And that, he said, was the last he saw of Ruth, until he visited her in Holloway after the murder.

So there it was. He hadn't given Ruth the gun at his home at Goodwood Court. He hadn't driven her to Hampstead. And he hadn't then driven away, leaving her near the public house where Blakely was drinking.

And there was one other allegation that he was at pains to deny. He did not drive Ruth and the child to Penn in search of Blakely that afternoon, nor did he stop near Gerrards Cross so that Ruth Ellis could get out of his car, walk into the woods, and take a practice shot at a tree. That is what, today, Mr Victor Mishcon, Ruth's lawyer in her divorce action, says Ellis told him when she gave the death-cell statement the day before she died. That is what, today, her solicitor throughout the trial, Mr John Bickford, says that Desmond Cussen blurted out to him only two days after the murder.

Two solicitors. Two uncannily similar stories. He dismissed them both. Of Bickford's allegations: 'I don't know why he's saying this after all these years. Is he trying to make money out of this? Is he writing a book?'

I assured him Mr Bickford wasn't.

'Well, what other motive could there be?'

'I suppose the obvious alternative motive is that he's telling the truth. And that he wants to set the record straight, as it were.'

'Well, I just don't see that.'

And of the death-cell statement that she gave Mr Mishcon: 'It could only have been a completely desperate effort to get herself a stay of execution.'

'But Mr Mishcon says he had the clear impression that she didn't care that she was going to die, that he had to drag that statement out of her, for the sake of her family, if for no other reason.'

'Well, what he dragged out of her just wasn't the truth.'

'But had she not said to Mr Mishcon: Yes, I will tell you facts

206

and I will tell you the truth which hasn't yet been completely known by any manner of means?'

'The statement she gave to Mr Mishcon implicating me is not true.'

For about two hours, we talked. Mainly, we explored the implications of Ellis's death-cell statement. With his permission, we recorded much of the conversation. I reproduce some of the exchanges, without comment except when a note of explanation is necessary.

On what he'd been doing on the evening of the murder:
You dropped Andrea and Ruth at Egerton Gardens. What did you do then?

I went back home.

What did you do for the rest of the evening?

Oh, good heavens. Probably had a drink. Might have done some office work or something.

You're not sure?

Well, you know, questions like this after twenty-two years . . .

It was a remarkable day, Mr Cussen.

I know but one wouldn't remember exactly what one did when one went home.

You don't remember where you were when Ruth Ellis shot David Blakely?

Well, I must have been at home.

You've never, in all these years, said: 'Good heavens, while I was doing so-and-so, she was actually shooting David?'

Well, I never thought of it that way.

On whether or not they'd been drinking Pernod together, as Ruth Ellis alleged:

In no way could the police have missed that when they picked her up. They're not fools. And, when they took her in, if there'd been any sign of her being intoxicated, or having any liquor, that surely would not have been overlooked or withheld by them. They would have made it clear at the time.

As far as we can gather, no medical examination was made of Ruth Ellis at Hampstead police station that evening.

Well, what I'm saying is that, if she'd been doing this drinking, as she claimed, the police couldn't have failed to realize it.

But there was an eyewitness to the shooting, there was an off-duty policeman to whom she handed the gun, there was a man dying in the gutter, there was the fact that she was taken to the police station and virtually admitted straight away that she'd done the killing – I would have thought perhaps that noticing whether or not there was a smell of Pernod on her breath would have taken a low priority from the police point of view.

Well, I would naturally assume the police would take notice of a thing like that. If she'd had a lot of Pernod, that would have clung to her breath for many hours – probably till next morning.

(I later spoke to two members of the police force involved in the arrest and charge. Neither could remember whether or not Ellis had been drinking. One, PC Alan Thompson, to whom she handed the gun, had only just emerged from the pub. 'I'd been drinking a couple of beers. I might not have noticed the smell of alcohol on someone else's breath.')

On Ellis's behaviour that day, remembering that she'd been 'stood up' by Blakely that weekend and had been so furious that, only two evenings before, she sought him out and smashed in the windows of his car as it stood parked outside a friend's house:

She seemed preoccupied . . . I can only say that the poor damned girl had it, had it on her mind.

Did you sense this (tragedy) coming? I mean, were you worried about this?

No, I wasn't worried. Although I thought it was odd (pause). I can't really explain.

You weren't perturbed?

No. No, no, not at the time.

And yet you'd been with her when she'd gone to Tanza Road, smashed in the windows of Blakely's car; the police had been called, the Black Maria had arrived – surely, you were concerned about this girl's state of mind?

It hadn't – hadn't entered my mind at the time.

But didn't you drive her there (that evening)?

Yes.

And you saw her state of mind.

Well, she was . . . I don't know how really to say this. She was highly temperamental at times.

I'm trying to ask you what your observations were on the extraordinary events of that weekend.

(Silence.)

I mean were you simply going along with what this powerful, determined woman was doing?

Well, I was trying to dissuade her from it.

From what?

From carrying on – the two of them. I mean I'd always tried to get them peaceably together. So that they should not be continually fighting.

You had? You had?

I think so. Some time or another I must have spoken to Blakely and to her about this.

Why did you do this?

Well, I wanted to help.

Did you love her?

I would say I must have loved her.

It's almost as if you were under her influence that weekend.

Well, partially. Probably (pause). It could have been. I wanted to help her (pause). Not to the point of giving her a gun, if that's what you're trying to get at. That's ludicrous.

I didn't suggest that.

I thought that's maybe what you were trying to get at.

When you say 'trying to help them', were you trying to get them to stay together or to part?

I was trying to get her to stop the futility of tearing off and spying on him. I didn't see what good it was doing. It was getting her more upset . . . but I think, now, I was just wasting my time. I think she was so infatuated with him, and vice versa, that I realize now that I was wasting my time.

When did you realize you were wasting your time?

I suppose very shortly before Blakely's death.

What made you reach that decision?

I suppose the futility, and the driving her around (after him) that I did. And trying to explain to her the futility of it all. And she seemed to be getting worse – and he wasn't any better. Well, the two of them, they just couldn't leave one another alone. In spite of the beatings.

And there you were – in the middle?

Mmmm.

What was that like for you?

Well, it wasn't very pleasant. You see, I had my feelings for her. I often wondered whether they weren't actually in love with one another.

What do you think she was looking for, from you?

Some sort of guidance – or stability. I think she'd been hurt so much in life by other incidents that she just couldn't find it in herself to trust a man.

She'd been hurt by men?

Yes.

Did you tell her she could trust you?

Well, I think, and hope, she knew that. I was trying to get her trust and get her to have some confidence in somebody. She had no confidence in anybody, really.

And what were you looking for in her?

Oh, it sounds stupid now, I know, but I was probably a bit of a knight in armour . . . trying to do the right thing by her.

Looking after the child?

Yes.

Giving him money to go to the zoo?

Mmmm.

Taking him to the pictures?

Well . . .

Making him breakfast?

Yes. Trying to make a home for them both, really.

Had you been in love before?

Not really, I don't suppose.

Why was Ruth Ellis so special?

I couldn't answer that. Are you married? What's so special about your wife?

That's the way you looked at Ruth?

Well, whether it was real true love I had for her, or whether I just wanted to help (pause). If you love somebody, you *want* to help.

210

On the situation in which his love for Ruth Ellis had placed him, in April 1955:

You were picking Ruth up [by car] every morning, to drive her to modelling courses?

Yes.

You were paying for those modelling courses?

Yes.

You were helping her to pay the rent on the flat in which she was living with David Blakely?

Mmmm.

You were buying clothes for her. You were paying school fees for her son. You were buying his school clothes. You were feeding them at your flat, and . . .

Not all the time was I feeding her at my flat. She could come and go as she pleased.

And yet, with all this, she was sleeping with David Blakely?

(Pause.)

That must have been difficult for you.

Well, it was always a question of whether or not their association would discontinue. And I was, I think, prepared to put up with it at the time, in the hope that it would discontinue.

But it wasn't a situation calculated to bring peace of mind to any one of the three of you.

No – I wouldn't say it was, really.

So – were you never angry?

Well, I was obviously angry on the occasion when I took him outside and tried to give him a good thrashing.

(*Note:* This was at the Bull public house, Gerrards Cross. Blakely declined the invitation to 'come outside'.)

But when you wanted to thrash Blakely, that was anger at what he had done to her.

Yes.

I'm talking about – were you never angry at what they were doing to you?

No, I wouldn't say I was angry. I wasn't happy about it . . . Oh, it seems ridiculous now (pause). Whether I was just hoping in those days that she would be as good as her word and would give him up. But, every time she tried to – one excuse or another, and they'd get back together again.

211

Would you have married her?

If she'd ... I think I would if she'd made a clean break with him.

When did you realize you'd lost her?

I suppose, really, when she went and killed him.

All of which brings us to the gun, the murder weapon itself. It was a .38 Smith and Wesson ex-service revolver. Ruth Ellis, remember, had held throughout her arrest, her trial, and the days leading up to the eve of her execution, that she had been given the revolver as a security on a debt. It had been given to her by a man in one of the night clubs. She was never more specific.

Interestingly, no one seems to have believed the story. Separately, I have asked the judge, a member of the jury, Ruth's own counsel, the prosecuting counsel, and two of the policemen most intimately concerned in the investigation. Each has said to me that they thought the story too far-fetched.

But, here again, we come back to the fact that this was an open-and-shut case. The source of the gun seemed to matter very little, in the light of the overwhelming weight of evidence against her – that she had committed the murder, and was admitting that she'd committed it.

The police, DI Davies and DC Claiden, assembled the evidence diligently and fairly. There is only one small doubt in my mind. And it concerns the evidence of Mrs Marie-Thérèse Harris, who, early in 1955, was giving Ruth Ellis French lessons at Desmond Cussen's flat. Lessons, of course, paid for by Cussen.

Mrs Harris visited the flat one day and Ruth was out. She wasn't the most enthusiastic or punctual student, so Mrs Harris decided to wait. Ruth's son Andrea was there. Mrs Harris, as she chatted to the lad, mentioned that they were troubled by pigeons near her home. Andrea said he might be able to help. He went to a drawer – and took two guns out. Mrs Harris was alarmed, naturally enough. 'It's all right,' said Andrea, 'they're not loaded.'

Mrs Harris told the police this story when she heard about the murder. The police went to Cussen's flat and, eventually, Cussen was able to find two guns: a starting pistol (which, incidentally, went off as he and the police handled it!) and a Webley air pistol.

The police then went to Mrs Harris. They took the firearms

with them. She was unable to identify either of them as being those she had seen in the flat, some months earlier.

But did the police take the murder weapon with them, to give Mrs Harris a chance to identify that? This is the crucial question – and there's some doubt about the answer to it. The records indicate that the murder weapon was taken to the Scotland Yard forensic laboratory immediately after the murder, and stayed there under examination. DC Claiden believes they must have gone to the forensic laboratory and taken the murder weapon from there – but cannot be sure.

I took photographs of three weapons to Mrs Harris, admittedly twenty-two years after the event. They were photographs of a starting pistol and a Webley air pistol, identical with those taken from Cussen's flat – plus a photograph of a .38 Smith and Wesson. Mrs Harris examined the photographs – and eliminated the starting pistol immediately. Andrea had certainly not taken *that* out of the drawer. Mrs Harris knows nothing about guns. But she is a careful witness.

Of the two remaining photographs, she picked out the Smith and Wesson revolver as having been the larger gun she'd been shown by Ruth Ellis's son that day early in 1955.

As far as I can tell, this is the only time, when questioned by police, solicitors, or journalists, that she has ever identified one of the weapons she saw in Cussen's flat. Could it be because it was also the first time she'd ever been shown it, since that day?

Mrs Harris was never called to give evidence.

John Bickford, Ruth Ellis's solicitor from the start of the case, went to see her in Holloway prison. The only remarkable aspect of their conversation that day was that Ellis wanted a message delivered to Desmond Cussen. She wanted him told that she had informed the police that she had been given the gun by a man in a night club, as security on a debt. Bickford had thought the message so peculiar that he had made a note of it in red ink . . .

Do you remember Mr Bickford bringing this message to you?

Yes. Yes. Something along those lines I think he mentioned to me.

Why did she want to get that message to you?

Well, I'd been wondering where she'd got the gun (pause). Her parents were.

Why didn't she send the message to her parents?

Probably because I was closer to her than her parents were, in some ways.

But why should you *be wondering where she got the gun? Wouldn't your chief concern be her well-being? Wouldn't it have been more likely that she would send a message out to you, saying: 'Don't worry, Desmond. I'm all right'?*

No . . . um . . . that she, she should send Bickford with that message is . . . strange. Insofar that she obviously wondered . . . I, she would have been thinking, I suppose . . . that I'd want to know where she got it.

Did you then say anything to Mr Bickford?

Obviously, I would assume, I would have asked if there was any way in which I could have helped her.

In what way – I mean, simple things like sending her a box of chocolates, or . . .

Oh no, it would have been a little bit more than that.

But what did you have in mind?

Well, possibly, any way I could have helped with the story of the gun.

What do you mean?

Well, he'd come and told me about this. There was this message, it was quite obvious I'd be interested where she got it . . . I suppose I was in a state where I could have said anything stupid.

Done anything stupid?

Well, I suppose there's a possibility. I was very upset about the whole matter.

What sort of stupidity? You say: 'I might have said anything stupid about the gun.' Such as what?

I don't really know.

Such as 'I gave her the gun'?

No, I couldn't have said a thing like that.

I must tell you that Mr Bickford is adamant that you did say a thing like that.

Well, my upset state . . . maybe I intimated something like that. There did appear to me that (she was giving) such a lame excuse for having the gun.

So, you might.

214

He (Bickford) must have intimated to me that he didn't believe her story about the gun.

So you might have said to him that you'd given her the gun?

I might have said it – but I can't believe it, somehow . . . In an upset state I might have accidentally said it.

Do you mean that, if you did say it, you didn't mean it?

I would say . . . yes, naturally I wouldn't have meant it (pause). I could have said it as, you know – 'would it do any good if I said anything like that (about the gun)'.

So that's what you said?

It would appear so, if Bickford is adamant I said it.

(Note: This is not Mr Bickford's memory of the conversation. He remembers Mr Cussen volunteering the information that he had given Ruth Ellis the gun.)

I don't know whether Desmond Cussen supplied Ruth Ellis with the gun with which she shot David Blakely. Perhaps no one will ever know where she obtained the gun. But of the tragic triangle, Ellis – Blakely – Cussen, only Cussen is still alive, and, however far he travels he will live in the shadow of the events that shattered the calm of that April evening in Hampstead, for the rest of his life. He said:

Looking back on it now, you know these have been difficult questions to answer. Because she's gone, and why speak evil of the dead? I've had misgivings and thoughts run through my mind since then. In those days I obviously acted like a bloody fool. But what I did, I did with the best of intentions.

She's still on your mind?

She always will be. I was very fond of her. You just can't cut a person out of your life.

The only woman for you?

I thought so at the time. I did meet somebody else, who shall be nameless.

What happened?

She unfortunately died of cancer, over East (in Eastern Australia). I was beginning to become very fond of her as well. And there's no doubt she was of me.

Life's hard.

Some find it easy. Some find it hard.

How about you?

Well, I wouldn't say I've found it all that easy. Specially with things like this cropping up.

Memories, repercussions – they won't go away?

Oh, there are always times when they go away. Fond memories always come back.

And erase the bad memories?

Not completely. But I think one likes to remember the niceties and forget the nasty side.

The same with your memories of Ruth Ellis?

Well, it's natural one would prefer to remember the good times with her. Sitting here now brings back the sadness of the whole thing. It's not been easy to sit here and talk.

I believe that. I believe that.

Only once more did we mention the subject before I left Australia. A clear, bright, new day in this country where Desmond Cussen has tried to find a clear, bright, new life:

I never thought she would hang, you know. I always thought she's get a reprieve, right up to the end.

Yet she made no effort to save her life. She wanted to die. And she'd told you that.

Yes. That's true.

That's what makes the death-cell statement so amazing. At the last minute, to change her story. If she'd made that statement even a couple of days earlier, that must have led to a stay of execution, so that further inquiries could be made. Inquiries that would have involved you, I'm afraid.

Well, I could only say what I'd said to the police already. That I'd no idea where she got the gun. And they'd believed me (pause). She was a dreadful liar, you know.

(Pause.)

Mind you, she's got her wish. She used to complain when I visited her in Holloway that they'd cut all the reports of her case out of the newspapers she was given to read. She wanted to know the headlines she was making. She loved the headlines. She always wanted to be a star. She achieved that, didn't she?

FOR THE BEST IN PAPERBACKS, LOOK FOR THE 🐧

In every corner of the world, on every subject under the sun, Penguin represents quality and variety – the very best in publishing today.

For complete information about books available from Penguin – including Puffins, Penguin Classics and Arkana – and how to order them, write to us at the appropriate address below. Please note that for copyright reasons the selection of books varies from country to country.

In the United Kingdom: Please write to *Dept E.P., Penguin Books Ltd, Harmondsworth, Middlesex, UB7 0DA.*

If you have any difficulty in obtaining a title, please send your order with the correct money, plus ten per cent for postage and packaging, to *PO Box No 11, West Drayton, Middlesex*

In the United States: Please write to *Dept BA, Penguin, 299 Murray Hill Parkway, East Rutherford, New Jersey 07073*

In Canada: Please write to *Penguin Books Canada Ltd, 2801 John Street, Markham, Ontario L3R 1B4*

In Australia: Please write to the *Marketing Department, Penguin Books Australia Ltd, P.O. Box 257, Ringwood, Victoria 3134*

In New Zealand: Please write to the *Marketing Department, Penguin Books (NZ) Ltd, Private Bag, Takapuna, Auckland 9*

In India: Please write to *Penguin Overseas Ltd, 706 Eros Apartments, 56 Nehru Place, New Delhi, 110019*

In the Netherlands: Please write to *Penguin Books Netherlands B.V., Postbus 195, NL–1380AD Weesp*

In West Germany: Please write to *Penguin Books Ltd, Friedrichstrasse 10–12, D–6000 Frankfurt/Main 1*

In Spain: Please write to *Longman Penguin España, Calle San Nicolas 15, E–28013 Madrid*

In Italy: Please write to *Penguin Italia s.r.l., Via Como 4, I-20096 Pioltello (Milano)*

In France: Please write to *Penguin Books Ltd, 39 Rue de Montmorency, F-75003 Paris*

In Japan: Please write to *Longman Penguin Japan Co Ltd, Yamaguchi Building, 2–12–9 Kanda Jimbocho, Chiyoda-Ku, Tokyo 101*

A CHOICE OF PENGUINS

The Secret Lives of Trebitsch Lincoln   Bernard Wasserstein

Trebitsch Lincoln was Member of Parliament, international spy, right-wing revolutionary, Buddhist monk – and this century's most extraordinary conman. 'Surely the final work on a truly extraordinary career' – Hugh Trevor-Roper. 'An utterly improbable story … a biographical coup' – *Guardian*

Out of Africa   Karen Blixen (Isak Dinesen)

After the failure of her coffee-farm in Kenya, where she lived from 1913 to 1931, Karen Blixen went home to Denmark and wrote this unforgettable account of her experiences. 'No reader can put the book down without some share in the author's poignant farewell to her farm' – *Observer*

In My Wildest Dreams   Leslie Thomas

The autobiography of Leslie Thomas, author of *The Magic Army* and *The Dearest and the Best*. From Barnardo boy to original virgin soldier, from apprentice journalist to famous novelist, it is an amazing story. 'Hugely enjoyable.' – *Daily Express*

The Winning Streak   Walter Goldsmith and David Clutterbuck

Marks and Spencer, Saatchi and Saatchi, United Biscuits, GEC … The UK's top companies reveal their formulas for success, in an important and stimulating book that no British manager can afford to ignore.

Bird of Life, Bird of Death   Jonathan Evan Maslow

In the summer of 1983 Jonathan Maslow set out to find the quetzal. In doing so, he placed himself between the natural and unnatural histories of Central America, between the vulnerable magnificence of nature and the terrible destructiveness of man. 'A wonderful book' – *The New York Times Book Review*

Mob Star   Gene Mustain and Jerry Capeci

Handsome, charming, deadly, John Gotti is the real-life Mafia boss at the head of New York's most feared criminal family. *Mob Star* tells the chilling and compelling story of the rise to power of the most powerful criminal in America.

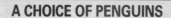
A CHOICE OF PENGUINS

Return to the Marshes Gavin Young

His remarkable portrait of the remote and beautiful world of the Marsh Arabs, whose centuries-old existence is now threatened with extinction by twentieth-century warfare. 'A talent for vivid description rarely found outside good fiction' – Jonathan Raban in the *Sunday Times*

Manhattan '45 Jan Morris

Disembarking with the victorious GIs returning after the war, Jan Morris takes us on a wonderfully nostalgic exploration of Manhattan in 1945; an affectionate portrait of an unrepeatable moment in history.

Britain's Poisoned Water Frances and Phil Craig

Every day millions of British families drink water containing toxic chemicals. But what are we doing about it? This startling investigation is essential and shocking reading for anyone concerned about our environment, our health, and the health of our children.

How I Grew Mary McCarthy

Mary McCarthy's account of her formative years possesses all the insight, wit and intelligence of her classic *Memories of a Catholic Girlhood* and her international bestseller *The Group*. 'Rich, generous stuff … it leaves one licking one's lips for what is yet to come' – Penelope Lively

Who Should be Sleeping in Your Bed – and Why James Oliver

Should a Little Princess be faithful to a Wimp? This series of simple quizzes and personality profiles devised by clinical psychologist James Oliver will show you why infidelity happens – and how to make sure it doesn't happen to you.

The Big Red Train Ride Eric Newby

From Moscow to the Pacific on the Trans-Siberian Railway is an eight-day journey of nearly six thousand miles through seven time zones. In 1977 Eric Newby set out with his wife, an official guide and a photographer on this journey. 'The best kind of travel book' – Paul Theroux

Trail of Havoc Patrick Marnham

In this brilliant piece of detective work, Patrick Marnham has traced the steps of Lord Lucan from the fateful night of 7 November 1974 when he murdered his children's nanny and attempted to kill his ex-wife. As well as being a fascinating investigation, the book is also a brilliant portrayal of a privileged section of society living under great stress.

Light Years Gary Kinder

Eduard Meier, an uneducated Swiss farmer, claims since 1975 to have had over 100 UFO sightings and encounters with 'beamships' from the Pleiades. His evidence is such that even the most die-hard sceptics have been unable to explain away the phenomenon.

And the Band Played On Politics, People and the AIDS Epidemic
Randy Shilts

Written after years of extensive research by the only American journalist to cover the epidemic full-time, *And the Band Played On* is a masterpiece of reportage and a tragic record of mismanaged institutions and scientific vendettas, of sexual politics and personal suffering.

The Return of a Native Reporter Robert Chesshyre

Robert Chesshyre returned to Britain in 1985 from the United States, where he had spent four years as the *Observer*'s correspondent. This is his devastating account of the country he came home to: intolerant, brutal, grasping and politically and economically divided. It is a nation, he asserts, struggling to find a role.

Women and Love Shere Hite

In this culmination of *The Hite Report* trilogy, 4,500 women provide an eloquent testimony to the disturbingly unsatisfying nature of their emotional relationships and point to what they see as the causes. *Women and Love* reveals a new cultural perspective in formation: as women change the emotional structure of their lives, they are defining a fundamental debate over the future of our society.

FOR THE BEST IN PAPERBACKS, LOOK FOR THE ⓟ

LITERARY BIOGRAPHIES AND AUTOBIOGRAPHIES

Sylvia Beach and the Lost Generation Noel Riley Fitch
Joseph Conrad Jocelyn Baines
The Making of Charles Dickens Christopher Hibbert
A Sort of Life Graham Greene
The Young Thomas Hardy Robert Gittings
Ernest Hemingway Carlos Baker
John Keats Robert Gittings
Rudyard Kipling Charles Carrington
How I Grew Mary McCarthy
Katherine Mansfield: A Secret Life Claire Tomalin
Prick Up Your Ears: The Biography of Joe Orton John Lahr
A Better Class of Person John Osborne
Ezra Pound Noel Stock
Sartre: Romantic Rationalist Iris Murdoch
Shelley Richard Holmes
The Autobiography of Alice B. Toklas Gertrude Stein
Lytton Strachey Michael Holroyd
Dylan Thomas Paul Ferris
Tolstoy Henry Troyat
Tolstoy A. N. Wilson
Anthony Trollope James Pope-Hennessy
The Diaries of Evelyn Waugh
Walt Whitman Paul Zweig
Oscar Wilde Hesketh Pearson
Oscar Wilde Richard Ellmann
Yeats: The Man and the Mask Richard Ellmann

FOR THE BEST IN PAPERBACKS, LOOK FOR THE 🐧

BIOGRAPHY AND AUTOBIOGRAPHY IN PENGUIN

Just for William Nicholas Woolley and Sue Clayton

Originating as a film for the award-winning BBC2 documentary series *Forty Minutes*, *Just for William* is the story of William Clayton, diagnosed with leukaemia at the age of nine – and the story of a family who refused to give up hope in the battle against one of the deadliest diseases of all.

The Secret Lives of Trebitsch Lincoln Bernard Wasserstein

Trebitsch Lincoln was Member of Parliament, international spy, right-wing revolutionary, Buddhist monk – and this century's most extraordinary conman. 'An utterly improbable story … a biographical scoop' – *Guardian*

Tolstoy A. N. Wilson

'One of the best biographies of our century' – Leon Edel. 'All his skills as a writer, his fire as a critic, his insight as a novelist and his experience of life have come together in this subject' – Peter Levi in the *Independent*

Fox on the Run Graeme Fowler

The intimate diary of a dramatic eighteen months, in which Fowler became the first Englishman to score a double century in India – before being cast down by injury and forced to come to terms with loss of form. 'One of the finest cricket books this year' – *Yorkshire Post*. Winner of the first Observer/Running Late Sports Book Award.

Backcloth Dirk Bogarde

The final volume of Dirk Bogarde's autobiography is not about his acting years but about Dirk Bogarde the man and the people and events that have shaped his life and character. All are remembered with affection, nostalgia and characteristic perception and eloquence.

Jackdaw Cake Norman Lewis

From Carmarthen to Cuba, from Enfield to Algeria, Norman Lewis brilliantly recounts his transformation from stammering schoolboy to the man Auberon Waugh called 'the greatest travel writer alive, if not the greatest since Marco Polo'.

PENGUIN TRUE CRIME

Crippen: The Mild Murderer Tom Cullen
The famous story of the doctor who poisoned his wife and buried her in the cellar.

Who Killed Hanratty? Paul Foot
An investigation into the notorious A6 murder.

Norman Birkett H. Montgomery Hyde
The biography of one of Britain's most humane and respected judges.

The Complete Jack the Ripper Donald Rumbelow
An investigation into the identity of the most elusive murderer of all time.

The Riddle of Birdhurst Rise R. Whittington-Egan
The Croydon Poisoning Mystery of 1928–9.

Suddenly at the Priory John Williams
Who poisoned the Victorian barrister Charles Bravo?

Stinie: Murder on the Common Andrew Rose
The truth behind the Clapham Common murder.

The Poisoned Life of Mrs Maybrick Bernard Ryan
Mr Maybrick died of arsenic poisoning – how?

The Gatton Mystery J. and D. Gibney
The great unsolved Australian triple murder.

Earth to Earth John Cornwell
Who killed the Luxtons in their remote mid-Devon farmhouse?

The Ordeal of Philip Yale Drew R. Whittington-Egan
A real life murder melodrama in three acts.

Famous Trials of Marshall Hall Edward Marjoribanks
The authoritative life of the most distinguished advocate of his generation.

The Dominici Affair Jean Laborde
French justice on trial.

Murder Not Proven? Jack House
Four notorious cases from Scotland.